CORRUPTED

CORRUPTED

A study of chronic dysfunction
in South African universities

JONATHAN D. JANSEN

WITS UNIVERSITY PRESS

Published in South Africa by:
Wits University Press
1 Jan Smuts Avenue
Johannesburg 2001

www.witspress.co.za

First published 2023

http://dx.doi.org. 10.18772/12023027946

978-1-77614-794-6 (Paperback)
978-1-77614-795-3 (Hardback)
978-1-77614-796-0 (Web PDF)
978-1-77614-797-7 (EPUB)

This publication is peer reviewed following international best practice standards for academic and scholarly books.

The names of individuals whose conduct and the details thereof already exist in the public domain have been retained. The names of individuals who have consented to being mentioned in the book have also been retained. Where individuals disclosed information to the author confidentially, their identities have been anonymised.

The views and opinions expressed in the book belong solely to the author. The publication of the book does not constitute an endorsement of the views by Wits University Press, the University of the Witwatersrand and its employees, subsidiaries or affiliate companies.

Project manager: Elaine Williams
Copyeditor: Russell Martin
Proofreader: Inga Norenius
Indexer: Margaret Ramsay
Cover design: Hybrid Creative
Typeset in 10 point Minion Pro

CONTENTS

ACKNOWLEDGEMENTS

This book would not have been possible without the colleagues named below making themselves available for interviews, some more than once and a few via email. Please accept my sincere thanks for sharing your time, expertise and insights into the subject. However, the curation and interpretation of the data, and the theses that follow, are my own.

Ivan Abrahams, Lucie Abrahams, Rob Adam, Hugh Amoore, Saleem Badat, Nasima Badsha, Narend Baijnath, Leslie Bank, Ahmed Bawa, Ramesh Bharuthram, Chris Brink, Vanessa Brown, Sakhela Buhlungu, John Butler Adam, Edwin Cameron, Randall Carolissen, Nico Cloete, Chris de Beer, Roy du Pre, Kuzvinetsa Peter Dzvimbo, Ahmed Essop, Judy Favish, Loretta Feris, Brian Figaji, Glen Fisher, Patrick Fitzgerald, Magda Fourie-Malherbe, Peter Franks, Michael Gering, Trish Gibbon, Erica Gillard, Jennie Glennie, Brenda Gourley, Adam Habib, Martin Hall, Fred Hayward, Cyril Julie, André Keet, Quintin Koetaan, Piyushi Kotecha, Tembile Kulati, Lis Lange, Lesley le Grange, Jim Leatt, Craig Lyall-Watson, Chief Mabizela, Bongekile Macupe, Botshabelo Maja, Louis Malomo, Vincent Maphai, David Maughan Brown, Peter Mbati, Rob Midgley, Antony Melck, Kirti Menon, Sarah Meny-Gibert, Letticia Mmaseloadi Moja, Naseema Mohammed, Teboho Moja, Mahlo Mokgalong, Nicky Morgan, Rob Morrell, Peter Morris, Sean Morrow, Themba Mosia, Ronaldo Munck, Prakash Naidoo, Dan Ncayiyana, Njabulo Ndebele, Heather Nel, Thandabantu Nhlapo, Loyiso Nongxa, Mario Novelli, Dumisa Ntsebeza, Thandi Orleyn, Angina Parekh, Diane (Di) Parker,

Gansen Pillay, Barney Pityana, Sipho Pityana, Larry Pokpas, Corina Pretorius, Molapo Qhobela, Rocky Ralebipi-Simela, Marcus Ramogale, Fazel Randera, Jairam Reddy, Vijay Reddy, Ihron Rensburg, John Samuel, Lavern Samuels, Oliver Seale, Sipho Seepe, Chika Sehoole, Camilla Singh, Mala Singh, Paul Slack, Edwin Smith, Dhiru Soni, Albert van Jaarsveld, Anton van Niekerk, Engela van Staden, Lourens van Staden, Christopher (Kit) Vaughan, John Volmink, Dianna Yach, Shirley Zinn.

ACRONYMS AND ABBREVIATIONS

ANC	African National Congress
BTF	broad transformation forum
CHE	Council on Higher Education
DUT	Durban University of Technology
DVC	deputy vice-chancellor
Gear	Growth, Equity and Redistribution
HDI	historically disadvantaged institution
HELM	Higher Education Leadership and Management
IF	institutional forum
MEC	member of the executive council
MUT	Mangosuthu University of Technology
NCHE	National Commission on Higher Education
NECC	National Education Crisis Committee (later, Coordinating Committee)
Nehawu	National Education, Health and Allied Workers' Union
NSFAS	National Student Financial Aid Scheme
SABC	South African Broadcasting Corporation
Sasco	South African Students' Congress
Sassa	South African Social Security Agency
SRC	student representative council
SU	Stellenbosch University
UCT	University of Cape Town

UDW	University of Durban-Westville
UFH	University of Fort Hare
UFS	University of the Free State
Unisa	University of South Africa
Unitra	University of Transkei
Univen	University of Venda
UP	University of Pretoria
UWC	University of the Western Cape
VC	vice-chancellor
VUT	Vaal University of Technology
Wits	University of the Witwatersrand

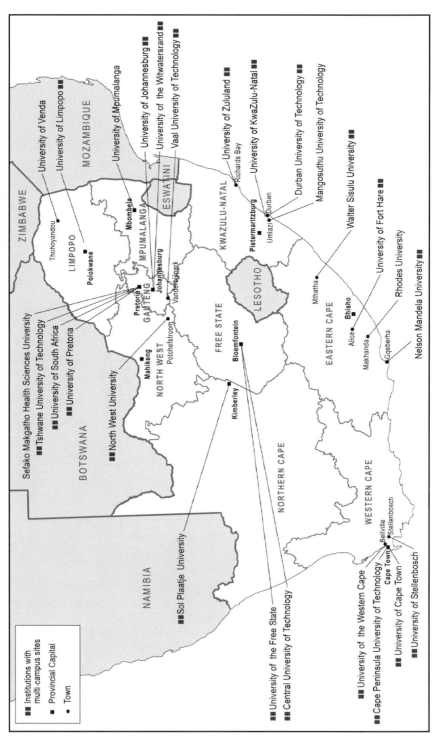

South African universities

1

A Study of Chronic Dysfunction in Universities

THE PUZZLE

In July 2021, a major South African newspaper ran the headline 'Is the Vaal University of Technology an Institution Bewitched?'[1] It was a strange question to ask of a modern institution, a premier site of higher learning. Yet a mere few weeks earlier, one of the country's most distinguished academics seemed puzzled during an interview about the campus citizens of another dysfunctional institution: 'If you were a Zulu, they'd tell you that you can't understand these people, they've been bewitched.' This former vice-chancellor and administrator of universities had seen his fair share of institutional implosion. 'Bewitched', in this context, expresses the frustration experienced when we struggle to explain why a university has a high turnover of vice-chancellors, why university councils regularly collapse, and why there is constant campus turmoil or shutdowns because of conflicts, protests and disruptions.

Such chronic dysfunction sometimes attracts the attention of the political head of higher education in government (now the minister of higher education and training), who will often dispatch an assessor to an institution to report on the situation. The assessor's report usually triggers the appointment of an administrator to take over key functions of the university and establish some semblance of order. When, despite ministerial intervention, the university falls back into dysfunction, some do indeed wonder whether the institution is under some spell.

There is no shortage of polemical writings on corruption and mismanagement in these dysfunctional universities. These tend to be exaggerated, self-aggrandising accounts of institutional malfunction, in which the evidence is slim, one-sided or nonexistent. Three book-length publications of note are Nithaya Chetty and Christopher Merrett's *The Struggle for the Soul of a South African University* [2] (concerning the University of KwaZulu-Natal), Aubrey Mokadi's *A Portrait of Governance in Higher Education* [3] (about the Vaal University of Technology), and Nhlanhla Maake's *Barbarism in Higher Education* [4] (documenting the author's travails at the Vaal Triangle campus of what was then Potchefstroom University).

There also exist at least three reviews of assessor reports that seek to extract key findings of value. These are straightforward summaries and extrapolations rather than empirical or theoretical treatments of the subject beyond what was already known. One of these was commissioned by the Council on Higher Education and titled *Institutional Governance in the Higher Education System in South Africa.* [5] Another was conducted by Higher Education South Africa (renamed Universities South Africa [USAf] in 2015) and titled *Analysis of Recent Assessor Reports of Universities in South Africa.* [6] A third report was completed by the Department of Higher Education and Training itself under the title *Summary of Recent Assessor Reports and CHE Publications on the Governance of Universities.* [7] However, such survey accounts of institutional malfunction are clearly not enough to understand deep, chronic dysfunction in universities; hence, this inquiry.

This book grapples with a simple but elusive question: what explains the persistent instability of a subset of universities in South Africa? The question has intellectual significance in that there are no major empirical studies of institutional dysfunction in higher education beyond single cases. It has social significance because the resolution of this problem has major implications for the roles of universities, especially in poor and rural underdeveloped communities. And it has practical significance for those who govern and manage these institutions, often under dismal conditions and, as we shall see, sometimes at risk to their reputations and lives.

The study also has personal significance. As someone who has been a professor, department chair, dean (twice), (acting) deputy vice-chancellor, vice-chancellor and administrator (twice), I have long been dismayed and intrigued by my direct experiences of recurring upheaval in some of the universities where I worked. I have been dismayed because of the high costs of institutional instability for staff and students, as well as for the disadvantaged communities surrounding the campus. I have also been intrigued because, in searching through the voluminous literature on higher education, I have yet to find layered empirical work or breakthrough theoretical insights that offer satisfactory explanations for institutional dysfunction. Having worked in highly functional former white universities as well as highly dysfunctional black universities, I could see first-hand how institutional inequalities were deepened by chronic instability in the less well-endowed institutions.

BEYOND BEWITCHMENT: EXPLAINING DYSFUNCTION

Since the end of apartheid in 1994, there have been no fewer than twenty government interventions that led to administrators or interim vice-chancellors taking over the governance or management functions of troubled universities. These include a presidential commission of inquiry at one university, a ministerial task team at another, and more than a few informal interventions by government to turn around failing universities.

The visible signs of persistent dysfunction are familiar to those inside and outside such universities: never-ending stakeholder conflicts, student protests, disruption of operations, violent confrontations, burning buildings, police presence, student arrests, campus closures and so on. The consequences are serious: teaching time is lost; funders withdraw; research is sidelined; leading academics depart; top students go elsewhere; staff morale drops; accreditation agencies threaten repercussions; government intervenes.

What underpins the very public manifestations of conflict and confrontation which lead to seemingly endless patterns of disruption and dysfunction from one academic year to the next? To simply dismiss ongoing dysfunction in universities as the result of a culture of violence or endemic corruption offers little insight into its root causes; that is, a radical explanation. Nor would any serious analyst accept an observed crisis as its own explanation.

No doubt, some of the deeper explanations for chronic dysfunction reside in the origins and histories of these institutions and their evolution over time. Consider, at one end, the rural black universities of the former bantustans, geographically isolated from the major urban industrial centres of the country. A history of deprivation, financial and intellectual, must contribute something to our understanding of chronic dysfunction there. Contrast, at the other end, the urban white English-speaking universities with their relative material advantage, organisational capacity and intimate colonial roots founded on the values of universities in the mother country. There is, undoubtedly, a 'present past' that is reflected in distinctions today between functional and dysfunctional universities.

Yet, to read the contrasting fortunes of universities in the present as a simple case of historical whiplash would count as sloppy social science. Institutions, after all, are not merely a reflex of history. They are also made and remade in the context of their times to produce particular social and academic outcomes.[8] There are real people in these universities, with real power to influence institutional fates and fortunes. Agency matters, even if under conditions not of its own making, to paraphrase Karl Marx.[9]

The ubiquitous 'lists of demands' that accompany protests of workers or students or other 'stakeholders' on campus may also offer some explanations for abiding crises. What do those lists say, for example, about the subjective meanings of the university for students, compared to the exalted mission and vision statements of higher education leaders? What does the appellation 'world-class university' mean when material want dominates the daily discourses of lament? Where material needs frame the almost daily demands on 'management', certain understandings of the university emerge among campus citizens. Indeed, I often heard in the course of this study a description of the university as an all-encompassing welfare station for students – or merely another 'Sassa distribution agency' (a reference to the South African Social Security Agency, which delivers welfare grants to poor citizens).

There are those who insist that the explanation resides in the lack of institutional capacity among the historically disadvantaged institutions. If only there was more capacity for governing complex institutions such as universities, or greater capacity for managing these billion-rand enterprises, then many of the problems of dysfunction would disappear. At first glance, it does appear that capacity is a problem in struggling institutions. For example, when millions of rands became available for a landmark expansion of campus infrastructures, little was spent because of the lack of capacity to manage such large amounts of state funds (see chapter 9). It was thought better to leave the money untouched than to risk becoming the subject of auditor reviews or worse. But is capacity really the whole explanation when some universities are found to be looting institutional resources on an industrial scale? In other words, is the problem of dysfunction one of capacity or of integrity?

Those who seek explanations for dysfunction through the lens of institutional integrity make a values argument. Strong, functional institutions are held together by a set of core values to which those who work and study there subscribe. For universities, the academic project lies at the centre of their commitment to values. Every governance action or management directive has in mind the core functions of teaching, learning, research and civic engagement. When critical decisions must be made, there is a foundational question that frames that moment: what is in the best interests of the university? When major disruptions to the university inevitably happen, it is this sense of shared values about the academic project that binds campus citizens together. Such an institution has integrity which is expressed in the everyday routines of university operations and which becomes even more visible when the academic enterprise is under threat. Dysfunctional universities seem to lack this asset called institutional integrity (see chapter 9).

Apartheid, as a point of reference, can be employed to explain away almost any kind of dysfunction, even three decades into South Africa's constitutional democracy. The burden of the past certainly rests heavily on the institutional contortions of the present. Yet there are historically disadvantaged institutions that have dealt the hand of history a lusty blow. The University of the Western Cape (UWC), for example, is now a highly rated institution of higher education in South Africa. Of course, it is an urban institution, which suggests relative advantage; but then there is also the University of Venda in the rural north of South Africa, which has made significant strides since a major turnaround led by a transformative outside vice-chancellor.[10] Similar advances are being made at the University of Limpopo, which at one stage was bankrupt and now boasts substantial revenues in its current account. Thus, the heavy hand of history cannot be the only explanation for dysfunction.

There must be some cogent explanation for persistent dysfunction that lies beyond the explanations generally proffered. In digging deep into the micropolitics of unstable universities, it became clear that there was one common thread running through all of them: the ruthless competition for scarce resources. For this reason, the present book offers an account of chronic corruption rooted in a political economy framework as an explanation for institutional dysfunction (see chapter 3).

KEY CONCEPTS IN THE STUDY

What is a dysfunctional university? For the purposes of this book, a dysfunctional university is defined as one in which there is a routine breakdown in one or more of the governance, management or administrative functions of the institution, such that it cannot perform even its most basic academic and operational responsibilities. This conception could be regarded as the threshold for classifying an institution as dysfunctional in this study. 'Routine breakdown' implies that such collapse is not a one-off event, like the occasional breakdown in the IT operations of a university, but happens on a regular basis.

The governance function refers to the council of the university, its highest decision-making body. Dysfunction in the governance arrangement is found in some of the following ways: the council is deeply divided into factions, so that almost every major decision is split among warring elements; the council is seldom quorate, sometimes by design, so as to give one faction an advantage over another; the council administration is chaotic, with scheduled and unscheduled meetings running for hours and sometimes days at a time, with inadequate documentation and last-minute changes in the agenda; and the council chairperson is at war with the vice-chancellor or with the management team as a whole.

The management function refers to the executive arm of the institution, including the vice-chancellor and the senior team responsible for managing the university in accordance with the policies approved by council. Dysfunction in the management function is evident when there is constant in-fighting among members of the senior executive team; budgets are not honoured; accounts are overdrawn; there is no effective internal audit function or, where it exists, there are a high number of irregularities reported but not resolved in successive auditing cycles; nepotism is rife; and there are never-ending conflictual relationships between management and stakeholders, such as trade unions or students.

The administrative function refers to the core administration tasks of a university, such as the management of meetings, the registration and graduation of students, the processes for the appointment, selection and promotion of staff and so on. Dysfunction becomes visible in a university when the basic documentation for meetings is routinely late, disorganised or inaccurate; the registration of students is chaotic, postponed or incomplete; systems that govern student applications and admissions are defective (for example, online sites crash regularly); and there is always a discrepancy between the record of students who qualify to graduate and that of those who show up for graduation.

Dysfunctional institutions are also described in this book as chronically unstable universities. This term describes the constant state of unsteadiness or unpredictability in the operations of a university. The most common manifestation of instability is the frequent closure of campuses due to disruptive protests. On routinely dysfunctional campuses, such protests often turn violent, thereby threatening property and lives. In response, the university repeatedly shuts down and reopens in seemingly interminable cycles of disruption. The loss of critical teaching time is a direct consequence of being a chronically unstable university, and this has direct consequences for the institution's reputation and the credibility of its degrees.

As regards instability, it is important to underline that this research distinguishes between chronic events and sporadic events in the assessment of dysfunction. The historic student protests of 2015–2016 affected most of the established research-intensive universities, such as the University of Cape Town (UCT) and the University of the Witwatersrand (Wits). This led to protracted interruptions and closures; but these were sporadic events, part and parcel of the protest movements on campuses throughout the world that are normally focused on one big issue at a time, such as the campaign for decolonisation in universities worldwide.[11] Sporadic events such as these may be impactful, but they are infrequent in the life cycles of the more established universities and attract much more public and media attention precisely because they are rare as major, disruptive events.

Chronic events, on the other hand, are defined as routine, persistent protests, disruptions and closures that happen in every academic year, and often more than once in a year, for a range of reasons that are often related to recurring material concerns of poorer students, such as fees, food and accommodation. It is because disruptions are so routine that they have become 'normalised' in the public mind and only gain national attention with a dramatic incident, as when a student tragically dies during a protest.

Institutional dysfunction is explained in this book in relation to two additional concepts: capacity and integrity. Capacity refers to the ability of a university to deliver on its core duties. However, capacity is problematised in this study to mean more than 'filling up' the lack of ability to deliver, for example, through training and development. The lack of capacity, as will be demonstrated, is also a learned incapacity; this means a deliberate incapacitation of the governance, management and administrative systems in order to enable corruption – a central focus of the book (see chapter 9).

Integrity, on the other hand, refers to the internal value system that holds an institution like a university together. The sense of coherence and shared purpose comes about through a binding commitment to the same core values, such as the centrality of the academic project in the life of the university. In the dysfunctional institutions included in this study, the focus on shared academic values is displaced by a preoccupation with the university as a resource for the benefit of corrupt individuals or syndicates. In such cases, institutional integrity is breached, and the university is vulnerable to predatory elements (see chapter 9).

To understand dysfunctionality, it is important to start with a concept of functionality in higher education institutions. A former vice-chancellor of one of South Africa's premier institutions, who was appointed to assess the University of Fort Hare (UFH), developed a concept of functionality in his report that underlined the interdependence between governance, management and administration:

> In order for a university to run smoothly as an academic organisation, a number of very basic, quite rudimentary administrative processes must be in place and functioning. Records must be kept. Policies and procedures must be in place. Data must be gathered. Reports must be produced. Resolutions must be tracked. Information systems must provide usable and reliable information.

Maintenance must be done. Health and safety regulations must be adhered to. Facilities for persons living with a disability must be created and maintained. In all these respects, operations at UFH are weak. A report by Ernst & Young rates the maturity level of both governance and finance at UFH as 'rudimentary' – the lowest of five possible ratings. Such administrative weakness has a knock-on effect in terms of management and governance.[12]

Compare this with the actual conditions prevailing at another dysfunctional university in the words of its vice-chancellor at the time:

How can we tell the world that we are doing well when we find it difficult to perform the simple professional act of acknowledging receipt of business letters; when it takes months to fill a vacant post; when we make decisions that we do not implement; when our campus protection service sits back and watches millions of rands' worth of goods being stolen from us? When staff in the kitchen fight over carcasses of meat; when pay day is a holiday; when a large number of teaching staff go home at midday; when some students think that to be radical is to be rude; when the failure rate is so high that some 3 500 students have to sit supplementary examinations; when the research and publishing rate is the lowest in the country; when some of us expect to earn higher salaries for low productivity.[13]

Some would argue that these two cases represent a narrow, technical view of dysfunctionality, focused on the maintenance of order and function. As the critical theorist André Keet argues, a broader conception of functionality would include 'the idea of institutional conservatism or racism in the formulation of dysfunction'.[14] The well-established, former white universities in South Africa could well be described as highly functional, by the definition pursued in this book, but they may have normalised other dysfunctions – such as feeding off predatory journals in their subsidy income (see chapter 6) – while still maintaining organisational stabilities in respect of governance, management and administration.

Conscious of these broader conceptions of functionality and dysfunctionality pursued elsewhere,[15] this work nevertheless focuses mainly on stable or unstable organisational forms and functions, because this kind of detailed empirical work has not yet been done on universities generally or on post-apartheid higher education institutions in particular.

A final concept central to the book is the micropolitics of universities. Micropolitics refers to the everyday uses of power within universities for achieving particular goals. With the focus on the micropolitics of corruption in universities, the goal is to capture in fine-grained detail the uses of power by individuals or groups to achieve corrupt ends. The book provides detailed accounts of the patterns and processes of corruption at the micropolitical level of universities to demonstrate how dysfunction comes about, how it is sustained in the everyday life of institutions, and why it is so difficult to disrupt (see chapter 8).

THE MACROPOLITICS OF THE MICROPOLITICS OF INSTITUTIONS

An understandable concern of the social scientist is that the intense focus on the micropolitics of universities should not be read in isolation from the broader macropolitics of the society that shapes institutional behaviour. In other words, there are social, economic and political contexts outside universities that play a critical role in influencing what happens inside them.

I agree. Macropolitical factors shape and influence the micropolitics of what happens inside institutions. Several examples would support this position in the context of South Africa's post-apartheid universities. For one, the economic policies of the first democratic government, especially the neoliberal programme called Growth, Equity and Redistribution (Gear), had the simple, practical consequence that there would be no significant financial redress in favour of the historically disadvantaged institutions (HDIs), which might, in theory, have brought them up to par with the former white universities. The broad policy of reconciliation imprinted on the world's newest democracy by its icon, Nelson Mandela, also meant that there was no radical redistribution of land, property or institutional resources from white to black hands. This kind of reconciliatory approach naturally applied to universities as well, in that none of the accumulated reserves and resources of the advantaged universities were transferred to their disadvantaged counterparts – even a one-off corrective allocation was off the table (see chapter 10).

Nor can one discount the class interests of the new elites that came to power in the post-apartheid government. As this research reveals, conflicts and tensions arose inside the new bureaucracy, not only with the remnants of the old order who stayed on in the Government of National Unity, but also between progressives in the Department of Education (the bureaucracy) and their comrades in the ministry of education (the political office). The non-redistributionists won, and there was no mass bailout of black universities, let alone redress funding to fundamentally reconfigure the prospects of disadvantaged institutions (see chapter 10).

Needless to say, the powerful Bretton Woods institutions, the World Bank and the International Monetary Fund, had warned the newly emergent South African government against radical redistribution of any kind and threatened repercussions if there were any such tendencies. 'We were captured before there was state capture,'[16] remarked an adviser to Nelson Mandela of those times.

In short, the macropolitical conditions in the state clearly set limits on the possibilities for a radical restructuring of higher education. In this regard, the positions taken in this book align with those of the more critical social science scholars of institutions. Accordingly, the analysis pursued in this research recognises the interplay between the macropolitics of society and the micropolitics of dysfunction that results from corruption in the sampled universities.

However, the book departs from the radical social science critique of the micropolitics of universities in that it does not allow the macropolitical to overdetermine what happens inside universities. Put differently, universities as institutions are not cold, unthinking machines whose functioning reacts mechanically to the switch of social, economic and political conditions in the broader society. To be sure, those macropolitical forces set the terms and map the terrain on which institutional behaviour unfolds. Yet, as will be shown, there is ample space within the authority of institutions to recreate themselves despite the legacy of apartheid history and the vicissitudes of government policy in the democratic era. To simply insist, without further reflection, that disadvantaged universities are victims of resource deprivation from the past, aggravated by neoliberal choices in the present, is far too deterministic an account of history and policy.

The analytical task is thus to determine what it is that institutions actually do under conditions in which some, undoubtedly, become or remain dysfunctional, while others make use of their agency to create different institutional futures. This is a potentially productive learning space, where macropolitics and micropolitics intersect, and it may yield new insights into institutional behaviour after apartheid.

METHODS

This 'deep dive' into the study of chronically unstable universities has the simple goal of explaining persistent dysfunctionality within these institutions. To this end, I conducted more than a hundred interviews with some of the most senior people involved in, and knowledgeable about, South African universities. These included assessors and administrators; chairs and members of university councils; subcommittees of councils; chairs and members of university senates; higher education researchers and evaluators; university management consultants; institutional forum leaders; university training and development specialists; ministerial advisers; international consultants; vice-chancellors and deputy vice-chancellors; higher education policymakers and planners in government; managers in accreditation agencies; leaders in science councils;

experienced journalists who report on higher education; and senior academics in various universities.

Each of the interviews was transcribed for purposes of a three-pronged analysis. First, what were the signal (that is, exceptional or unusual) issues raised in the interview (for instance, the way taxi operators see a public university)? Second, what thematic concerns recurred in the interviews (for instance, the way multimillion-rand infrastructure grants triggered widespread corruption)? And, third, what comparative insights emerged (for instance, different viewpoints among respondents about the efficacy of institutional forums)?

The specific form of the data-gathering method employed can be described as peer conversational interviews (PCIs). The PCI has three features that distinguish it from standardised interviews. First, by virtue of context, the interviewer and the respondent are both experts in the area of inquiry, whether by training or experience or both, and this sets the terms and boundaries of the conversation. Second, in relation to content, the questions are intended to be evocative: both the interviewer and the respondent are drawn into a conversation which brings up issues that might not have been raised in a straightforward question-and-answer format. Third, in terms of construction or design, the format is interactive, allowing the interviewer and respondent to engage in a two-way conversation, even as the interviewer presses the respondent for information on the topic under discussion.

In addition to the interviews, I conducted a close reading and analysis of the 17 assessor reports on troubled universities produced between 1996 and 2021 (see Appendix A.1, A.2); ministerial reports on other universities; and 'non-assessor-type' interventions, from accounts of the elusive 1996 report of the Gautschi Commission[17] on the University of Durban-Westville to the 2021 *Report of the Ministerial Task Team to Conduct an Independent Review of the University of South Africa.*[18]

As an additional source of documentation, I led an analysis of the audit reports for all universities conducted by the Higher Education Quality Committee (HEQC) of the chief accrediting agency, the Council on Higher Education, between 2000 and 2012. The HEQC has a statutory duty to conduct what are called institutional audits according to criteria that include the 'fitness-for-purpose' of the institutional mission, the quality of the assessment system, the adequacy of staffing, and the links between planning and resources.

The remaining documentation examined included media reports; foundation reports (for instance, the Helen Suzman Foundation ran a series of commentaries on each investigated institution);[19] council and management reports (where available to the public); annual reports of universities; court documents (where the ministerial intervention, in process or content, was challenged in court); and any other public records that shed further light on the problem of dysfunction.

Both interviewees and institutions are represented anonymously, except in cases where persons or universities are already identified in the assessor reports, which are public documents published in government gazettes, or in cases when names have appeared in the media.

HOW TO NAVIGATE THE BOOK

Chapter 1 has outlined the basic thesis of the book, the intellectual justification for the inquiry, its perspectival approach to the subject, and the methods deployed in making the evidentiary case for a deeper understanding of chronic dysfunctionality in universities.

Chapter 2 gives a brief historical and organisational account of South African universities since their origins in the colonial period,[20] and the ways in which the racialised lives of the different institutions cast a long shadow in the present.

Chapter 3 gives a detailed presentation of the conceptual framework deployed in this study. It argues for viewing dysfunction through the perspective of political economy, defined simply as the relationship between power and resources. Resources are not only material (like money) but also symbolic (like certificates), political (for instance, party politics), and cultural (including values) – all assets that can make or break institutions. When universities are perceived primarily as a concentration of resources that must accessed by all means possible, then the dark side of political economy manifests itself in staggering levels of corruption. To understand the workings of political economy, I start with the micropolitics of everyday life in institutions and then work outwards to demonstrate how this is conditioned by the macropolitics of the broader society.

Chapter 4 introduces a personal account of political economy into the narrative of institutional dysfunction, drawing on my own experiences working inside broken universities. The idea is to give the mainstream (often plodding) structural accounts of political economy a more human face by revealing encounters with real people whose lives were ruined when the complex of power and resources was unleashed on their bodies – sometimes literally. This biographical account of political economy illuminates the more personal and painful renditions of its operations in ways not always elicitable from respondents.

Chapter 5 places the conflict and contestation that plague dysfunctional institutions in historical context. How did unstable institutions become this way? The roots of instability lie in the very origins of these universities as white-determined and white-controlled institutions, whether it be the University of South Africa in its colonial founding in 1873, or Fort Hare in its missionary-inspired beginnings in 1916, or the high-apartheid creations of the 'bush colleges' in the late 1950s. The chapter illustrates how legitimate anti-apartheid resistance shaded unproblematically into anti-institutional hostilities in the democratic period; indeed, a line of unbroken resistance in the most vulnerable universities continues to this day. Nowhere is this more evident than in student and trade union politics; in this regard, the chapter traces the de-fanging of institutional forums in South Africa's flat stakeholder model of politics, and its consequences for universities.

Chapter 6 presents in considerable detail the ways in which universities stand out as powerful, concentrated resource centres in all communities, especially in the impoverished areas where most of the dysfunctional institutions are located. It unpacks one of the few systematic studies of the economic impacts of a university on its surrounding community, in this case Stellenbosch University. Then, using recent data, the chapter details the role of a public university as a resource accumulator through three revenue streams (government subsidy, student fees and private income) and a resource distributor through its impact on the local economy (by such means as procurement and employment). This sets the stage for an analysis of four highly exploitable resources in a university: financial aid, council remuneration, research funding, and the student residence market.

Chapter 7 lifts the lid on the criminality that marks everyday life in dysfunctional institutions. Murders, beatings and stabbings, on the one hand; surveillance, humiliation and dismissals, on the other. Within the university, the chapter narrates the actions of two rogue vice-chancellors alongside that of a rogue chair of council to give a sense of the depth of criminal activities in the selected universities and the ways in which the power–resources complex sustains such dysfunction. Outside the university, the chapter also shows how the taxi industry (providing student transportation) and municipal council members came to claim a stake in the resources of several broken universities. The chapter is therefore able to demonstrate how the academic project becomes marginalised in dysfunctional universities as the criminalisation of institutions takes centre stage in the business of higher education.

Chapter 8 begins to synthesise the analytical accounts of corruption into categorical descriptions of how dysfunctionality happens and how it is sustained. It identifies twelve specific micropolitical strategies through which power is exercised within institutional life. These include the use of the disciplinary function; the uses of rumour and gossip; tripping-up tactics; the promise of rewards; the politics of the proxy function; and the outright threat of violence. The power of such strategies lies not in the individual instruments but in their collective impact on the psyches and behaviour of staff and students, thereby keeping everyone in their institutional place. As in the criminal world outside universities, the repercussions for those who dare to call out corruption are intended both to discipline the whistleblower and as a warning to everyone else.

Chapter 9 draws together evidence presented in the previous chapters to pin down two particularly powerful concepts on which hinges the explanation for chronic dysfunction in South African universities. 'Capacity' is the organisational ability to get things done effectively and efficiently, whether in campus operations (for instance, finance and IT) or the delivery of academic programmes. 'Integrity' is the commitment to a binding set of shared values (such as honesty and transparency) that steers the organisation and to which there are significant levels of 'buy-in' from those inside. When capacity is low and integrity is weak, the result is dysfunctionality. The chapter shows how these two vital concepts are related, and how learned incapacity stands in the way of the simplistic view of capacity building as 'filling up' what is missing in an organisation's ability to do things right.

Chapter 10 draws together the different threads of the study in order to answer the vital question: how can dysfunction be disrupted in chronically dysfunctional universities? The chapter starts by laying out the deeper reasons for dysfunction, including the emergence of informal institutional rules; institutional dissociation on the part of staff and students; and the politicisation of the everyday in university life. It then argues that durable change requires – more than short-term government interventions – a focus on changing the rules of the game that sustain institutional dysfunctionality. The book concludes with a critical assessment of the value and limits of political economy for explaining ongoing dysfunction in South African universities.

2

Historical Roots of Dysfunction: Shaping the South African University

The first South African university was the University of the Cape of Good Hope, which was established by an Act of Parliament of the Cape Colony in 1873. It was not a teaching university, but set standards and examinations for what were known in those early years as 'university colleges'. It was renamed the University of South Africa in 1916, relocated from the Cape to Pretoria in 1918, and only started to offer 'postal tuition' about three decades later, in 1946.[1]

The South African College, established in 1829, was a high school for boys, but it contained within it a small tertiary education component, which developed into a fully fledged institution, the University of Cape Town (UCT), in 1918. The Victoria College, so named in 1887, also developed out of smaller constituent parts, including an arts department, and became the University of Stellenbosch (now Stellenbosch University [SU]) in 1918. It was not, in fact, uncommon in those times for ordinary schools to have 'university college departments' as part of their facilities.[2]

Apart from the two former colleges that became independent teaching universities (UCT and SU), the rest were organised as a 'federation of colleges' under the aegis of the University of South Africa (Unisa). These included Natal University College in Pietermaritzburg, founded in 1910; Grey University College in Bloemfontein, founded in 1906; Transvaal University College in Pretoria, founded in 1910; Rhodes University College in Grahamstown, founded in 1904; the School of Mines and Technology in Johannesburg, founded in 1910; and the Potchefstroom University College for Christian Higher Education, founded in 1919.[3]

These affiliate colleges of Unisa would in time gain independent university status – as the University of Natal in 1949; the University of the Orange Free State in 1950; the University of Pretoria in 1930; Rhodes University in 1951; the University of the Witwatersrand in 1922; and Potchefstroom University for Christian Higher Education in 1951. All of these were racially segregated white universities.

The first black institution of higher learning was the South African Native College, founded in 1916, which became the University College of Fort Hare in 1951, and the University of Fort Hare in 1970. Unlike the white colleges, this 'Native College' was not a constituent college of Unisa, but it did prepare its students for Unisa's external examinations. It was also a university that, since its inception, enrolled some white students and appointed black academic staff, despite its 'native' designation. (It was very rare for black universities at their point of origin to hire black academics.) And from its renaming as a university college in 1951, it was – with undisguised racial paternalism – affiliated to Rhodes University for the purpose of setting common academic standards; students of the two institutions wrote the same examinations.[4]

With the rise of Afrikaner nationalism in the mid-twentieth century, new Afrikaans universities were established with strategic political intent. One of these was the Rand Afrikaans University, founded in 1966 for urban Afrikaans speakers in Johannesburg, which was meant to be an ideological counterweight to the liberal Wits University across the freeway. Similarly, the bilingual University of Port Elizabeth, founded in

1964, offered a home for white Afrikaans speakers on the east coast as a counterpoint to the liberal Rhodes University further inland.

With the National Party government firmly in the political driver's seat after 1948, higher education was radically disfigured, in accordance with the racial fantasies of the apartheid state. The Extension of University Education Act of 1959 created four new 'university colleges' (also called 'bush universities' or 'tribal colleges' by their critics). These were the University College of the North, founded in 1959 for Sotho, Tsonga, Tswana and Venda ethnic groups; the University College of the Western Cape, founded in 1959 for coloured people; the University College of Zululand, founded in 1960 for Zulu and Swazi ethnic groups; and the University College for Indians, founded in 1961. All of these would eventually become autonomous universities (see Appendix B), disconnected from Unisa as the examining authority.

It was also around this time that the Fort Hare Transfer Act of 1959 placed the University College of Fort Hare under the Department of Bantu Education and required it to serve the Xhosa ethnic group exclusively. Though all black, these five university colleges would be stamped with an 'Afrikaans orientation' and Afrikaner control: in addition to its rectors (vice-chancellors), the 'chairmanship of each college council was given to a professor or rector from one of the Afrikaans-medium universities'.[5]

Extending the government's ideological machinations even further, additional black universities were created within the apartheid 'homelands' for other tribal groupings – with the university name being that of the homeland, except for the older Fort Hare University. These were the University of Transkei, founded in 1977; the University of Bophuthatswana, founded in 1979; the University of Venda, founded in 1982; and the University of Fort Hare (renamed in 1970), for the Ciskei homeland.

Gradually, other black universities were established, such as the Medical University of South Africa (Medunsa), in 1976, and Vista University, in 1981, for urban blacks. Vista had seven city campuses spread throughout the country, along with a head office and distance education centre (Vudec) in Pretoria.

South Africa also had an extensive network of segregated black and white technikons that provided career-oriented technical and vocational education, many of them being much younger than the traditional universities surveyed above. These technikons would, in the democratic (post-1994) era, be transformed into universities of technology, and most of them were 'merged' with traditional universities. How did these mergers change the higher education landscape?

THE SOUTH AFRICAN UNIVERSITY SYSTEM ON THE EVE OF DEMOCRACY

At the point of transition from apartheid to the new democracy in 1994, South Africa had 21 universities (10 'black' and 10 'white') and 15 technikons (7 'black' and 8 'white'). Then came a massive restructuring (if not reculturing) of these 36 higher education entities through what is often still called 'the mergers' of 2002–2005; however, these mergers were, in reality, a mix of actual mergers (between large institutions) and incorporation of smaller institutions into larger ones. The official arguments for the mergers included efficiency (for instance, where two technikons lay across the road from each other and duplicated each other's programmes) and equity (for instance, where unequally resourced black and white universities existed a short drive from one another).

Out of this rescrambling of 36 institutions emerged 23, which in turn consisted of 11 traditional universities, 6 comprehensive universities (with a mix of traditional university and technikon programmes), and 6 universities of technology.[6] Importantly, a few of the more established universities were left largely untouched by the mergers, such as UCT, Wits and Stellenbosch as well as the University of the Western Cape and the Vaal University of Technology. Some of the major mergers involved the creation of a single distance-education institution, with Unisa merging with Technikon South Africa and incorporating Vudec; the universities of

Durban-Westville and Natal joining to form the University of KwaZulu-Natal; and the Rand Afrikaans University and Technikon Witwatersrand combining and also incorporating two campuses of Vista University to form the University of Johannesburg (see Appendix B).

Subsequent to the mergers, three more universities were added to the existing 23 institutions. Medunsa, which was once an independent medical university, merged with the University of the North to form the University of Limpopo (UL), with its main campus in Polokwane, even though the medical campus was situated 260 kilometres away in Pretoria. In 2015, however, the Medunsa campus was 'de-merged' from UL to become part of a brand-new institution, the Sefako Makgatho Health Sciences University. Two additional universities were also established in provinces that previously had none: the Sol Plaatje University in the Northern Cape and the University of Mpumalanga in the province of that name.

In short, while South Africa had 36 universities at the end of apartheid, those were reduced to 23 through the mergers of 2002–2005, and today there are a total of 26 public higher-education institutions. There are also 50 TVET (technical and vocational education and training) colleges completing the post-secondary education landscape, but these lie outside the scope of this study.

What is the significance of this brief history of South African universities for a book on institutional dysfunctionality in the present? First, it highlights the deeply racialised and fragmented histories of South African universities, as reflected in the embedded inequalities between them. Resources built or denied for more than a century have cast long shadows which are visible in simple things like the contrasting physical infrastructure of UCT and the University of Zululand.

Second, it draws attention to the manufactured instabilities engineered by the apartheid regime to keep black universities from a steady development path like that enjoyed by their white counterparts. No institutional case presents such contrived precarity more clearly than that of the University of Fort Hare, which went from offering a 'wider intellectual world'[7] to a liberal, mission-educated elite to becoming a tribal college under the Ciskei's homeland government. What was once a place of higher learning for Africans, coloureds, Indians, some whites and Africans from other countries became little more than an ethnic college serving up an intellectually anaemic curriculum for Xhosa students.[8] The lack of medical schools, engineering faculties and architecture departments in black universities is a direct consequence of discriminatory curriculum emphases from a segregated and unequal past.

Third, it throws light on the European colonial roots of South African universities. Unisa, the founding university, was modelled on the University of London (chartered in 1836), which at that time was also a non-teaching institution that functioned as an examinations board, offering a cheaper and nondenominational alternative to Oxford and Cambridge.[9] In character, culture, staffing and curriculum, the early South African universities bore the imprint of imperial Britain and, in particular, of Scotland.[10] The entrenched academic values and orientations of especially the established English universities continue to reflect those European intellectual and ideological orientations – a legacy that had a direct bearing on the fierceness of the decolonisation protests on those campuses (especially at UCT and Wits) during the 'Fallist' campaigns of 2015–2017.[11]

Fourth, it exposes the shortage of critical histories of universities in South Africa, as the vast majority of existing accounts 'possess a commemorative character … remarkably insular and inward-looking'.[12] It is therefore important for this account of the political economy of universities to dedicate a full chapter to 'how we got here' (see chapter 5). As will be seen, the history of the contested arrangements that birthed and shaped South Africa's universities stretches well into the present – in debilitating ways.

THE BASIC STRUCTURE AND ORGANISATION OF A SOUTH AFRICAN UNIVERSITY

To grasp the nature of dysfunction in South African universities, it will help to understand their basic structure, for therein lies a complex politics embedded in the history of these institutions.

The chancellor is the titular head of a university. His is a largely ceremonial position with the main function of conferring degrees and diplomas at graduation ceremonies. Chancellors are often prominent public figures in government, business or industry whose stellar accomplishments enhance the reputation of the university in the public eye. Contrary to popular opinion, the chancellor has no authority over what happens in a university, although vice-chancellors and chairs of council do sometimes bend the ear of the ceremonial head for wisdom and advice on one or other institutional matter.

The vice-chancellor (VC) is the academic head of the university, though some institutions have opted instead for 'chief executive officer' (CEO), which aligns with a corporate understanding of the business of higher education. The VC has an executive management team of anywhere from two to five deputy vice-chancellors (DVCs), who are also called vice-rectors in the Afrikaans university tradition. Sometimes, the extended title of vice-chancellor and principal (or vice-chancellor and rector) is used to refer to the head of the university.

The council is the highest decision-making body of a university, and is responsible for the governance of the institution. It approves important policies, such as student admissions and language policy; considers and signs off on the annual budget; and approves the fees for tuition and accommodation set every year. The VC and DVCs are senior appointments made directly by the council of the university, and the council delegates to them the execution of its policies.

In South Africa the council is, in effect, a body of stakeholders, even though they are ostensibly not there to represent their constituencies, for 'council members must participate in the deliberations of the council in the best interests of the institution'.[13] The stakeholders typically include the vice-chancellor, deputy vice-chancellors (one or two), senate members, students, ministerial appointees (no more than five), academic employees, non-academic employees, convocation (alumni) members, and members with specific skills and competences. Specific categories of membership within these designations vary from one university to the next, so that some councils include, for example, members of religious organisations, donor representatives or municipal representatives. The registrar serves as the secretary of council, and at least 60 per cent of council members must be external to the university, neither students nor staff.

The senate is the senior academic body of the university, and traditionally consisted of the professors of the various faculties (historically, mainly white men), but with the pressure for transformation, various universities have increased the number of non-professorial senators. The senate approves the academic business of the university, including curricula, professorial appointments, examinations, academic timetables, and the establishment (or disestablishment) of academic units and centres.

The institutional forum is a body that advises council on matters such as senior management appointments, language policy, transformation issues (such as race and gender equity), institutional culture and codes of conduct. Members typically include representatives of various stakeholder groups (like students and trade unions) and of council and senate.

Convocation represents the alumni of the university and elects one or two members to council. The student representative council (SRC) is the body elected by students annually, and two SRC leaders also participate in the council. Every university has at least one union representing academic and administration and support staff. Union representatives are elected to council by way of the academic and non-academic staff membership categories.

What are the potential and actual lines of conflict and disrepair in these structures that are relevant to this inquiry into dysfunctionality in universities? The main sources of tension lie in the breaching of the line between governance (the role of council) and management (that of the executive); the merely advisory role of the institutional forum; the potential for senate, as an academic body, to be marginalised from the operations and resources of a university; the organisation of student representation around external party-political affiliations; and the election of members to council by way of various stakeholder categories, whether or not they have the skills, experience and competence to be effective. As will be shown, in dysfunctional universities, these multiple pathways onto council are also potential avenues for bringing corrupt and destructive elements onto the governing body of a university.

As indicated in the discussion above on methods, assessors' reports provide raw detail of the operation of dysfunction with universities, but they are constrained both by the lack of organisational expertise on the part of the interveners and the brevity of their engagement. At the same time, the depth of dysfunction in many institutions has meant that even the energetic engagement of an administrator was not able to resolve complex and long-standing institutional problems within two years. Hence, the need for this study as a 'deep dive' into the reasons for chronic dysfunction beyond the surface features of the more obvious problems in evidence at the sampled universities.

3

Dysfunctionality in Universities: A Political Economy Perspective

In its simplest form, political economy can be described as the relationship between power and resources. More extensive reflections on the subject define it as 'the study of the social relations, particularly the *power* relations, that mutually constitute the production, distribution, and consumption of *resources*'.[1] Yet another authority places emphasis on the processes that constitute political economy: 'all the activities of cooperation, conflict and negotiation involved in decisions about the use, production and distribution of resources'.[2]

With these framing ideas in mind, this work applies a political economy perspective to investigate the micropolitics of a particular institution, the university. It examines not only the relationship between power and resources, but how that interaction contributes to chronically dysfunctional institutions. However, in the course of this study, existing conceptions of political economy were found to be somewhat too restrictive for the study of universities in highly contested environments in developing countries like South Africa.

A review of standard texts on the subject typically takes the reader on an intellectual tour of the major traditions, starting with the classical political economy of Adam Smith and David Ricardo, and including the Marxian political economy first developed by Karl Marx and Friedrich Engels. Between and beyond these two well-established traditions, there are variations, critiques and departures, including feminist political economy,[3] environmental political economy,[4] and moral political economy.[5] In these readings, and their rebuttals, the state and markets feature prominently as the focus of analysis. There is seldom any attention paid to school education as the subject of political economy outside the interests of government funding agencies.[6] One exception is the landmark study of Samuel Bowles and Herbert Gintis, *Schooling in Capitalist America*,[7] which remains a classic reference point for students of the political economy of education.

On the other hand, the term 'political economy of higher education' is often loosely applied to externalities such as the global knowledge economy or the financing of higher education.[8] But there are few studies that turn political economy inwards, to the study of the nexus between power and resources inside higher education institutions. By applying a political economy analysis to dysfunctional universities, therefore, this book expands the perspective to a specific kind of institution (the university) by undertaking an in-depth examination of the interplay between power and resources.

In brief, political economy is employed here as a perspective, a way of seeing things, that brings into clearer focus the relationship between power and resources. Accordingly, a political economy approach to the analysis of institutions in general starts with questions like: Who produces the resources? Where do they come from? Who owns them? Who lays claim to them? How is access to resources formally and officially adjudicated; in other words, what are the institutional rules that govern access to resources? And, finally, what institutional consequences result from the scramble for resources?

THE MICROPOLITICS OF POWER AND RESOURCES INSIDE UNIVERSITIES

Deep inside the daily operations of a university, there is a constant struggle for access to and control over finite resources. It is a struggle largely invisible to the outside observer, because it plays out within the routines of institutional processes such as the deliberations of tender committees or the registration of new students or the approval of staff travel. These are regularities in university life that proceed like clockwork from one day to the next, mostly within the formal rules of the institution. What is less visible is the constant internal struggle to influence the allocation and distribution of such resources in favour of some groups or individuals, outside or despite the institutional rules. Also less evident are the powerful informal rules that govern resource decisions (see chapter 10).

With a starting focus on the micro-institutional level, political economy can be understood as a framework that draws attention to the rules, norms and values that govern and guide people's choices and actions.[9] Such an approach allows us to understand human behaviour close-up, through the study of 'the rules of the game', both formal and informal, governing decision-making to do with resources in universities. A political economy analysis therefore gives insight into 'the underlying reasons why things work the way they do' inside institutions.[10]

What are some of the foundational questions that a political economist would ask of the workings of power and resources in universities in particular? Who are the power-brokers in a modern university and how are they organised? What interests and motivations drive the claims on university resources? How do the power dynamics around resources play out among various stakeholders, such as unions, students, staff, management and councils? What contestations for resources occur, both inside and outside meetings? In what myriad ways are university resources accessed outside the rules?

Further, how are the exclusive claims on resources made and justified by influential groups in universities? Who are the 'good guys' when it comes to protecting university resources; when do they win or lose, and why? Why, how and when are institutional rules governing resources – such as procurement policies – invoked, ignored, amended or resisted outright? What is the role of authority figures (such as chairs of council and vice-chancellors) in prohibiting or enabling the irregular use and distribution of university resources? What are the formal and, especially, the informal rules by which access to resources is facilitated and sustained by competing groups on campuses? And, most importantly, what maintains 'the way things are done' when it comes to the use and abuse of university resources?

THE DARK SIDE OF POLITICAL ECONOMY

Simply to dismiss wrongdoing in dysfunctional universities as corruption is to miss the opportunity to understand root causes and, therefore, durable solutions. It is the task of the scholar to understand 'how people get what they want even when others do not want them to get it'.[11] Or, in Harold Lasswell's classical formulation of the science of politics, the task is to determine 'who gets what, when, and how'.[12]

There is, to be sure, a burgeoning literature on corruption in higher education across the world,[13] but what is often lacking in this research is fine-tuned empirical work that documents in detail how the abuse of resources happens, and provides coherent explanations of how corrupt behaviour is sustained within a political economy approach to institutions.

There is certainly no shortage of corruption in universities worldwide. The kinds of corruption documented include degree fraud, plagiarism, cheating, predatory publication, nepotism, admissions bribery, financial diversions, conflicts of interests, academic dishonesty and embezzlement.[14] These can be viewed as examples of the dark side of political economy, a world in which power and resources are harmfully entangled.

Consider, by way of illustration, three cases easily recognisable from the media: the celebrity parent who uses her influence to buy a place for her daughter at an elite university; the staff member in administration who uses his position of influence to sell fake certificates to 'students' who graduate without having spent a day in classes; and the councillor who sits on university tender committees to ensure that the successful bid for student transportation services goes to his business partner outside the institution.

In each of these cases, the link between power (influence, authority, position) and resources (status, certification, money) is clear. Power, in these examples, is not simply raw political power, but also social, economic or positional power that can be wielded to influence a particular outcome. It follows, therefore, that resources are not simply material but also symbolic: consider, for example, status enhancement as the result of an unfair or illegal intervention by someone with power. In other words, the cases illuminate connections between power and resources that lend themselves to a political economy analysis.

What does political economy therefore look like in the shadows of institutional life? When one examines the micropolitics of institutional corruption close-up, it becomes clear that these are not simply individual acts by wayward academics or incompetent clerical staff, but rather vital elements of a culture, a way of doing things in universities where corruption has become the norm. Put differently, in such contexts corruption cannot be dismissed as exceptional instances of wrongdoing, but is embedded within the fabric of institutional life. In our sample of universities discussed in this book, everyday corruption is routinely performed in academic and administrative departments, as well as in the governance and management functions of the institutions. Who in authority at universities benefits from the everyday nature of corruption is the substance of a political economy analysis.

Such an approach to political economy is therefore a departure from its uses in mainstream positions on the subject. 'Political economy' often appears as a signifying tag or title in an article or book on higher education without any attempt to fully exploit its analytical power. This perspective is more often used, as suggested earlier, in relation to the broader social, economic and political conditions that impact on higher education, such as changes in technology and new knowledge economies.[15] From the left, political economy is invoked to signal a critical perspective on mainstream economics, for instance, a Marxian view of society; such work tends to be largely theoretical and normative in its claims about what is wrong and what should be in society and its institutions.

The approach taken in this book, however, turns the light of a political economy analysis inwards on the daily operations of universities as institutions, with a particular focus not on what should be (normatively) but on what actually happens (empirically) in ongoing contests among powerful groups for access to valued resources.

THE MACROPOLITICAL ECONOMY THAT OVERSHADOWS THE MICROPOLITICS OF INSTITUTIONS

None of this means that institutional corruption can be isolated from an analysis of the broader social, economic and political context. Our application of political economy in the South African context acknowledges that corruption is generalisable across institutions. In fact, it is impossible to understand corruption inside universities without understanding corruption outside them.

The members of council, the highest governing body of a university, come, for example, from municipalities where they are managers; from cities where they are mayors; from companies in which they are business dealers; from political parties where they might be officials; and from self-owned businesses dependent on income from public institutions. When those entities or their leaders who serve on university councils are themselves corrupt or corruptible, they bring into the institution values and behaviours that further contaminate the higher education environment. In this way, there exists a symbiotic relationship between corruption on and off campus which embeds the culture of wrongdoing in institutional life.[16]

This means that the connections between power/influences and resources/assets are tightly coupled across institutions, from inside the university to local government and small business ventures outside it.

At some point, those couplings of agencies become consolidated and even subject to role reversal, as in the extraordinary case where one South African university runs the sewerage system on behalf of the impoverished town in which it is located.

This example raises important ethical questions for political economy in contexts of underdevelopment. How does one make sense of ostensibly corrupt behaviours in deeply unequal societies? More pertinently, how should one understand the claims on resources in communities where a well-resourced university exists within eyeshot of the tin shacks where students and workers live? In these contexts, common to South Africa's rural universities or peri-urban campuses, the university stands out like a sore thumb amid abject poverty.

Invariably, the university in such a community is the primary employer. In this context, a very important perceptual change takes place in which the university is seen as the one resource that can alleviate poverty where there is, quite literally, nothing else. For poor students – a fast-growing constituency especially in rural institutions – the university is a place of residence, accommodation, stipendiary income and food security. For poor workers, often the majority of staff, the university is an employer and little else. In such conditions, the university becomes a perennial site for contesting low wages (by workers) or for demanding more funding (by students), or both at the same time, when alliances between workers and students form to strengthen each other's causes.

When students therefore press for more resources, typically through student representative councils, that is often a reasonable demand from the poor. When staff agitate for higher wages, often through their unions, that too is an understandable claim on public resources. If all political demands for more resources were as simple as that, the political economy approach could make its case comfortably by means of, for example, (neo-) Marxian theories about the exploitation of labour or the underdevelopment of society.

It is, however, not only the poor who demand resources within universities. There are also powerful people and groups within institutions who use their influence not only to demand more funds but also to extract vital resources for their own benefit. Ethical questions thus become complex in cases where it is difficult to distinguish the legitimate concerns of the poor from the corrupt behaviours of well-placed institutional actors. This book presents rich case studies of such blurring of the lines between legitimate and illegitimate or illegal attempts by influential actors to extract resources from institutions.

But cultures of corruption are not simply embedded within a university and its surrounding community. They often stretch much further, into the national government itself. When there are waves of corruption within the state, those tendencies filter down to all institutions, including public universities. Indeed, in a short period of time, state capture in politics found its match in the institutional capture of South Africa's largest university.[17]

A corrupt government sends a signal that corruption is tolerated, that the powerful can evade accountability, and that wrongdoing can be explained away. Historical suffering casts a mist over what should be moral clarity about corruption within universities – this is what the literature calls rational-choice corruption.[18]

The nested nature of corruption is standard fare in analyses of political economy. Yet this perspective can be held and at the same time strengthened by fine-grained empirical studies of how the political economy of corruption plays out within institutions. Put differently, the ways in which the power–resources contestations come to be expressed are institution-specific in nature, and therefore their resolution depends on understanding the political operations within particular institutions – in this case, the public university.

PUTTING POLITICS BACK INTO POLITICAL ECONOMY

Bringing the political back into political economy[19] simply means accounting for the full range of actors involved in the competition for institutional resources. In the South African context, it is worth identifying these competing actors to understand them on their own terms and in relation to their allies and enemies.

Students in South African universities are highly politicised, partly as a result of historical factors and partly because of existing political arrangements (see chapter 5). Whereas in most universities around the world students' interests are primarily confined to matters of student affairs (for instance, governance, outreach, media and activist projects like climate change), in South Africa student politics are at the centre of continuous campus activism.

As is typical of other African universities, questions of immediate material interest are a constant source of student mobilisation in South Africa: for example, the quality of food, transport for commuter students, accommodation and safety concerns. But, as in Uganda, student organisations in South Africa are also thoroughly politicised.[20] What does this mean?

Student bodies on most campuses are organised along the same party-political lines as found in the national parliament. This means that there is a high degree of influence, both financial and strategic, from the external political parties on their campus affiliates. It also means that the annual campus elections for student representative councils become very competitive – and sometimes violent – as the political parties vie to dominate university politics.

Why is winning on campus so important to outside political parties? Because, especially in chronically dysfunctional universities, election to the student council offers an entrée to institutional resources. How does this happen? In several of the universities, students sit on important decision-making bodies. Sometimes, they also participate in tender committees that make decisions about the allocation of multimillion-rand contracts to companies. In many of the dysfunctional universities, these students are lobbied by competing entrepreneurs for the award of contracts. In such cases, the student representatives on tender committees become important brokers on behalf of outside interests.

Students also sit on senates and councils, where their voice can play a decisive role in the appointment of executives, such as the vice-chancellor, deputy vice-chancellors and other senior officials. Once again, students can be lobbied directly by applicants for these senior positions in exchange for reward. When students belong to a particular political party, they can also be influenced by their party to press for a particular set of appointments.

Many universities have clamped down on student participation in tender committees by writing or rewriting the institutional rules to exclude their involvement. But where student representatives do participate in such crucial committees, they can still play an influential role on behalf of businesses in search of university contracts.

Since student representation on important committees like council is normally limited to two persons, how can they be so influential? For one thing, they seldom act on their own: they often ally with workers, represented through one or more of the unions on campus that also enjoy representation on council. Thus, the combined force of student and union representatives on councils and other committees strengthens their role in decision-making.

Unions have come to play a dominant role in the politics of dysfunctional universities in South Africa. Often, there is more than one union, with the staff being split between academics and workers, on the one hand, and between rival workers' unions, on the other. The union with the majority of support becomes the recognised union, but this does little to reduce the on-campus political contestations targeting university management. The union is represented on the council as a stakeholder grouping, but, especially in dysfunctional universities, it often insists on having a seat on the appointments and tender committees as well.

With one or two union representatives on these resource-related committees, union leaders exert their influence on distributional outcomes in three ways: through alliances with the student representatives; through connections with other stakeholders on council; and through political pressure on, if not outright intimidation of, other members of committees. No union has been more powerful in the politics of dysfunctional universities than the National Education, Health and Allied Workers' Union (Nehawu); in some institutions, it is openly acknowledged that 'Nehawu runs the university'.

The distribution of power on campuses is, however, not only concentrated among internal stakeholders like students and unions, but also among the other stakeholders represented on councils in South Africa's flat and inclusive model of democracy. One powerful constituency is convocation, a body representing alumni, which, at most universities, elects one or two members to council. While sometimes the convocation's representation on council can be relatively weak, at other times it becomes a major mobilising factor in placing pressure on the university and its resources.

Two examples will suffice. At one university, a person who was elected chair of council on a convocation ticket became a major force in the destabilisation of the institution by constantly undermining the authority of the executive management. In another case, at a former white institution, the convocation representatives of the older alumni became a bulwark on council for maintaining the domination of Afrikaans in the face of the changing language policy of the university. Thus, older, experienced and politically connected convocation members can interfere directly in the resource or policy decisions of the institution. And, again, convocation members can ally with other power groups to drive decisions of council in a preferred direction.

There is, however, another important power group within councils, and that is the members chosen by council itself from the external community, for their specific areas of expertise. In this way, council members can jockey to bring in allies from political or union groups to strengthen their voting blocs on matters of resource allocation. A typical external stakeholder in this category might be a senior business executive, a legal expert or 'a representative of the community'.

Where there are strict criteria and high standards set for council appointments from the outside, much of the political power of external stakeholders is constrained; but where the bar for appointments is low or loosely applied, these outside interests can play a disproportionately influential role in council politics. One of the most significant of such external power groups comprises members of local government authorities, such as municipal council members or provincial government officials. These are often individuals whose appointments are tied to membership of the dominant political party in the region. In the democratic ideal, they represent local government in the university community. But, as will be seen, in the dysfunctional universities they are often the same officials accused of rent-seeking behaviours; that is, politically connected individuals or groups who seek out institutional contracts for work for which they lack the necessary competence (see chapter 7).

There is yet another group of power-holders within councils that receives far too little attention in institutional analyses of higher education. These are the maximum of five members of a council appointed by the minister responsible for higher education. In a perfect world, these ministerial appointees would be chosen simply for their skills in fields like auditing, planning or human resources. In a highly politicised environment like South Africa, and depending on the minister in place at the time, these may also be prominent politicians or union operators brought in to execute a political role on the council.

Sometimes, these senior people are called on to play a stabilising role in the governance function of a turbulent university. At other times, they are appointed to 'sort out' a particular set of political problems among various stakeholders on council. And there have also been instances where a comradely connection seeks and obtains a seat on council regardless of qualification or other disqualifying factors (see chapter 10). Normally, these appointees are there to be the eyes and ears of the minister in respect of the business of a particular university. In well-functioning universities, the ministerial appointees add value to institutional governance without carrying any specific mandate other than the broad transformation of higher education.

Some of the groups named here hold 'the best interests of the institution' as their essential governance commitment. They see themselves as a moderating influence in turbulent universities and are alert to the requirement that the institutional rules be respected. However, other groups among them arrive as contestants for power and resources within fragile universities.

Where ethical and responsible members of council are a minority, they soon find themselves confronting resource-hungry constituencies who act directly for themselves or on behalf of client groups. In such cases, there is a constant struggle for power and influence, as we shall see. When corrupt individuals or groups win, and rent-seeking behaviour becomes the norm, the few good people leave, in order to protect their personal and professional reputations; at this point, institutional capture becomes a reality.

Given the inevitable changes in a council over time, a well-functioning governing authority at one point can become a dysfunctional body at another. For example, when councils are dissolved by ministerial fiat, there is normally a period of stability in the governance arrangements as a new authority is established, granting the institution two vital qualities: high-level capacity and deep-level integrity.

Institutional capacity is the ability of an institution to achieve its goals through the available skills, knowledge, values and systems available to it. Institutional integrity, on other hand, is 'the robust disposition of a public institution to legitimately pursue its legitimate purpose … consistent with its commitments'.[21] Institutions of integrity, it follows, are those with 'social norms and codes, including legal rules, that "bind" individual behavior'.[22] Put simply, whereas capacity refers to the ability to do a job, integrity means doing that job according to a set of binding rules and values that hold an institution together.

Over time, however, good council members depart, and new ones are appointed through the stakeholder community system, rather than by such exceptional actions as ministerial intervention. In fragile universities, this means that once again resource-hungry groups could become part of the council and the old problems resurface.

A political economy analysis recognises the primacy of politics in universities, accounting for the contests, conflicts, compromises and contradictions that bring rival groups into competition for authority. With that authority in place, access is obtained to institutional resources, thereby igniting a constant struggle within the university. In this kind of rivalry over resources, the very meaning of a university is disfigured.

THE SUBJECTIVE MEANINGS OF THE UNIVERSITY

To take a step back, where do institutional resources come from and to whom do they belong? In South Africa's 26 public universities, a significant proportion of resources come in the form of state subsidies for teaching, research, development and infrastructure; in 2019, that amounted to more than R42 billion in 'grants', while 'other receipts', including tuition fees, stood at R46.4 billion.[23]

In the poorer universities, state subsidies constitute the largest share of all funding, while in the more established institutions there is a larger degree of private funding, including monies received through research grants (see chapter 6 for a more detailed analysis). For example, the proportion of total income from direct state subsidy is 50 per cent or higher for 14 of the 26 institutions, and ranges from 34–38 per cent for the elite universities (such as the University of Cape Town, Wits and Stellenbosch) to 86–87 per cent for the newer universities (such as Mpumalanga and Sol Plaatje).

This funding reality – that the university is a state-funded enterprise – has significant meaning for how stakeholders, especially in the historically black and underdeveloped institutions, see universities in relation to governmental resources. Since universities are public institutions, they exist to serve the needs of the public, and in this respect they are no different, perceptually, from the local municipality or any other state-owned enterprise. This perceptual shift in the understanding of the university is something that has become more pronounced over time – to the point that the institution, and its resources, are seen as something that needs to be 'paid over' to students, workers and the community. Elsewhere, I have called this the welfarisation of the university.[24]

For the elite universities, the purpose of the institution centres on its academic mandate. Here, the university is a place where high-quality teaching exists alongside world-class research, a place in which grants, publications, ratings and results determine the standing of the university in the global ranking tables. In other words, the academic project is at the centre of all institutional endeavours. It is this commitment that drives the allocation of resources and the agendas of departments, schools, faculties, senates and councils.

In dysfunctional universities, the academic project enjoys much less attention, being replaced by ongoing contests and squabbles over power and resources among competing stakeholders. Council meetings run for hours, often for a whole day, and in some cases they reconvene the following day. On the agenda are endless numbers of items that have little to do with the academic project. Instead, there are never-ending tussles over everything from the suspension of the vice-chancellor to forensic audit reports on one or other alleged act of malfeasance. In this way, inefficiency becomes part and parcel of the mismanagement of the university, with the focus being on matters material rather than academic.

What this all means is that in a political economy analysis of institutions, it is important to take account of the subjective meanings of the university for its stakeholders. There is, indeed, far too little work on what has been called 'cultural political economy' in universities, where culture is defined as 'the ensemble of social processes by which meanings are produced, circulated and exchanged'.[25]

If the university is seen primarily as a place in which to find a job or a contract, a scholarship or bursary, or a degree certificate, then its more profound meaning as a place of higher learning becomes less important in its operations. This is not to say that there is anything wrong for someone in an impoverished community to apply for work or seek funding relief for studies; it is simply to recognise that the sheer act of human survival, experienced in the desperate search for resources, will be reflected in how the institution is perceived and does its work.

It is with this idea of the university as a resource to be captured through rent-seeking or clientelism that power-brokers enter the gates of the institution for purposes that completely distort the deeper academic purposes of higher education, especially in terms of teaching and research. One way in which this develops at some dysfunctional universities is the insistence by community-based gangs that, of the millions made available through the government infrastructure grant, they obtain 30 per cent of the work or revenue in up-front cash. These so-called business forums have been dubbed 'the new construction mafia',[26] and they control the building of new infrastructure at some universities through what amounts to extortion. Here, too, the university is not seen as a place for advancing new ideas or producing work-ready graduates, but as a place from which to extort resources in the name of community development.

Such a perceptual shift in the view of the university means that its executive gets tied up in dealing with the constant clamour for resources. More and more complex rules must be formulated to protect vital resources; trust dwindles as everything disappears, from toilet rolls in the lavatories to the books in the library. It is, however, the tender committees where the real competition for resources plays itself out, and management has to remain on constant alert – if it is not itself, on occasion, implicated in some of the schemes. In short, the more the managerial leadership of a university is preoccupied with managing and protecting institutional resources, the less it is able to focus on the academic project. This implies that astute university executives need to understand how power works within institutions.

THE OPERATIONS OF INSTITUTIONAL POWER

What are the mechanisms by which groups with power in universities unlock institutional resources? One of the most common strategies is to collapse the distinction between governance and management in institutional operations. Councils are responsible for institutional governance, meaning they are broadly concerned, among other things, that the university has a full and complete suite of policies; that plans are adequately budgeted for; and that the university is built on strong ethical foundations. Once institutional policies and plans are approved, it is the duty of management to execute those commitments in the light of agreed goals and outcomes. Again, the council makes senior appointments; the management provides their contracts of employment.

The problem arises when governors try to manage the university or when managers seek to govern the university. This collapse of the lines between governance and management is the single most important cause of institutional dysfunction in South African universities, and often the reason for ministerial intervention (see chapter 4). Contrary to interventions that assume that such infringement is a weakness of understanding that can be corrected through 'capacity building' for council members (in this regard, millions of rands have been spent), I will instead argue that the crossing of the lines is often intentional, as a means for accessing and controlling institutional assets.

Consider the following examples: a chair of council opens an office on campus from which to direct his work; council members arrange and attend multiple committee meetings to boost their incomes; council members become involved in influencing appointments beyond the scope of their authority, which is limited to senior executive positions; council members lean on students or union members to influence contractual awards; council members meet with some factions within management to steer appointment outcomes; managers ignore the authority of their councils and proceed to increase their own salaries; both council members and executive managers disregard the institutional rules on the delineation of powers.

When such things happen, it is only a matter of time before institutional dysfunction sets in and the university becomes ungovernable. The minister, in accordance with legislation, then appoints an assessor as a prelude to the administrative takeover of high-level functions at the university concerned. There is no question that while the appointment of an administrator can turn a faltering university towards full functionality, the extent to which this can happen depends on powerful political forces both inside and outside the institution. That is why some dysfunctional universities have had two or more ministerial interventions in the form of assessors and administrators.

All this raises the question of not only the origins of the resources being competed for, but also the nature of the resources themselves. Much of the analysis of political economy assumes that it is only material resources that are the subject of competitive power plays within a university, with access to financial income through the tendering process being the most obvious example.

THE NATURE OF INSTITUTIONAL RESOURCES

Material resources

In any institution with a budget in excess of R1 billion, there is a lot of money spread across the university for access by legitimate as well as unscrupulous operators. After all, universities need 'service providers' for everything from catering, gardening and cleaning to supplies, transportation, security, auditing, legal services and maintenance. Many of these services are outsourced to external companies and therefore subject to competitive bids, most of which run into millions of rands. With that volume of public money on the table, the system of procurement is under scrutiny by two groups of people: those with a determination to ensure fairness and honesty, and those with an equal determination to gain unfair and dishonest access to those resources.

The question of fairness, an otherwise straightforward pursuit, comes with an interesting and potential twist for corruption. In many of the former white universities there were established networks of 'providers', which were typically white and had long connections to their institutions; these closed networks were not without their own corrupt relations with the university, at least in the sense of being racially exclusive over decades. With the transition to democracy, those close ties needed to be broadened for greater inclusivity or, more directly, to bring in black companies as competitors. Indeed, equity in procurement is still a major issue. When, however, the equity partners become corrupt partners, their defence is often that they are under investigation because they are black, or that they were excluded for the same reason. In short, the lines are once again blurred between the necessary quest for racial justice in procurement and the corrupt practices of competitors striving to access institutional resources.

What emerged over time therefore was a new dimension of the struggle for institutional goods: the contest for material resources between the older white networks of privilege and a class of newly emerging black contractors. The white networks (the insiders) would stake their claim to institutional resources on loyalty, affinity and supposedly superior expertise; the black contractors (the outsiders) would make their case on grounds of equity, transformation and inclusive contracting policies. It was perhaps inevitable that race would feature prominently in public and private discourses in the competition for material resources. The resolution of these contests lies in the hands of the institutional tender committees, which then become a site of contestation, often on behalf of one or more of the competitive bidding partners.

Symbolic resources

There are also symbolic resources which become the target of corrupt groups claiming a role for themselves as powerful operators on campuses. Such non-financial resources matter. Indeed, 'symbolic resources are valued because disciplinary communities and the broader public have come to see them as representing unique expertise or intellectual achievements'.[27]

One of the most important symbolic resources is certification. By producing and selling diplomas and degrees, influential groups can provide desperate students, staff and community members with qualifications they have not earned. A particularly powerful example in this study will reveal the high stakes involved, extending to violence and even death, when access to symbolic resources is threatened with disruption (see chapter 7).

In a country where symbolic resources such as certification can make a major difference in social status and personal income, gaining control over these assets is an important goal of influential groups on campus. These actors are typically members of staff who have privileged access to symbolic resources like certificates or duplication facilities in the university administration. Needless to say, stripping such symbolic resources erodes the credibility of institutions, as unearned certificates flood the street market. The demand for such resources continues unabated, despite the risks entailed.[28]

In corrupt institutions, symbolic resources that enhance status are also to be found in the arrangements for advancement and promotion. The mechanisms for this include the lowering of academic standards in order to advance staff on grounds, for example, of political transformation. Such actions work within the institutional rules, however bent towards a social objective that diminishes the value of the academic estate. Nowhere is such appropriation of symbolic resources more evident than in the scramble for doctorates and honorary degrees. Time after time academics have been caught out in the media for faking a qualification they did not earn, including scholars who use titles like 'doctor' or 'professor' without merit.

One important strategy in the abuse of symbolic resources is to circumvent the senate. As described earlier, the senate is the body responsible for the academic business of a university, including the awarding of degrees and certificates. If political operators can make certification awards outside the authoritative approval of senates, their grip on symbolic awards is strengthened. In every one of the dysfunctional universities covered in this book, the senate has been marginalised in important academic decisions.

A less obvious, but recently more prominent, form of corruption in the quest for symbolic resources occurs when individual academics seek subsidy-generated resources through questionable publication practices, for example, publishing articles in journals of dubious standing and quality, which have become known as predatory journals.[29] On the one hand, these tactics are concerned with personal advancement and the achievement of status – not at all strange within the academy, for 'researchers engage in academic discourse as an ongoing, publication-based positioning practice in which symbolic positions need to be gradually turned into institutional positions'.[30] On the other hand, the exploitation of this expensive state resource (a R4.9 billion industry in South Africa)[31] to optimise personal and institutional benefit through near-impossible levels of publication output in predatory journals is a clear case of corruption (see chapter 6).

There are two important observations to be drawn from this particular example of the academic claim on public resources. First, the relevant material resources – government subsidies – lie outside higher education and are competed for by all public universities. A greater or lesser proportion of them come into the institution to benefit the individual and the university itself. Second, symbolic resources and material resources are intertwined in the scramble for these assets by both the individual and the institution.

Political resources

No political economy analysis of universities would be complete without recognising a third and powerful set of resources for which influential actors compete: political resources. In South African universities, where youth organisations are often structured as affiliates of political parties off campus, students become a vital and replenishable resource for political operators.

In the first place, students, who are concentrated in their thousands on campus and who become eligible to vote in national elections as they enter tertiary education, represent a captive audience for astute politicians on the outside. The major political parties go as far as designating specific politicians with the singular task of winning over as many students as possible to their organisations. One way to demonstrate success is by ensuring that their party-aligned candidate wins the annual election for leadership of the student representative council.

Students captured by a party often become long-term adherents and activists for its political cause. At the same time, students with political ambitions see their campus activism as a launching pad for lucrative careers within politics; they become student leaders and seek prominence and recognition for themselves from the provincial and national party bosses. A kind of political symbiosis therefore develops between the student leaders and party leaders whose futures, quite literally, depend on each other.

For the external party operators, the students generally – and the student leaders in particular – are little more than political assets to be captured, nurtured and deployed to advance the interests of the party. In some dysfunctional universities, student leaders serve not only as recruitment agents for the party but as corruptible surrogates who can influence the award of material resources, such as contracts out for tender. These are the factors that explain the intense competition for power in student elections.

POLITICAL ECONOMY AS IF INSTITUTIONS MATTER

I have made a conscious decision, in framing this political economy approach to institutions, to start with a detailed examination of the micropolitics of higher education and how the contestation between power and resources proceeds within public universities. In other words, rather than start with the selection of a preferred theory of political economy and 'apply' it to institutions, the approach has been to begin with institutional practice and then work backwards to the larger questions of state, economy and markets in the macropolitical environment. In his now classic study of education policy, Richard Elmore called

this 'backward mapping': one starts with what teachers actually do prac-
tise and then see whether the schools' formal policies cohere with what
happens inside classrooms.[32] Ours is a backward-mapping approach to
the study of institutions, which does not privilege formal theory over
theory-in-practice, so to speak.

Such an approach to the study of the political economy of universities
has three advantages over the traditional application of a favoured theory
to institutional cases. First, it allows the institutional case to speak for
itself rather than being required to 'fit' the framing theory as a starting
point. Second, it allows for an existing theory or perspective on political economy itself to be reframed on the basis of empirical data from
the institution studied. And, third, it allows for a diversity of institutional experiences of the interplay between power and resources to be
accommodated under the same umbrella.

That diversity or differentiation requires further deliberation in political economy, even when the same kinds of institutions, universities in
this case, are under investigation. Clearly, there are universities that can
be regarded as stable and functional by our starting definition; that is,
these are institutions where, although they also experience major turbulence in governance and management from time to time, those functions
do not collapse to the extent that governmental intervention is required.
It is also evident from this research that highly stable and functional
institutions are not limited to the former white, privileged universities,
but also include traditionally black universities with their own histories
of underfunding and inequality.

Nor are the dysfunctional universities, as defined here, exclusively ones
in rural areas or the former bantustan institutions of the apartheid era.[33]
Some are large and others smaller urban universities in the major cities
of South Africa. To classify dysfunctional institutions by race, region, size
or even merger status (some of the larger universities are products of
multi-institutional mergers in the period 2002–2005) is therefore to mis-
calculate the common and different ways in which the power–resources
complex develops in various institutional contexts.

In this regard, there is no question that the three types of what I call negative resources (material, symbolic and political) go some way to explaining high levels of dysfunctionality in institutions. What they cannot explain, though, is what keeps institutions together; that is, high levels of functionality. For this, it is important to understand the power of a positive resource within institutions: culture.[34]

Cultural resources

It is useful to differentiate higher education institutions by a fourth class of assets, which we call cultural resources, defined as those 'cultural values, rites, norms, or actions which lead in a subculture to a common understanding, and which can be used to legitimize meanings, interpretations, and actions'.[35] Whereas material, symbolic and political resources are things to be seized for the benefit of influential groups, thereby triggering further dysfunction, cultural resources are assets that institutional actors draw on for maintaining function. Cultural resources, therefore, carry a positive benefit for stable institutions by allowing them to maintain a semblance of order and functionality under threat of instability.

At the heart of the cultural resources available to a stable, functioning university are the values and norms upheld in the name of the academic project. In such a university, there is an institution-wide understanding that the academic project cannot be undermined by the threat of instability in the environment. When such a threat happens, a set of institutional actions is triggered to prevent the disruption of the academic project at all costs. And as this study will demonstrate, those actions are rooted within a value system that privileges stability over turmoil, certainty over unpredictability, and control over chaos.[36]

How do these actions reveal themselves in the daily operations of a highly functional university? Some real-life examples from stable universities are presented here, with elaborations in the evidence-led chapters that follow.

At an elite university there is a serious confrontation between a popular vice-chancellor and an influential, well-respected senior administrator. The council is split on the matter, and a decision on the vice-chancellor could go any one of three ways – retention, dismissal or sanction. Never before has this university faced such a crisis with respect to the head of the institution. Some council members resign, and the newly constituted governing body retains the vice-chancellor and allows the influential administrator to leave as her term comes to an end. A potential crisis is averted, and the institution continues on its stable academic path, even if shaken to its roots.

In another university, there is a major crisis involving the chair of council and the vice-chancellor. All the ingredients are present for institutional collapse and ministerial intervention. The conflict spills into the open and ends up in the courts. Irregular meetings are convened, and some of their decisions upheld and others dismissed. The confrontation continues for months, then years. Influential public figures are brought in to resolve the impasse, without success. But there is no collapse in governance or management. The vice-chancellor continues to lead and eventually retires as planned. A new council chair is in place. The crisis is managed, even if legal struggles continue.

In neither of these institutions, one white and one black, are the vital functions of the university disrupted. Neither of the two is subject to government intervention in the form of assessors and administrators, or even an external task team to bring things to order. Both institutions recover from potentially damaging threats to the core academic and administrative functions. Why? In both universities, the academic project is employed by institutional leaders as its stabilising rudder.

The white university, more than a hundred years old, has embedded the norms and values of the academic project in everything it does. It is understood by campus citizens that this is the leading university in Africa according to the global rankings; that many of its former and current professors are superstars in the international academy, among them Nobel laureates; and that its students typically go on to achieve great things in the worlds of commerce, engineering, the arts and the sciences. That understanding filters up and down through the university administration. In fact, as this study will show, it is the capability and commitment to the academic project in middle-level management that make these institutions resilient in the face of disruptive threats (see chapter 9).

The black university, by contrast, is a creature of apartheid, established in 1960 as a training facility designated for so-called coloured people. It was, in the language of the day, a typical 'bush college' that was under-resourced and had low-level ambitions for training the future civil servants of the apartheid government; there was no medical faculty or engineering school, for those were allocated to the white universities.

Despite the odds, a succession of outstanding academic leaders transformed the institution into a highly regarded university, with solid rankings in fields like biology and the humanities. Over time, the academic project became deeply entrenched at this university, an achievement made concretely visible in a massive, state-of-the-art life sciences facility that cost R550 million. These academic achievements became a defining cultural resource which the institution would use to shape its post-apartheid identity and on which it could draw in times of crisis.

In universities that draw their academic identity and stabilising focus from such a deep reserve of cultural resources, other things fall into place as well. The senate, responsible for the academic project, maintains a central place in the functioning of the institution. The competition for major academic awards and grants anchors the research ambitions of such institutions. The ratings of scholars and the rankings of the university are essential elements in the pursuit of academic standing and prestige. These are cultural resources that stabilise institutions under threat.

By contrast, universities trapped in dysfunctionality pay little attention to the academic project. When crises hit and dysfunctional institutions descend into chaos, there are no cultural resources to tap into as a way of refocusing the academic mandate and mission of the university. Everything is politics in the never-ending quest to extract more and more resources from a depleted institution.

CLOSING ARGUMENTS

It would have been tempting to pursue this analysis of the political economy of universities from where many others start, with the macro-economic options available to the South African government at the dawn of democracy and their consequences for institutions. For example, critical perspectives on those early years would argue that the post-apartheid government made poor policy choices for the economy and, by extension, for higher education. Government could have followed the progressive advice of the ruling party's economic think tank, the Macroeconomic Research Group (MERG), which argued for a massive state-led investment programme that would advance economic growth and reverse racial inequalities.[37] The position of MERG was that the state should actively drive a mixed economy in which the policy emphasis would be on redistribution, empowerment and equity.[38]

The Reconstruction and Development Programme (RDP) launched under President Mandela in many ways encapsulated the ideas outlined by MERG. It acknowledged the importance of economic growth but put emphasis on reconstruction and redistribution through a gigantic infrastructure programme focused on things like water, transport, health and, of course, education. But two years after coming into power, the ANC-led government abandoned the RDP and instead chose a very different macroeconomic framework, which came to be known as the Growth, Employment and Redistribution (Gear) policy. Rather than embarking on ambitious expenditures as envisaged by MERG and the RDP, the government would act to dramatically reduce budget deficits through actions that included cutting expenditure and lowering inflation. The economy would be deregulated, and government would give up on any ideological pretensions it might have had in favour of nationalisation of the private sector. It was argued by influential voices that if the government followed the neoliberal policies of the Washington Consensus, then foreign direct investment would increase, thereby creating conditions for growth and job creation. In this model, the government's role was not to intervene in the economy but to step aside and allow the market to do its work. Clearly, the RDP did not fit in with this austere vision for the economy, and so it was scrapped.

The relevant question is this: would the trajectory of higher education development in the post-apartheid period have looked different if government had pursued the more radical ideas of MERG and the RDP rather than those of Gear? Put differently, would the macropolitical economy of South Africa have determined more equitable and just institutional outcomes across the 26 public universities?

The premise that 'more resources should have been unleashed' for universities and, in particular, for the historically disadvantaged institutions continues to underpin arguments in favour of a more radical path for South Africa's political economy in the early years of democracy. However, the evidence presented in this book suggests that such a view is wrong, and for a simple reason: it is based on a rational, economic analysis of political economy that cannot account for the dynamic and complex social, cultural, historical and political factors that conditioned existing institutions as they moved into the democratic era. Ongoing academic research on bantustan institutions,[39] and analyses of conditions in universities at the point of transition, all make this point well.[40]

Universities did not start as blank slates in the transition of the 1990s but as compromised institutions that, on the one hand, carried the ideological baggage of a colonial and apartheid past and, on the other hand, were already deeply contested social institutions unlikely to be whipped into democratic shape by a straightforward calculation that more resources equals smarter policies, equals better outcomes.

Nonetheless, among progressives the question persists: what if smarter government policies had been chosen that deployed more resources to overcome the institutional inequalities that still mark the white–black divide in universities? To begin with, much of the distributional logic of government policy was, in fact, gradually embedded in university funding from the time of the transition to democracy. For example, equity funding is heavily invested in instruments like the Historically Disadvantaged Institutions (HDIs) Development Grant (more than R2.414 billion since 2016/2017);[41] earmarked infrastructural allocations that focused on HDIs came to R4.142 billion during the seven-year period 2008/2009– 2014/2015, covering seven disadvantaged universities with 36.7 per cent of total infrastructure spend;[42] and national student financial aid to poor and working-class students amounts to R28.581 billion (2021/2022 allocation), which covered 755 116 students in the 2020 academic year,[43] an increase of more than 67 per cent in the number of disadvantaged students.[44]

In addition to these equity-driven investments, there are grants favouring universities with large proportions of disadvantaged students ('the disadvantage factor');[45] teaching and research grants now under the University Capacity Development Programme; the earmarked GAP grant for poor and missing students; the earmarked foundation provisioning grant; and other smaller corrective funding commitments.

The questions whether such corrective funding was adequate and whether it sufficiently identified individual and institutional equity targets are worth considering. Yet there is ample evidence that there are serious problems of capacity and integrity within institutions that limit their ability to translate resources into results; in this regard, the state had very little infrastructural power to ensure such translation. Infrastructural power is defined as the institutional capacity of the state to logically implement decisions. As empirically demonstrated for other inherited educational institutions – schools – such power requires 'some degree of cooperation … in the form of institutions that enable the state to regulate and obtain the cooperation from social groups'.[46]

By starting our analysis with the micropolitics of institutions, then, it is possible to see close-up the continuities in 'political corruption before and after apartheid',[47] which are to some extent independent of the size of state funding or the progressive intentions of new social policies. These settled arrangements are best explained by the history of institutions like schools and universities, and they play a powerful role in constraining the positive reach of power and resources in contexts of deprivation.

It is not only corruption that constrains an institution's reach but also capacity. As one senior government official responsible for institutional funding commented, 'There was a season (2008–2014) in which earmarked infrastructure allocations was mainly (but not exclusively) focusing on HDIs. However, building projects did not materialise as expected owing to lack of capacity at most HDIs.' He later reflected on meetings of senior government officials: 'The nagging issue with those who are closely involved … is that lots of additional state funding resources cannot flow towards the HDIs until the issue of capacity to effectively use the funds within these institutions has been addressed properly.'[48]

What happens in institutions with broken systems due to problems of capacity and integrity? Exactly what happened in the apartheid administrations of bantustan institutions, so deftly captured by Sarah Meny-Gibert: 'The presence of patronage in a bureaucracy does not necessarily prevent the average citizen from accessing state services; rather, it makes this more dependent on informal networks and the power of local leaders in a given area.'[49] It is this central weakness in political economy analyses of higher education that underpins our conceptual framework: the need to restore politics when it comes to making sense of the macroeconomic choices facing governments with the daunting task of transforming institutions.

In sum, it is the macropolitics at the point of transition that explains why the new democratic government made the choices that it did – the sanction, or threatened sanction, of the markets, the lobbying of capital, and the fear of failure at a time of collapse of the European socialist regimes. It is the micropolitics inside universities that explains the chronic dysfunction that results from the endless pursuit of resources outside the formal institutional rules of good governance and management. And it is the connection between them – the macropolitics of the state and the micropolitics of institutions – that best explains chronic dysfunction in the universities under study.

4

A Personal Journey through the Political Economy of Universities

The personal is political economy.[1]

'The Minister has instructed us to give you a bodyguard; the guard will come from the group that provided security to President Mandela.' The announcement landed with a thud, made worse by the fact that someone thought a simple professor from the University of Pretoria needed to know the elite security stable from which his protection was to come. Why would the administrator of a troubled university need armed bodyguards?

My initial reaction was to resist. After all, I had grown up on the rough streets of the Cape Flats and had seen my fair share of ruthless gangsters; 'I can handle this,' I tried to reassure myself. But the minister's envoy made it clear that this was not something to be negotiated. I *would* have a bodyguard.

Late that night, as I finished work on the main campus of the Mangosuthu University of Technology (MUT) in the township of Umlazi, the armed guard was waiting outside my fortified office. I was tense on the short trip of about 18 kilometres to my hotel on the Durban beachfront. 'Wait outside please,' ordered the guard as he walked through my hotel room, checking cupboards and lifting lampshades. After a few minutes, I was allowed in and ordered to double-lock the door. I fell on the bed emotionally exhausted.

Then a strange realisation came to me as I reflected on the situation. This was wrong. As a scholar, I treasure the idea of a university as a place where one is free to think and to act in accordance with academic values. The notion of being accompanied by armed guards onto and off campus was inimical to the very idea of a university. I was disturbed about what this unwanted security detachment would signal to the community of students and academics whom I was expected to lead out of trouble. For the first time it hit me: this might not be a university after all, only an organisation in which staff came to earn a living and students came to obtain a certificate that might one day earn them a decent income. The routines of administration were certainly there – registration, instruction, examination, graduation – but the true essence of a university was not at all evident in those moments, and even less so as I entered the belly of the institutional beast.

THE WARLORD WHO BECAME A VICE-CHANCELLOR

When I first gained sight of the assessor's report on MUT that had led to the suspension of its vice-chancellor (VC) and my appointment as administrator, it seemed completely unreal, even a bad joke. I learned that the VC had spent much of his time inside his fortified office with a heavy steel door and a peephole through which he could see who was on the other side. Few, I was told, ever came inside. After his departure, it had taken days for the *muti* (traditional medicinal herbs) to be cleared from the many cupboards in the dark-panelled office with its private toilet. The VC would regularly consult with sangomas (traditional healers) ahead of difficult council meetings; the council meeting room would smell badly on such occasions, a senior staffer told me, after some sangomas had spent the previous night there to ensure outcomes favourable to the university leader.

In the VC's office were closed-circuit cameras from which he could watch staff come and go, including an angle on the toilets. The assessor's report revealed that 'special software was secretly and illegally installed on the PABX to record the telephone conversations of some 20 staff members' even as they engaged with the assessor's team;[2] unsurprisingly, many of them were dismissed. Control was the VC's thing, and the great leader knew the comings and goings of the people who worked for him. Every account of his leadership was one of autocratic rule, and those who dared to cross the man would get a written warning, instant dismissal or, as we shall see, sometimes something much worse.

I was given a tour of the main floor of the administration building and shown an elevator that only the VC was allowed to use. The lift brought him from the basement, where he parked his gold Jaguar, straight up to the executive floor, where it released him a few steps from his fortified office. The Jaguar, more than one person whispered, had a stock of AK-47s in the boot. I could not confirm this, even though it was rumoured that the man had been a warlord during his time at the University of Zululand, where he had been a political science lecturer during the many years of deadly violence between the Inkatha Freedom Party (IFP) and the African National Congress (ANC), before things settled down in the new democracy. This was, after all, the ANC's front man north of the Tugela, who once told John Carlin of the UK's *Independent* newspaper that 'in the past, we participated fully in the peace accords. But it never worked out. We miscalculated and the carnage just continued. I felt we should devise another strategy – a strategy to avenge the deaths of our comrades and a squad to protect people from Inkatha. We trained a squad, local guys, not MK [the ANC's military wing], and it has repaid us handsomely.'[3] During the informal briefings about the VC and his tactics, I tried very hard not to show signs of utter dismay or any measure of fear.

The lift carried another shock. Welcoming council members to my first meeting of the governing body, I was told that a councillor in a wheelchair was going to come upstairs using this lift. I waited for the person, introduced myself and welcomed him to the meeting. Once we were comfortable in conversation, I asked him how he had ended up in a wheelchair. Without blinking, he told me that while he was serving on council, his company won a tender for one or other university service. After he left that meeting and while driving down the highway past the campus, a rival sprayed his car with bullets, leaving him paralysed from the waist down. Word had got out that he was the successful bidder. Stunned, I did not think it was the right time to ask whether it was appropriate for a council member to participate in a governance meeting about his own company's bid for a university contract.

I sat down in the suspended VC's office and wondered why on earth I had agreed to the MUT assignment, and how any university leader could possibly do the kinds of things described to me or live this kind of life. Even the official website seemed to be in on the act, declaring that 'in 1997 [the leader concerned] assumed reign as the Vice-Chancellor & Principal'.[4] Reign!

More importantly, I started to wonder what kind of power arrangements inside and outside MUT had kept the VC in such a dominant, authoritarian and frankly scary position of leadership for so long. Things would become much clearer as I began my work in 2009 at this semi-rural university in the heart of an African township.

AN OPEN AND REVEALING DOOR

I was so perplexed by the secrecy of the VC's office that I swung the door wide open and invited any staff member or student to come in, take a tour of the shrine, sit down and, if time allowed, have coffee with the administrator. People started to share unbelievable stories about their lives on this university campus. The invitation became public knowledge, and slowly people started to arrive with their own stories. I simply could not believe what I was hearing, and here I limit myself to one particularly disturbing account shared with me.

The young white man who came through the door was visibly trembling as he sank into the comfortable brown leather couch in the former VC's office. Thin, wide-eyed and clearly scared, he did not speak for several minutes. I waited. Then, he did something completely unexpected; he took off his shirt to reveal deep marks running across his back. What on earth was this about, I wondered.

He had been an academic engineer at MUT but was fired by the VC. He made the mistake of confronting the latter in the parking lot of a local shopping centre. As video footage showed, a seemingly infuriated VC opened the boot of his car and descended upon the academic with a sjambok,[5] beating him to the ground. His friend, a staff member at MUT, recorded the brutal attack and sent the chilling video of the screaming academic to a deputy vice-chancellor (DVC), pleading for help. Nothing happened, and the bloodied academic was left to fend for himself.

I was so emotionally affected by this tragedy that I walked across to the office of this DVC (since deceased) and asked him pointedly: Why, upon receiving the anxious message, did you not respond? Did you ever confront the VC about what happened? He looked at me with what can only be described as an embarrassed smile, tearful emotion in his eyes, and a clear suggestion in his facial expression that I simply did not understand the situation. I was furious, even as it became clear why he had done nothing: to stand up in defence of an academic and for the academic rights of the young engineer would in an instant have cost him his livelihood. The DVC was not willing to risk his career by doing the right thing.

That was not the only account I heard of someone who had been ejected from campus on the instruction of the VC. But this kind of autocratic authority was also wielded to facilitate the VC's access to the university's resources. A typical scenario was described to me.[6] The VC would apparently be driving to his farm in Estcourt on a Friday afternoon and call the head of finance at the university. He would issue an instruction for money from the university coffers to be transferred into his personal account. And the instruction would be carried out. How could such an obvious crime even happen? I naturally asked the finance man. He shrugged his shoulders, and I read in his body language the same kind of message as in that of other senior colleagues: fear of intimidation and the potential loss of a job. These instructions to transfer university money into the account of the VC would apparently happen time and time again.

Or somebody would notice the agricultural sciences department's tractor travelling north towards – as it turned out – the VC's farm. Other kinds of university equipment were likewise going down the highway. This was corruption on wheels. No staff member can legitimately take home university equipment for purposes having nothing to do with the academic business of the institution. The great leader could, however, order this to happen.

How did the VC of one of the smallest universities in the country, the one with the lowest academic output in terms of research publications, manage to award himself the highest salary of all the vice-chancellors in the country? He earned R3.68 million, more than the leaders of the major research universities with three or more times the number of students.[7] Clearly a VC cannot determine his own salary; it is the prerogative of his nominal boss, the Department of Higher Education. In short, the great leader had made the public finances of the university his personal bank account.

There is one positive element of the MUT story that merits recognition. The dysfunction would have continued had it not been for 'the good guys' on council who raised the alarm directly with the minister of education. Led by the deputy chair of council, a highly regarded judge, this small group realised that the destruction of the university could not be halted within a corrupt and divided governance structure. Their case was persuasive and their insistence paid off when the minister intervened. But the corrupt faction would live to fight another day.

Preparing for the job of administrator, I knew what had to be done. My first task was to restore some measure of confidence among the staff and students of this beleaguered university. I felt that I had to quickly change five or six big things that would stop the leaking away of vital resources through a broken institutional net. And it was important to break the circuitry of power and resources that flowed through the formal and informal structures of the institution in order to give the university even the slightest chance of success.

But there was one thing that made those goals very difficult to achieve. The minister was under pressure from provincial politicians not to dissolve the council, the very body that had enabled the corruption and incompetence. I was appointed only as the replacement VC, or administrator, reporting to the very same council. Inevitably, by 2018 a third government intervention was required, after another VC had been removed in 2016. (At the time of this writing, the current VC was also under suspension.) The influential chairman of the MUT council, who also served as the mayor of the Durban municipality (eThekwini), was eventually posted as the South African ambassador to Germany, where he was promptly accused of corruption and recalled to South Africa.[8] Most of these developments after I left MUT were predictable, since the root causes of dysfunctionality, the power–resources conundrum, had not been addressed. There was a different outcome with my earlier posting as administrator of the Durban University of Technology (DUT), to which we now turn.

THE FIGHTING ELEPHANTS AND THE AFRICAN GRASS

A few days before taking up my posting as the administrator of the DUT in 2006, a report appeared in the national newspapers in which the president of the student representative council (SRC) made it very clear I would be made to feel unwelcome upon arrival from my base in Pretoria, where I was 'a mere Dean'.[9] I found it strange that someone I had never met could be so firm in his judgement about a stranger; he must be afraid of something, I said to myself. So, the first thing I did when I arrived early one morning at the Steve Biko campus of the newly merged institution was to request a meeting with the SRC leader.

He dutifully arrived at my office in the basement of the administration building, a curious location but one that other administrators often found to contain an unsubtle message: know your place. I welcomed the young man warmly and asked about his family, and he produced a lovely picture of his baby daughter. Then we talked business. I asked about his concerns regarding my assignment; he spoke about the university's problems in general. At the end of the meeting, I put my arm around the young leader's shoulders and assured him that I would do everything to ensure that the students were well served during my tenure, and that I expected his full cooperation.

The DUT saga had erupted suddenly, and it could have been avoided altogether. After the merger of two former technikons, one for whites, Technikon Natal, and one for Indian South Africans, ML Sultan Technikon, staff relations were always going to be difficult, socially, culturally, politically and, of course, academically. But that was not the main problem.

One moment the university was running along just fine. The council had an excellent chairperson, who knew and respected the boundaries between governance and management. Council governed by setting institutional policies and expectations, and management executed them accordingly. And then, all at once, a large number of inexperienced councillors joined the council, and a weak, inexperienced and corruptible deputy chair saw the opportunity to advance herself. She became the acting chair of council and then the permanent chair. She was also the chair of the executive committee of council, a subcommittee that often does the grunt work of governance and then brings considered proposals to the full council for deliberation and decision.

Unsurprisingly, governance and management deteriorated. The new chair started to attend meetings of academics, a highly unusual move for members of a governing body unless they are invited to attend. She also interfered openly in the daily operational activities of the university. As chairperson, she delayed senior executive appointments needing the approval of council. There were lengthy email spats between the VC and the chair, which were described in the assessor's report as 'the blurring of boundaries' between management and governance. The chair bypassed the functional audit committee of the university and set up her own task team. The VC, a professor of theology, was at his wits' end and threw his own metaphorical punches in what was now an open brawl between the two most important leaders in the university.

When the elephants fight, says an African proverb, it is the grass that gets hurt. Staff were distraught, writing to the minister directly through one of the unions. Students, who had their own concerns, were left stranded. Fights in council over a forensic audit dragged on for months, then years. The last thing on the minds of campus citizens was the academic project. Teaching, learning or research did not feature in any of the submissions to the visiting assessor and his team. The university as an academic institution was clearly on the ropes.

In the case of DUT, one thing stood out in the parlous state of a university: the quality of its council leadership. Here was a small-time businesswoman trying to make a living by calling 'endless special meetings' (in the words of the assessor's report) for which she was paid. This was a practice she continued at the South African Broadcasting Corporation (SABC) as its board chair, where she convened 35 meetings (4 per year is common) and earned close to R1 million in all, or about R27 000 per meeting.[10] After the chair left DUT, it was found that she had lied repeatedly about her qualifications from the University of South Africa (Unisa), and in 2020 she was on the run from the police for degree fraud, for which an arrest warrant had been issued.[11]

Back on campus, I was appointed administrator of both council and management, which meant there was much less politics or subterfuge around urgent decisions that needed to be made. I led the completion of the long-delayed forensic audit, with great expertise on offer from the Durban-based KPMG accounting firm. We appointed a full complement of competent executives at the senior level and, once a brand-new council was in place, I announced my departure. It was a rich and fulfilling experience from which I learned a great deal.

Even with the enormous power of an administrator, how does one rebuild confidence in an institution and its rules? This was a question

I thought about carefully. It was important to respect committees in making key decisions, such as the appointment of executives: none of these were made without the full participation of the existing senior management and the senate. Similarly, the new council appointments were made through a consultative process in which the institutional forum (IF), headed by one of the most impressive leaders in higher education, became an invaluable ally. The role of the administrator was to serve as the guardian of democratic practice on campus and to ensure institutional integrity in decision-making.

We advertised in the media for new council members, setting the highest criteria for expertise in law, auditing, accounting, marketing, leadership and, of course, higher education management. We interviewed every candidate and headhunted some of the best people in and outside the province and asked them to apply. Eventually, DUT had arguably the most highly accomplished governing body of any South African university at the time. It was led by Jairam Reddy, a former VC and one-time chairperson of the National Commission on Higher Education, which provided the foundation for higher education policy in a democratic South Africa. His deputy was John Volmink, a highly regarded professor of mathematics, who also was an executive leader at the nearby University of Natal (later, the University of KwaZulu-Natal). And on the board sat some of the most impressive and accomplished leaders in the corporate world, for whom the university was not a feeding trough.

Just as importantly, our recruitment of the best governors for a university satisfied that other imperative of democratic South Africa – equity and diversity in appointments. None of the appointees were political operatives 'deployed' by the ruling party. All were consummate professionals who had already achieved great heights in their various careers. There was no need for any further ministerial intervention at DUT – because of the capacity and integrity of the new governing council.

While my time as administrator at both MUT and DUT marked important moments of my career, my personal journey through the political economy of universities in democratic South Africa started much earlier with my first academic post in 1994 as the chair of curriculum studies, and later as dean and acting DVC, at the University of Durban-Westville (UDW).

A SHOCK TO THE SYSTEM, AND TO MY SENSE OF ACADEMIC POLITICS AND ECONOMICS

I had arrived back in South Africa in 1991 after completing doctoral studies at Stanford University. You could not find a more calm, stable and wealthy university than 'The Farm' in California. A private institution, Stanford had one of the largest endowments in the world and could outcompete almost any other university in recruiting prized scholars and smart students.

When there was conflict at Stanford, it was resolved through deliberation. With the outbreak of war against an American enemy, there would be lunch-time talks to packed audiences on the language of conflict. A linguistics professor would unpack the political meanings of 'surgical strikes' or 'smart bombs'. Any student action would be the outcome of thorough debates from all points on the ideological spectrum, mostly polite. Staff protests were rare, except for the divestment campaign to pressure the university to withdraw its stocks from companies doing business in apartheid South Africa. The only time in four years that I witnessed anything close to a police presence on campus was when students were arrested for occupying the administration building to protest against apartheid; it was over before it had even begun.

After a short spell working with non-governmental organisations to undertake training and 'capacity building' in preparation for a new government in South Africa, I joined UDW in 1994. My first academic posting in the new South Africa was both exciting and exasperating. Exciting, because here was a university with some very strong academics and an even stronger sense of its transformation mandate. Originally established for Indian South Africans, UDW quickly moved to open its doors to all students, and enrolments grew, especially of African students.

These were exciting times, and I revelled in my leadership role among some of the most talented young academics I have worked with, before or since that time.

But the experience was also exasperating, because there were dark forces determined to make this campus a radical project of the ultra-left to advance the material benefits of workers on campus. These were the cleaners, caterers, gardeners and security staff, who were paid much less than academic staff; some of them were also outsourced workers. Most of these staff came from the large Indian townships, such as Phoenix and Chatsworth, and they would fill the main hall for what appeared to be daily remonstrations on behalf of workers against 'management'.

On the face of it, this sounded like progressive politics by the mass union called the Combined Staff Association of academics and staff. It was a small but highly organised outfit; at one meeting, I stared in amazement as a young man was introduced to the senate as the recently hired full-time organiser of the union. Even then, I did not realise that this was the start of war on campus.

I would soon discover that this movement was neither radical nor ultra-left; rather, the union was led by a group of anarchists determined to destroy the university and, in the revolutionary imaginary of some of their leaders, rebuild the institution from the ruins of its fall. In the process, the poor and working-class Indian staff became the fodder for union leaders playing with their lives and livelihoods.

What I witnessed next shocked me to the core. Every other day brought high levels of political energy to the campus, mostly around the compensation and working conditions of the majority Indian workers. Things often turned violent, with marchers regularly descending upon the offices of the VC, terrifying the secretary in charge, and rubbishing the entire place outside and inside the oak-panelled offices of the university's senior leadership. The shock reverberated throughout the campus.

Even more serious was the vilification of anyone who dared to counter or criticise the union. There was no doubt that the union had an insider in the local press, and every day the paper carried an anti-management account of the struggle, combined with highly personal and vicious attacks on individuals on campus. These defamatory attacks continued for weeks, then months, and into the next academic year.

A particular target singled out for violence and vendettas was Professor Ronaldo Munck, a top-flight (white, male) sociologist from South America, who was hired to head the sociology department. His first mistake was to require his staff to carry out their academic duties, such as showing up to teach their classes. His second mistake was to ask uncomfortable questions of the dominant union, whose charismatic leader happened to be a member of his department.

All hell broke loose upon the head of the Argentine scholar. His antagonists made his life a nightmare, both on and off campus. They followed him home to threaten and humiliate him; they burgled his home, urinated on his furniture, and spread faeces on the walls of his apartment. In addition, offices were vandalised. There were death threats. Car tyres were slashed. Smear campaigns were conducted by means of anonymous campus leaflets and in the local newspaper. Inevitably, prominent academics, several aligned with the ANC, resigned to work elsewhere. Intelligence agents from both the old and new regimes were rumoured to be working on campus. A *Times Higher Education* journalist found Munck and his partner 'hiding on a boat in Durban's marina, living in fear of their lives. They are being protected by an armed guard provided by the University of Durban-Westville.'[12] When his child was threatened at his preschool, Munck resigned from the university and left with his family for Ireland.

There was little question in my mind that three dangerous crosswinds had collided to create the political turbulence at UDW in the mid-1990s. The first was an anarchistic political project determined to destroy management and governance at the university in order to rebuild it in the name of radicalism. The second was a personal vendetta by a powerful, charismatic union leader apparently hell-bent on ejecting the foreign sociologist who was making academic demands of his staff and questioning the political project of the union. The third was an ethnic mobilisation of

Indian workers to front the union's cause, inevitably fuelling racial conflict with the growing number of African students on the campus.[13]

With the campus in serious dysfunction, UDW became the first university in the democratic era where government intervened by instituting an external inquiry. The upheaval at UDW demonstrated how a powerful stakeholder on a university campus, a rogue staff union with ulterior motives, could work to destroy one of the country's most promising universities while, in the process, undermining confidence in its governance, management and administrative systems.

Because the Gautschi Commission was focused largely on the actions of individuals (several of whom were later suspended), it failed to account for the institutional conditions that made such renegade behaviour possible in the first place. One unaddressed matter was the compromised governance structure of the university, which did not have enough independent councillors of sufficient quality to effectively govern the institution. As a result, less than a decade after the Gautschi Commission, another minister of education was forced to appoint an assessor at UDW to report on, among other things, 'the reason for the serious lack of confidence in the governance structures of the University and the apparent inability of the Council to address these matters'.[14]

When I moved from my position as dean and acting DVC at UDW to take up a deanship at the University of Pretoria, in the administrative capital of the country, the relationship between power and resources took a completely different form at my new university. Here, my experience of the political economy of higher education was the complete opposite of what I had lived through at UDW.

INSIDE THE ROCK-SOLID SHIP

The main administrative building of the University of Pretoria (UP), where the senior executive and top-level administrators sit, is called 'The Ship'. Its solid, concrete structure is matched by an institutional steadiness when it comes to politics, resources and the relationship between them.

The first thing I noticed as the new dean of education was that at UP power is comfortably centralised in the senior management of the university. There is a long history of command and control at this century-old university, with administrative surveillance over every aspect of university life.[15] Rules and regulations are followed meticulously, and every statutory committee functions strictly within its mandate.[16] The annual budgetary cycles are managed with military precision. Fine-tuned faculty budget schedules are announced in advance. Each academic dean and administrative director has to justify every item of spending to management committees and then to larger meetings of the university's senior administration.

In this elaborate structure managed from 'The Ship', everyone knows their place. Council governs and approves major policies; management executes them. Deans get their marching orders from their assigned vice-rector. On receiving their *opdrag* (orders), deans depart to carry out the teaching, research and service duties of their various faculties. Fixed biweekly meetings of deans, directors and senior executives keep everything in line; a favourite management term during my tenure was the *belyning* (alignment) of policy, planning and programming.

There is little consternation in 'The Ship'; everything seems to work. The modus operandi of management at all levels is to seek consensus, not conflict. Like all institutions, before and after apartheid, UP has had its fair share of scandal, but unsavoury incidents seldom appear in the media; they are managed internally and resolved efficiently. Open confrontations between stakeholders are extremely rare, even if there are sometimes intense private tussles at all levels of the university.

In this highly structured environment, the connection between power and resources is tightly managed. Management control has its own inward-looking logic. Efficiency trumps equity, and effectiveness matters much more than the deep transformation of the institution, because the habits of *bestuur* (management) are more easily and routinely performed than the complexities of transforming academic appointments or decolonising the curriculum. Any threat of radical change is deftly managed, in ways that secure institutional stability; how exactly this is done has been empirically laid out in recent research.[17]

The control over political elements is therefore totalising. When there are campus-wide protests, there is visible overkill in the level and intensity of almost military-style policing. As a seasoned internal observer of the Afrikaans universities commented to me, 'even in their reporting documents the securitised response was foremost'. The groundwork for securing the campus was done in peacetime, through access control technologies. When there is a threat of loss of control, as in the student protests of 2015–2016, it is both disorienting and disconcerting for the university's traditional community, and the management takes unusual strain, since such movements are exceptional rather than routine, as at nearby institutions like Unisa and the Tshwane University of Technology.

Again, the political contestations inside the institution are not visible but are contained within the agency of conservative bodies such as alumni, donors and staff, who steer their authority through formal channels, such as convocation and council; the meticulous organisation of conservative politics is carried out behind closed doors. Scheduled meetings are not for fighting or contesting anything, but for affirming the political will of organised lobbies of white conservative forces. At the old Afrikaans universities, there is seldom blood on the floor.[18]

The management control over party-political student bodies is invisible but highly effective. For example, whereas the outcomes of student political elections are regularly questioned and challenged in other universities, at institutions like UP the administration of these annual events is nearly flawless because of the technologies of oversight employed. Things work, at least in a narrowly technocratic sense.

The centralisation of power means that the bulk of institutional resources are directed towards the managerial imperatives of the senior leadership, which tend to be innovations in technology and business enterprises rather than, for example, a fully funded gender institute or a centre for decolonisation studies. Radical change, even in its mildest or liberal versions, will not find much support from central coffers; if approved at all, that funding must come from external sources, as staff from the Aids centre or gender studies projects will attest. In other words, the commitment of vital institutional resources to social justice projects does not enjoy priority in this kind of institution, even as they build reputations based on well-managed resources and reserves.

On the positive side, what these conservative political economies allow for is a highly competent set of management arrangements when it comes to government-mandated change. This was especially evident in the period of mergers and incorporations, when the black Mamelodi campus of Vista University was incorporated into UP and transformed into a high-quality, second-opportunity science and commerce stream for disadvantaged students. In the same way, the white Normaal Kollege Pretoria in Groenkloof was also incorporated and transformed into a leading research and teaching facility for education students.

What these high degrees of functionality also reveal is that where management and administrative systems are strong, the opportunities for political operators at the local level are greatly diminished. But the clamour for resources by corrupt means never rests, as I was to find out in my next posting.

THE POOR WHITE UNIVERSITY OF SOUTH AFRICA

In my new position as rector (vice-chancellor) at the University of the Free State (UFS), I had a much more intimate view of the power–resources complex at an institutional level. But this was the UFS, a university in rural South Africa that made the transition from apartheid to democracy without the substantial resources and reserves of either UP or its even more wealthy Afrikaans cousin, Stellenbosch University (SU).

You do not have to spend too much time at any of these three universities to become aware of the troubled political economies of the white Afrikaans universities. Yes, there remain powerful systems for effective and efficient control, but many of these administrative routines have their origins in racial exclusion and minority rule. Put bluntly, some of these institutions felt they needed to keep the accumulated resources of white institutions out of black hands.[19] This is, of course, a special case of corruption, if not outright racism, in well-endowed public universities trying to retain power and resources.

The simple point being made here is that an honest account of the effective and efficient management of institutional resources would not yield a simple, uncomplicated story of power and control; it would, inevitably, also be an exposition of the racial politics of the exclusionary uses of public resources for the social and technocratic ends of the apartheid state.

And yet, it is the case that the white Afrikaans universities were not all the same. The UFS is essentially a rural university with three campuses. There is the old historic campus in Bloemfontein, the main campus, as students call it; a campus in the south of the city that was the old Vista University campus before it was incorporated into UFS; and a third campus, QwaQwa, about three hours' drive away in the eastern Free State. The original UFS campus, also a centenarian, was well managed and administered, like its Afrikaans counterparts, but it is certainly not wealthy. In fact, just before I arrived in 2009, the university faced a serious financial crisis and had to make major budgetary cuts, involving staff lay-offs, in order to survive that familiar problem of high expenditures and dwindling revenues based on falling student enrolments. The UFS was fortunate to have a Harvard-trained economist at the helm as VC, who was able to steer the ship back into safer waters.

MANAGING THE HISTORICAL POWERLINES

The power lines at the UFS were clear to me upon arrival. At its heart was a well-entrenched and conservative white Afrikaans establishment with a mainly pragmatic approach to institutional transformation. There were some hardliners on the staff, but many more in the alumni community who demonstrated their defiance through an almost daily attack on changes at the university through the local Afrikaans newspaper, *Die Volksblad*.[20] At times, their position would be expressed at special meetings of convocation that were marked by bitter, angry and resentful outbursts against the trajectory of change at the university.

The political actions of conservative staff, students and alumni would, over time, be managed, if not neutralised, through the considered actions of an astute team of strategic leaders. One strategy was to ensure that competent and progressive white and black council members would constitute the majority in the governing body; the conservative members would over time come to realise that there was little appetite for conservative racial politics, and eventually resign or retire from council at the end of their terms.

A second strategy was to ensure the new members of council were people of impeccable integrity and considerable skill. Our chair of council, for example, was a justice of the Appellate Court, and our deputy chair was the CEO of Alexander Forbes, the financial services firm (he now heads the South African Revenue Service). The chair and I, as VC, were charged with searching for and receiving nominations of potential council members, outside the stakeholder nominees, to present to the full council for approval. We chose highly qualified persons who were experienced in matters of governance and were financially self-sufficient, and who could be counted on to exercise political independence on council.

A third decision was to build a strong relationship between the chair of council and the vice-chancellor. We would meet regularly for an early breakfast at a Wimpy restaurant near the campus and engage each other in a respectful but forthright discussion of university business. There was a necessary routine in which we participated in almost every meeting – to remind ourselves of the line between governance and management. He would govern the university with council. I would execute council's mandate given to the senior executive team. When one of us seemed to stray across that invisible line, we would gently remind each other of the boundaries.

There was, however, another dimension to the assertion of power at UFS, and that was through the growing black constituency in the student body and, more slowly, in the staff complement. This was where I witnessed first-hand the enormous influence of the ruling party in the province, which exerted pressure on students (and, to a lesser extent, staff) in an effort to extend its political influence over this captive audience of more than 30 000 students in a relatively small city.

The primary vehicle for power on campus was the student representative council. As black student numbers grew, the conservative bloc in charge of the SRC, representing the Freedom Front Plus (VF+ in its Afrikaans abbreviation), was permanently displaced by the South African Students' Congress (Sasco) of the ruling ANC. To replicate politics on the outside, there was a student parliament, which included minority organisations from the student body, such as the Democratic Alliance Students' Organisation (Daso), representing the Democratic Alliance on the outside.

The student parliament on campus tried to mimic in style and content the vicious and sometimes violent rhetorical practices that marked the national parliament. The consequences of those power struggles and political performances were greatly damaging to the university and to the health and well-being of students from the non-majority parties.

UFS had just emerged from a racial tragedy in which four white male Afrikaans students humiliated five black workers (this was known as the Reitz affair after the student residence where it happened). The campus was deeply scarred. In this sensitive environment, the student parliament pitted black students from Sasco against white students from the VF+, and there was absolute mayhem as a result. Then I discovered that many of the white students who signed up for the VF+ were not, in fact, conservative diehards, as in the mother body; there simply was not another student body representing the interests of white students. Nor were all the Sasco students radical representatives of the ANC; there was no other major body taking care of the needs of black students. As a result, with the opening up of the campus to all students, whites went with the VF+ and blacks with the ANC-aligned Sasco by default. In short, the political organisation of the students along party lines fuelled racial division, with the inevitable conflict that followed.

In response, we decided to do away with student politics organised on a party-political system; the damage to race relations and to the future of the university was simply too great. There was a fiery reaction from outside the university, as the ruling party realised that it would lose the most important vehicle for pursuing this rich and captive set of political resources, the black student body. With council's backing, we stood our ground as senior leaders, and slowly the hatred and divisiveness on the main campus started to dissipate.

This did not mean, of course, that there was no student politics on campus. Our view was that any university without student politics was failing in its mandate to provide students with ample opportunities to learn 'the habits of democracy'[21] and the skills of activism on a range of fronts. The decision was a more limited one: to do away with party-political structures as the sole means for doing politics on a university campus. Students were now more likely to vote on the basis of issues and ideas than only on the racial identity of a political party operating on the university campus.

MANAGING THE MONEY

UFS, like its Afrikaans counterparts elsewhere, had a rigorous infrastructure for auditing, accounting and financial management that made it very difficult for any individual or group to gain unlawful access to institutional resources. That is not to say that there were no incidents occasionally picked up by the internal auditors, who reported to me directly on a monthly basis; all universities experience such testing of their systems by unscrupulous individuals. But those incidents were the exception, and were quickly identified and resolved.

I soon discovered the difference between scandal at the historically black universities, like UDW, and that at the former white institutions, like UP. In the former, the scandal is quickly publicised, as rumour or fact (it does not matter which) in order to give the political upper hand to one faction or another; indeed, every meeting of the university was like a sieve, with important information leaking to the press while the gathering was still in progress. In the Afrikaans universities, by contrast, the scandal is a matter of shame, to be quietly managed and resolved through internal processes. You do not hang your dirty washing on the line, I would often hear in Afrikaans.

Throughout my tenure, the UFS ran a tight ship when it came to resource management. I had a crack team of senior managers in finance who would tell me what was possible, and what innovative projects would unduly stress the public purse. Not once did I challenge their advice, because I knew that they acted in the best interests of the university and that ignoring them would court unnecessary risk – and the loss of their confidence. For several of these projects, it was better to find the resources from outside the university, since a growing number of foundations and corporations were now willing to support the UFS as it emerged from its racially afflicted past.

It was also important to lead by example, given the inescapably visible role of the university leader.[22] The ethical tone of an organisation is set at the top; or, in that vivid expression I heard from my white Afrikaans-speaking colleagues, *'n vis vrot van die kop af* (a fish rots from the head down). Simple things mattered. I never claimed money back for expenses of a few hundred rands, such as for airport parking or a meal on the go. When the marketing department suggested that we use my book *We Need to Talk* as part of a corporate sponsorship gift set, I paid the R100 000 in royalties over to the No Student Hungry Campaign, which we had launched to address the problem of food insecurity among students. The public messaging of these larger actions on the part of the leadership team mattered in an environment where so many young people struggled to survive while pursuing higher education. But public acts of leadership also relay to the broader community of staff important messages about personal and institutional ethics, the values and commitment that underpin leadership behaviour in a university.

One of the most difficult transitions from the apartheid era was felt by the traditional service providers to the university: those small to medium-sized contractors who had for decades enjoyed the racial privilege of preferred contracting for institutional resources. Here the struggle was intense. My vice-rector in charge of procurements, a man dedicated to both the equitable and accountable allocation of the institution's resources, was being harassed by a former contractor of the university; the vice-rector was black, the contracting firm white. The issue was one of those cases of embedded corruption from the apartheid past, in which white contractors (in this case, catering services) were allowed to operate on campus, with the university paying their utility bills while they raked in the money from students.

There was an exchange of words on the telephone and then the matter was over, but the contractor did not know that his phone was still on. He swore at my colleague with some of the worst racist epithets I had heard. To the credit of my senior team, contracts were openly and fairly adjudicated, sometimes in favour of black contractors, sometimes to the benefit of white firms. Fairness and consistency marked all university business, even as we understood the need for empowerment and opportunity for those previously kept out and at a distance from competing for institutional resources.

Throughout my seven years as VC at UFS, I understood that our most powerful resource was our academic credibility or worthiness as a higher education institution. Our ability to attract resources from outside government was dependent on whether we could be taken seriously as a degree-awarding institution. In addition, our ability to benefit from performance-based subsidy funding from government also depended on student success rates and research productivity.

You soon realise as a university leader that perhaps your most important job is to bring vital resources into the university from the outside and to manage those resources well on the inside. Whether you liked it or not, you as the leader stood at that interface between the subsidy from government and the sustainability of the university. You are tempted to optimise the subsidy income by artificially inflating the pass rate or turning a blind eye to increasing publications in predatory journals. The very serious risk, of course, is that both personal and institutional integrity are at stake. Yet, there are some vice-chancellors who do this routinely, as examples in this book will demonstrate. Such behaviour is not only wrong, but dangerous. And yet the pressure on university leaders to find ways of coping under conditions of declining state funding (in real terms) and uncertainties around tuition income is not to be underestimated.

Of course, the state is not the only source of external funding. The UFS was very fortunate to be one among a few universities, normally the well-established elite institutions, that are recognised among private and international foundations as a worthy investment for research and development funds. There was no doubt that following the Reitz affair, the UFS was seen as offering leadership in racial reconciliation and educational innovation, and therefore it was attractive to potential funders. With training and finances from a major United States foundation, we set up our first Advancement Office. A veteran of philanthropy left me with a sobering message: foundations and corporations do not simply give resources to a university; they must be convinced about the leader. Resources, I came to understand, could be given or withheld on the basis of an assessment of a university's leadership.

With this in mind, I proposed that the university's entire mission revolve around two commitments, which we called the academic project and the human project. The first was to deal with the low academic standards of the UFS and the second with its troubled racial legacy. The aim of the first commitment was to significantly raise academic achievement for staff and students; and the second, to pursue racial reconciliation as the basis for a more just university.

I soon became aware of the power that resided in the settled arrangements for academic work and promotion. There were threats of legal challenges, as the academic standard for promotion to the professoriate was sharply increased. Some confrontations in my office were most uncomfortable. Protesting staff had a point: the old standards made many people professors, while the new standards disqualified up-and-coming academics; then came that inevitable South African expression: 'you shifted the goalposts'.

Not getting easy promotion meant the loss of status and the loss of money that comes with moving into higher academic ranks. I tried to argue that the new standards elevated successful candidates to potentially world-class status – they could be proud of their new titles. It was a hard sell. All of this played out against the backdrop of a racially fuelled complaint I had encountered before as the incoming first black dean at UP, and now as the first black vice-chancellor at the UFS: 'standards will fall'. Now (mainly) white colleagues were complaining that standards had soared!

We also decided to raise the standard of admission to our degree programmes; by the time I arrived, the UFS had the second-lowest progression rate among undergraduates at the public universities in South Africa. Letters started to come in from the political parties on the outside: I was anti-black because it was now harder for black students to enter the former white university, obtain a degree, and earn good money from respectable jobs. My response was sharp and simple: 'No, *you* are anti-black because you do not believe that black students can achieve as well as or better than white students, whether in school or university, given the same opportunities.'

Of course, lifting admission standards was a gamble. The school system was broken as a result of the apartheid legacy, but also because of the ineffectual policies of the post-apartheid government. Since 1994, about half or more of the learners who started grade 2 did not make it to grade 12 (the final year of school), and those who passed did so on the basis of a low passing standard (30 per cent or 40 per cent), with very few gaining solid university entrance qualifications, especially in science and mathematics.[23] In theory, UFS's intention to increase the qualification standards for admission could threaten enrolment growth and therefore subsidy income.

In anticipation, the plan was to aggressively market the university through school visits and a plethora of other strategies to bring the best black and white students into the UFS. Situated in the heartland of the country, the UFS was not a first choice for middle-class students from most of the provinces. 'No sea, no mountain,' my marketing team explained, and there was also the perception that this was an Afrikaans-medium institution. But we worked hard on changing the image of the university in the mind of the broader public. I reassured my colleagues of a paradox that had long fascinated me from observation and research in the United States: when you raise academic standards, you recruit more and better students. That is exactly what happened at the UFS.

Nor did we abandon those who did not make the cut. The South Campus was transformed and became another route into mainstream academic programmes for talented students failed by the school system. In other words, those who missed the mark could attend the UFS on an extended programme for one or two years, after which successful students would study for degrees on the main campus. The success rate was astonishing across the disciplines. There need not be a trade-off between equity and excellence.

Despite the steady progress with the social and academic transformation of the university, I would learn a costly lesson about politics: power does not yield without a fight. Student factions were constantly mobilising to gain the upper hand on campus for their masters off campus; there was no question in my mind that some were not only lobbied but manipulated by outside forces with the promise of jobs in the provincial and, eventually, national structures of both the party and the government. In fact, it was fascinating to witness how seamlessly student leaders moved from campus into employment in local or national politics.

Towards the end of my term, I noticed what had become an institutionalised form of corruption at the UFS. Some academic departments, under political pressure, had allowed for the re-registration of several student leaders, despite their having repeatedly failed courses. The rules were that you could re-register for a failed course once, or at most twice, and only for a third time by special appeal on grounds of illness or disability. Here were students failing multiple courses four or five times and staying in the system. I then noticed that many of the repeat failures were student leaders (or their friends) from the main political-party affiliate on campus. This was surely wrong, and so we ended the practice. The reaction was swift and violent.

The charismatic student leader of the SRC had persuaded some of his comrades and older workers to march towards a rugby match that was already in progress. Halfway on their route, he called my acting dean of students with an offer. They would abandon the march to Shimla Park, the rugby stadium, if we allowed the repeatedly failing students back onto campus. She conveyed the offer to me and, as a matter of principle, I said it was not going to happen.

The small group of students and workers then proceeded to march onto the rugby field, overwhelm security and disrupt the game. Some parents, visitors and students in the stands descended onto the pitch. The student leaders could run away, while the older workers were stranded and attacked. It was a tragic and heart-breaking incident, but its roots lay in the discontent with our insistence that rules that applied to all students would not be bent for those with political connections.

Where the university did not have much control over politics and resources was in the hospitals where our academics worked and our students trained. South Africa has an arrangement in which doctors in medical schools are partly employed by the state. These so-called joint appointments mean that the costs are shared for, say, a professor of immunology who teaches students on campus and treats patients at hospital. In the Free State province, this arrangement was a complete disaster.

The National Treasury channels state funding through the provincial department of health, which, in the case of the Free State, has been one of the most corrupt and inefficient of government entities – to the extent that it was placed under administration and managed by the national government.[24] Vital resources for the medical school came late or not at all, and funding for patient care and student training was completely inadequate.

The result was constant confrontation between very angry medical school academics and the inept politicians and bureaucrats of the provincial department of health.[25] To cut a very long story short, corruption in local government threatened to collapse the training platform for our medical school; the accrediting agency, the Health Professions Council of South Africa, noticed this and placed the university on notice. What made matters worse was that the appointment of the hospital administrators in the province was itself heavily politicised. As a result I had to spend about 20 per cent of my time managing the chaos in the health department and its hospitals in a desperate attempt to stave off the loss of accreditation for our medical school.

How was this chaos and corruption possible? Quite simply because the oversight and management of the hospitals and our medical school academics lay outside the supervision of the university's managers and its internal systems of control. In the terms of this book, there was a separate political economy operating alongside that of the UFS, which nevertheless had significant repercussions for the reputation of the university and its capacity to deliver on its academic mandate.

It was one of the hardest relationships to manage, as I moved between the relatively stable political economy of the UFS and the thriving corruption in the political economy of the provincial government. One day, in desperation, I went to a meeting at the home of the then member of the Executive Council (MEC) responsible for health, who was recovering from a leg injury. The guards let me into her bedroom, and there I sat as a vice-chancellor on the edge of a politician's bed pleading for the outstanding resources for my medical school staff while her plastered leg dangled in the air.

A decent and astute politician, the MEC was as honest as she could be to a political outsider about the corruption within her own department. In another world, she told me, you could manage this place and make a success of it. It was a somewhat odd and unexpected comment. The MEC then told me how hard it was to simply keep the predators at bay as officials tried constantly to loot state resources that lay within her department. She promised to fight these forces with all her might.

A few weeks later, the MEC was dead. The official story was that on returning from an engagement in a rural area, a tyre burst, and her luxury car crashed into a concrete bridge pillar, killing the bodyguard driver and the politician.[26] However, more than one of my friends in the Free State government privately questioned the official account of what had happened. In any case, a new MEC was appointed to fill her place, though not long afterwards he was arrested by the Hawks for corruption.[27]

WHAT DID I LEARN ABOUT THE LIVED EXPERIENCE OF POLITICAL ECONOMY?

The capacious definitions of political economy and the extensive theoretical treatments of the subject have their place. There is, however, little available in the literature on what it means to personally live through and experience the interminable struggles over power and resources within institutional life. Political economy, when viewed through the microscope of university politics, makes visible the sometimes intense interpersonal and intergroup emotions, interests, rivalries, compromises, conflicts and contestations which yield particular social and academic outcomes.

I have learned on this journey through the political economy of higher education that, even when talking about the same kind of institutions (universities) in the same national context, the ways in which relationships between power and resources are forged and experienced can be completely different. In fact, the nexus between power and resources can also change over time within the same institutions; an example here is the seamless transition made by some who served the apartheid masters at one point and then went on to do duty under the post-apartheid masters.

The moral unscrupulousness especially of white institutions in transition from one regime to the next is unsettling. What wrestlings with conscience were made in that radical shift from dutifully serving one regime of truth to another as if nothing had happened? What are the costs of such an unconscientious migration from tyranny to democracy? The resources deployed for one purpose on one day were simply redeployed for another purpose the next day. The same power that authorised institutional behaviour before 1994 was still there in the years following 1994. This is a problem that requires further inquiry beyond this book.

What I have also experienced is the remarkable agility of institutions in responding to the challenge of transition. That response is, however, often skin deep in this racially ordered society. The external representations of the power–resources nexus should be approached with caution. On the one hand, the image projected of stability and predictability in the astute management of institutional resources is something to appreciate, even admire, in the context of widespread corruption in South African universities. On the other hand, stability has its own pathologies.

Here is a conundrum for political economy in transitional societies in the global South. How does a new country draw on and benefit from those power–resources arrangements inherited from former white institutions even as the terms of those relations are deeply transformed? Destroy the inheritance as given, and institutions collapse. Preserve the inheritance as received, and institutions ossify. Maintaining a balance is perhaps one of the most challenging responsibilities of a transformative university leader in the aftermath of our divided past.

5

Casting Long Shadows: How History Shapes the Politics of Universities in South Africa

By any measure of social change, the end of apartheid appeared suddenly, even if, in the *longue durée* of southern African politics, it was inevitable. Given P. W. Botha's calamitous Rubicon speech of August 1985, which some had expected to move the country towards the end of racial rule, political observers had grounds to be cautious when the so-called reformer F. W. de Klerk replaced the Old Crocodile. For this reason, the announcement in February 1990 of the unbanning of black political parties and the release of Nelson Mandela and other prominent prisoners caught most citizens off guard.

In the middle of an ongoing anti-apartheid struggle, the announcement meant that new strategies and tactics had to be adopted by the liberation movements outside the country, and by the democratic opposition on the inside, even as negotiating parties started working on the terms of the transition to democracy. How do you resist even as you cooperate? How do you reconcile and repair in the face of a low-intensity civil war, from the streets of Johannesburg to the lush green fields of the Natal Midlands? And how do you build democratic education institutions while the old structures are still in place?

In this period of high uncertainty about South Africa's political future, much conciliatory symbolism was offered for the public mind: from the fish hook caught in the hand of one of the negotiators and taken out by the other,[1] to the imagery of a rainbow nation touted by the popular cleric Desmond Tutu, and the symbolic act of Nelson Mandela donning the jersey of the white Springbok captain during the rugby World Cup of 1995. Antonio Gramsci's notion of interregnum was no longer a theoretical construct invoked by the more intellectual comrades, but the lived experience of leaders and institutions struggling to make sense of the old that was dying and of the new not yet born. The former liberation movement and soon-to-be ruling party felt compelled to put out an unbidden pamphlet intended to reassure, called *Ready to Govern!*

As elsewhere in the society, this anxious transition was made with great difficulty in South Africa's public universities. And, as this chapter will demonstrate, the roots of the ongoing crises at the sample of universities studied in this book lie within the history of these institutions and the kind of politics they brought into the highly unstable transition of the early 1990s.

THE ORIGINS OF RESISTANCE IN SOUTH AFRICAN UNIVERSITIES

The 'roots of resistance' on black campuses, as Mokubung Nkomo once documented, lie at the very point of the creation of these institutions.[2] They were brought into existence with an apartheid euphemism, the Extension of University Education Act of 1959. Black communities expressed ambivalence about how to relate to the new ethnic universities: desiring to access them, whatever their limitations, to pursue advancement, but resisting and seeking to change them at the same time. As a result, explains Nkomo, 'since their inception' the black universities 'have been in constant turbulence',[3] marked by cycles of closures, suspensions, expulsions, reopenings and so forth. For a long time, added Njabulo Ndebele as he recovered from his stint as vice-chancellor (VC) at the very turbulent University of the North, 'South Africa's historically disadvantaged institutions of higher education (HDIs) … were major sites of student anti-apartheid revolts'.[4]

Whatever the apartheid planners had in mind, therefore, tertiary education did not produce loyal and obedient civil servants to manage the segregated racial and ethnic departments of government. It spawned, instead, multigenerational activism that would extend over the decades, through and beyond the end of apartheid. What started with protests around internal issues – whether the forced wearing of ties, the quality of hostel food, or the racism of lecturers – would gradually extend to resistance against the apartheid state and its racist education system.[5] For students of the University of the Western Cape (UWC), the rallying cry 'Hek toe!'[6] was emblematic of that shift – to take the protest movement to the very gates of the university with a broader public argument about social change.[7]

University campuses in the decades after their creation would develop into hotbeds of student activism, marked by familiar routines of student protest on some issue or another. In the process, repertoires of protest and resistance were ingrained in institutional cultures, becoming as commonplace in the regularities of university life as attending classes, writing examinations or participating in graduations. In the early years of their origins, many of the protests targeted 'management', since the heads of the black universities were at the time mainly white and Afrikaans, and therefore seen as representatives of the apartheid state. As the seasoned university leader Ndebele once wrote of those times, 'A protracted conflict between students and management became a guaranteed feature of institutional life.'[8]

Sometimes, a dramatic moment in the broader society would draw national attention to the student protests. The Soweto uprising of 1976, though its focus was on the use of Afrikaans in black schools, quickly drew in the universities, which stood in solidarity with the school students. Universities became a major focal point in national protests, with shutdowns lasting months and many students having to repeat the academic year. These protests signalled a turning point in the national revolt against apartheid.

Two years earlier, another major event had brought campus politics to national attention: the pro-Frelimo rallies of 1974. Students on several campuses celebrated the rise to power of the revolutionary Frelimo movement in Mozambique and the ousting of the Portuguese colonial administration in that country. The arrival of black majority rule in a neighbouring state, and its potential implications for apartheid South Africa, were no doubt on the minds of both the student protesters and the white government. The University of the North was one of the key sites for these rallies, and the government acted swiftly with banning orders and arrests of Black Consciousness-aligned groups, such as the South African Student Organisation (Saso), which led the protest celebrations.[9]

More than one scholar has documented, and indeed underlined, the continuities of student activism over the decades, including the so-called period of quiescence between the Sharpeville Massacre (1960) and the Soweto uprising (1976). In this narration of unbroken student struggle on campuses, place names like Atteridgeville, Alexandria and Athlone feature prominently, all the way through to the historic 2015–2016 social movements known as Fees Must Fall and Rhodes Must Fall.[10]

Nor were white students on the English campuses uninvolved in anti-apartheid struggles.[11] The English universities, though politically ambivalent at the best of times, always carried within the student body a strain of activism against the apartheid government. What were the issues for white students? Describing their institutions as 'open universities', they demanded the non-racial admission of students. There were also regular protests against the arrest of student activists or the imposition of banning orders on student leaders. Activist staff and, on occasion, university leaders would protest against restrictions on student admissions and staff appointments in the name of institutional autonomy and academic freedom.[12] The National Union of South African Students (Nusas) was at the forefront of white student politics, and its leaders became ready targets of police action, which included spying, harassment, imprisonment, banning and expulsion.[13]

In addition, the protests against the policies of the apartheid government could sometimes turn inwards, when the university found itself in collusion with the state. In this regard, there was no greater scandal than that caused by the government's refusal to allow the University of Cape Town (UCT) to appoint the black, Cambridge-trained anthropology lecturer, Archie Mafeje. The university council, instead of acting on the decision of senate, and its own decision to appoint Mafeje, bowed to the dictates of the white government and rescinded his invitation. A nine-day student sit-in at the administration building followed, but it ended with no concessions on the non-appointment.

Before and immediately after the Mafeje affair, the English universities certainly experienced an uninterrupted tradition of student activism, though it was less frequent and less intense than on the black university campuses. As apartheid crumbled and a democratic government came to power, there emerged an interesting split among the former English universities, which was a consequence, in part, of changes in the racial demographics of the student body.

Wits University, for example, quickly became a majority black campus, and by the time of the historic protests of 2015–2016, the issues for students were largely material – the need for more money to pay rising fees. It is no accident, therefore, that the Fees Must Fall movement started on Wits campus. At UCT, on the other hand, students were mainly middle class, and the relatively smaller enrolment of poorer black students there meant that the university could comfortably cover their financial needs. Unsurprisingly, the issues that sparked the historic protests on the UCT campus were largely cultural – the need for symbolic restitution and transformation in the institution's representation of itself; hence the Rhodes Must Fall movement.

Now, as then, there remains a clear line of differentiation in student activism across the different higher education institutions. At black universities, the protests are constant, and focused almost exclusively on students' material concerns, such as accommodation, fees, food and transport. At the former white English-speaking universities, the protests are sporadic, and often based on a specific complaint or issue that is seldom material in nature. When black universities shut down, the events hardly gain media attention, partly because of their frequency and the familiarity of their routines. Conversely, when former white universities threaten to shut down, the media make it a major story.

The Afrikaans universities do not have strong traditions of protest, since these institutions were little more than servants of the apartheid state. These universities understood their role to be that of a *volksuniversiteit* (people's university) loyal to the government of the day,[14] although there were rare instances of dissent by individuals.[15] When students from the Afrikaans campuses did express any activism, it was to break up protests, for example, the violent attack by Stellenbosch University students on their UCT counterparts during the pro-Mafeje sit-ins,[16] the disruption of Nelson Mandela's address to the University of Pretoria community on his release from prison,[17] or assaults on a picket line of Wits students outside the Braamfontein campus in 1976.[18]

In short, protests on Afrikaans campuses were extremely rare, and mostly in defence of apartheid policies. As the student demographic changed after apartheid from exclusively white to majority black – as at the University of the Free State – protests became more common, and were focused on the material needs of disadvantaged students, as at the historically black universities.

In sum, it is impossible to understand the ubiquity of student protests in the post-apartheid period without recognising their roots in institutional pasts. What is also evident in this short review of the history of student activism is the continuity of traditions of protest across the higher education system from the past to the present. And we have seen the dissimilarity in protest traditions, then and now, which can be explained by the racial origins and changing demographics of various universities, as well as their spatial geographies.

THE SPATIAL GEOGRAPHIES AND POLITICS OF THE BANTUSTAN UNIVERSITIES

What was the nature of student politics in the rural bantustan universities? How was it similar to or different from resistance on urban campuses? And what are the consequences of those configurations and contestations for the political economy of institutions in the present?

The plight of the bantustan institution is best understood through the spatial politics of the apartheid order.[19] Rural, isolated and dislocated from the national economy, the universities were left stranded within their so-called homeland areas. Not only were the bantustan institutions isolated physically from major city centres but also socially and intellectually from what was happening in the urban universities.[20] An authoritative study on the subject concluded of one of the largest homeland universities that 'The structural location of Unitra [University of Transkei] in the post-apartheid landscape meant that it catered for the poorest and academically most disadvantaged. This is the foundation of Unitra's institutional crisis.'[21]

While in theory the bantustan governments had some autonomy in dealing with their universities, in the bigger scheme of things they were under the control of the apartheid government.[22] Stuck amid rural poverty, the university stood out as a major resource for the attention of bantustan politicians and bureaucrats, the surrounding community, and any number of power-brokers inside it.

The spatial location of the universities therefore made for a particular kind of politics and economics in relation both to the bantustan administration and to those who opposed it. As Nkosinathi Gwala observed, the rural university also provided advancement opportunities for the Afrikaner petty bourgeoisie: 'One feature of the bantustans [was] to create unprecedented sources of personal accumulation and upward mobility, not to mention potential for corruption. The result has been a never-ending series of secondments and internal promotions, thus ensuring permanent control of institutions originally designed to be taken over by blacks.'[23]

While the homeland university was a resource to be controlled, it was also, inevitably, a convenient site of resistance for anti-apartheid and anti-bantustan activism. Unsurprisingly, 'unrest centered on the bantustan universities. In fact, within the bantustans, the universities were the only centers of organized resistance.'[24]

There were several ways in which the bantustan universities expressed and experienced their own political economy differently from their urban counterparts. First, there appeared to be a much stronger consciousness of the ethnic character and identity of these institutions. Here, more than elsewhere, the sense of attachment to a particular tribal or ethnic identity was very strong.[25] This was reinforced through the regular deportation of 'foreign' academics who did not belong within the territory of the bantustan state and its higher education institution.[26] Foreign academics in such cases were mostly other South Africans who were not Tswana, Xhosa or other in apartheid's ethnic imagination. In addition, once a student was expelled from a homeland university, she or he could not be enrolled at one not designated for his or her tribal group.[27]

Second, it was not unusual for the president of the homeland to be directly involved in the detailed affairs of the university. The university was 'owned' by the bantustan leader, and seen as his property to be managed and controlled. 'The root of the [Bophuthatswana] university's problems', held one academic, 'is that Mr. Mangope [president of that homeland] regards it as just another department of his government.'[28] It was Mangope, for example, who marched onto the University of Bophuthatswana (Unibo) campus with his cabinet and riot police in tow to break up a nationally called prayer meeting of students.[29] Studies of another homeland university make the same point: 'In a very real sense, Unitra was simply another line item in the budget of the Transkei's Department of Finance.'[30]

Of course, there was not much else to be in charge of in the economically destitute homelands, and so the university as a concentrated resource was precisely the kind of institution a rural leader would want to lord over. In addition, there was pressure on the homeland leader, as a political vassal of the apartheid government, to keep the lid on supposed security threats to 'South Africa' (outside the balkanised territory) that might emerge from these rural universities.

Third, there was a highly personal and vicious approach to dissent; student activists spoke of the often extreme and sustained methods of torture visited upon individual protesters.[31] In the homeland territories, it was not at all unusual for the defence force to encamp on university grounds in order to intimidate and control; in the case of the University of the North this lasted for two years. Similarly, in 1986, at the University of Fort Hare, the Ciskeian police occupied the campus for most of the academic year.[32]

Fourth, because of their spatial location, the bantustan universities were particularly vulnerable to shifts in regional and national politics. So, for example, when democracy arrived in 1994, and universities opened admission to all, middle-class students left in their droves for former white institutions like Rhodes, UCT and Pretoria. These white universities were at pains to burnish their fragile transformation credentials in the new democracy, but it came at the expense of enrolments in the rural black universities. This had immediate and severe financial consequences for the latter. In a different case, the decision to move the post-apartheid administration of the Eastern Cape to Bhisho had a seismic impact on the resource base of the city of Mthatha and its university; instantly, many middle-class families left the area.[33]

And, fifth, the bantustan bureaucracy created particular forms of patronage that gave access to resources outside what would be regarded in modern, efficient organisations as the institutional rules.[34] Existing networks of patronage in bantustan institutions, including universities, did not miraculously dissolve with the transition to democracy.

In the former homelands, local leaders, including chiefs, stood as powerful mediators between the university and the community. In more than one institution in our study, the university is actually located on tribal lands, with the result that to this day there is no fence between the campus and the community. More recently, the abaThembu king Dalindyebo led a violent attack on campuses of Walter Sisulu University (the former University of Transkei) in an attempt to take back the land on which parts of the institution are built.[35]

Administrators from the big cities who ventured into some of the bantustan universities soon discovered that they could not make any major decisions without consulting the local chiefs and the communities they represented. An interim vice-chancellor at the University of Venda (Univen) recalls:

> We discovered that the land on which the university was built didn't belong to the university, it belonged to the traditional chief. And [the previous vice-chancellor] had put the chief off quite seriously. I have a video of me almost on my knees before the chief, pleading the case for the university and asking him to transfer the land, because without the ownership of the land we couldn't raise funds to do some of the things we needed to do. We needed to have the real estate transferred so we spent three years of very difficult work trying to get a change in the ownership of the land.[36]

What does all of this mean for the political economy of the present? It requires that any analysis of institutional dysfunction take account of the spatial politics of universities. As a rule, it could be argued that the further a university was situated from the major centres of South Africa, the less able it was to obtain resources to sustain the academic enterprise. And the location of educational institutions within the homelands brought particular forms of patronage politics that continued to shape them well into the democratic period.

An observer of homeland politics in the Transkei, Clive Napier, once wrote that the alliance between homeland functionaries and the apartheid government meant that leaders of the bantustans were invested in 'material interests in the status quo, like good salaries, positions of power and business opportunities'. At the other end of the pecking order, those who fell in line with the authority of the homeland leader became 'recipients of patronage from Matanzima and his functionaries', such as 'high positions in government [and] the allocation of scarce resources like housing loans, land, and trading rights'. [37] With these enveloping networks of patronage firmly in place, the same kinds of transactional arrangements became embedded in the bantustan university. An attempt at Unitra, for example, 'to investigate allegations of corruption and mismanagement within the administration of the university' was met by brute force from the homeland authorities.[38]

The critically important point is that the built-in corruption that characterised political–financial transactions in the educational institutions of the homelands (schools as well as universities) left an enduring mark on how their citizens came to understand the nature and purposes of the university, which, from the viewpoint of the homeland leaders, was little more than an extension of the civil service. Put differently, the contemporary demands on the resources of a university represent an uninterrupted pattern of behaviour which carried across the transition of the 1990s and which is highly visible in, though not exclusive to, the rural black universities of the post-apartheid period.

And, finally, this brief survey also demonstrates that it is impossible to understand or transform the former bantustan universities without considering the spatial geographies that produced particular forms of political economy, throwing long shadows into the present.

The historical stage now set, the key to understanding the transition in student politics under and after apartheid is to examine closely what happened in the mid-to-late 1980s, as South Africa hurtled towards democracy.

STUDENT POWER ON THE VERGE OF DEMOCRACY

By the mid-1980s, schools were once again at the centre of popular struggles for change. Within student ranks, there were calls for 'liberation now, education later'. A committee of concerned parents in Soweto, the Soweto Parents' Crisis Committee, recognised the danger this had for setting back education even further than the Soweto uprising had. In response, a National Education Crisis Committee (NECC) was formed in early 1986, representing students, parents and workers. There was now a new slogan, 'People's Education for People's Power'. Rather than being abandoned, education would be embraced as a vehicle for political change. The rising militancy in schools nevertheless continued unabated.

In a panic, the apartheid government announced a reformist ten-point action plan for black education in 1986, but it was too late. The NECC roundly rejected these plans, pushing forward with its agenda for alternative education to apartheid schooling, signalled by the concept of People's Education. Shortly thereafter, the leaders of the NECC were arrested and in 1988 the organisation was placed under restriction. The following year, the Mass Democratic Education Movement was formed, and under this broad banner the NECC operated in an unrestricted way.

The cycle of militant protest and state repression continued through the late 1980s, until the ban on all organisations was lifted in the historic speech by President F. W. de Klerk of 2 February 1990, which set the stage for the installation of a democratic government four years later. In his same speech, De Klerk unbanned the liberation movements, including the NECC, and the body changed its name to the National Education Coordinating Committee.

The change of name, in itself, suggested that a change of strategy was under consideration – less 'crisis' and more 'coordinating'. The NECC announced 1991 as 'The Year of Mass Education' in an attempt, alongside allies in the Mass Democratic Movement, to bring some degree of normality back to education. Activism now had to shift from protests alone to preparing policies and plans for taking over the government of the country.

Incidentally, around this time I was asked by the NECC to help the organisation think through its future options. Travelling around the country, I interviewed the constituent components of the NECC (student, teacher and worker organisations) to gauge their views on the current status and future strategy of the parent body. Rather than giving directions to the leadership based on extensive interviews, I laid out various options for the future, including the so-called Nixon strategy: declare victory and go home.

There is no question that student struggles were a vital component of the campaign to bring the apartheid government to the negotiating table in order to end apartheid. But the costs were high. One observer made the understated point that 'As a result of the disruption of schools (mainly of a political nature) the black youth is among the most politicized groups in South Africa'.[39] There were other consequences.

With schools at the centre of national protests, chronically underfunded public institutions became completely dysfunctional in parts of the country. The authority of teachers was diminished, even as student voices and representation gained more and more pre-eminence in the political sphere. Government control of and influence over schools were severely curtailed, and the inspection system, a specific target of protests, lost all legitimacy in so far as the supervision and assessment of teachers and teaching quality were concerned. The political language of making the country or its institutions 'ungovernable' would cross unquestioned from apartheid to democracy. Thus, an analysis of the institutional consequences of student resistance helps explain, if only in part, the continuing dysfunction of schools and universities almost three decades since the end of legal apartheid. At the point of transition, however, there was a new country to anticipate and build.

STUDENT POLITICS FROM RESISTANCE TO RECONSTRUCTION

In a relatively short period of time, and into early 1990s, the NECC redirected its activism from anti-apartheid protests and alternative education to playing a significant role in preparing the policy groundwork for a new South Africa. Some of those initiatives included the establishment of education policy units in selected universities and participation in developing a series of policy papers under the auspices of the National Education Policy Investigation (NEPI). Inevitably, the NECC's continued involvement in the Education Desk of the now unbanned ANC became a matter of deliberation, if not dispute, as the country prepared for the first non-racial, democratic elections. After the elections of 1994, there really was no need any longer for the NECC, which formally disbanded in 1995.

As the smoke of decades of anti-apartheid resistance began to clear in the middle 1990s, it became evident that there was a rich vein of student organisations that had, over the years, sustained student politics in higher education. Some were discontinued and others had merged or realigned their politics, while a few smaller organisations, like the Pan African Students Organisation, with strong pan-Africanist standpoints, and the Azanian Student Convention, with its Black Consciousness orientation, emerged from these difficult years.[40]

The most prominent of the student organisations still standing at the point of transition was the South African Students' Congress (Sasco), aligned to the NECC and, by extension, to the ANC. Sasco itself was the product of a merger in 1991 between the South African National Students' Congress (Sansco) and Nusas.

Sasco's affiliation with the ruling party would give it much prominence as a major campus presence for student politics, even as smaller bodies associated with new political parties came into existence in the years after the democratic transition. Newcomers included the Democratic Alliance Students' Organisation, associated with the Democratic Alliance; the South African Democratic Students' Movement, associated with the Inkatha Freedom Party; and the Economic Freedom Fighters (EFF) Student Command, associated with the party of that name.

As the country was about to become a democracy, it was not only student organisations like Sasco that were to lead campus politics into the new South Africa, but also a major trade union called the National Education, Health and Allied Workers' Union (Nehawu). The union was founded in 1987 by workers from the education sector, among others, and was affiliated to the Congress of South African Trade Unions (Cosatu), which, in turn, was an ally of the ruling party, the ANC. Filling out this ecology of activist organisations at the moment of transition was an influential staff association called the Union of Democratic University Staff Associations (Udusa), from whose quarters important figures in higher education policymaking would soon emerge.

The stage was now set for a transition in which the majority party in government would play a major role through organised campus affiliates – Sasco, Nehawu and Udusa. One of the critical issues at that point in the transition was who had the power to make decisions in universities. As a result, when South Africa transitioned from apartheid to democracy, there was no small measure of confusion on the ground about the question of institutional decision-making. This issue lay at the heart of what was now a widely used political keyword, 'transformation'. The sensitivity of activists on this important issue was born of long experience and intense contestations around the hierarchical, authoritarian and exclusive practice of decision-making within university managements, as well as the bicameral governance arrangements (senates and councils) that defined higher education under apartheid. Unsurprisingly, the first major policy paper on higher education elevated the issue of democratisation to the second 'fundamental principle' (after equity and redress) for higher education transformation after apartheid. It is worth quoting in full.

> The principle of democratization requires that governance of the system of higher education and of individual institutions should be democratic, representative and participatory and characterized by mutual respect, tolerance and the maintenance of a well-ordered and peaceful community life. Structures and procedures should ensure that those affected by decisions have a say in making them,

either directly or through elected representatives. It requires that decision-making processes at the systemic, institutional and departmental levels are transparent, that those taking and implementing decisions are accountable for the manner in which they perform their duties and use resources.[41]

Leading into the transition, however, there was a major stumbling block to attempts to democratise decision-making in the ways envisaged. The management, senates and councils of universities were largely white, male and, in many cases, conservative with respect to the democratic agenda of activists among the students, staff and workers of the ANC-allied organisations on campuses. How would the governance and management of universities proceed in this vexed transition period?

The answer was transformation forums, more commonly called broad transformation forums (BTFs) on campuses. As the country prepared for democratic transition, the idea of a forum emerged as a kind of negotiating site for almost everything, as an unpublished study from the period summarised: 'National and provincial transformation forums emerged in critical areas of the South African political economy between 1992 and 1994. Forums, viewed as catalysts for democratic change in the transition period, emerged in agriculture, housing, electrification, local government, education and other areas. The motivation behind creating forums was political and consistent with political and economic negotiation processes occurring at a national level.'[42]

It was apparently Sasco students who, in December 1994, pressed the first minister of education to introduce legislation to force universities to establish transformation forums that 'would include all institutional stakeholders and supersede councils as the highest decision-making structure'.[43] Minister Bengu did not legislate, but he did send a communiqué to all universities (and technikons) imploring these institutions to set up transformation forums. This move was historically unprecedented and politically risky because it meant, in effect, that there would now be parallel governance structures responsible for decision-making in public universities: the BTF, on the one hand, and the executive management, senate and council, on the other.

In one of the rare studies of the operations of these transitional arrangements, it was found that, inside this 'shadow governance structure', each university had its own arrangements for the composition of the BTFs.[44] In some cases, management formed part of the BTF structure; in other cases, they were excluded. Sometimes only internal stakeholders constituted the BTF, but there could also be external community representation. Some BTFs were small and manageable, while others were really 'broad', with close to a hundred members.

Negotiation became a major objective of the BTFs, and gave opportunities for stakeholders to be involved in important decisions made by the university concerned. As a result, the senior structures of the university could not make 'unilateral decisions' (a familiar charge of activists) without involving all stakeholders – students, staff, workers and, on occasion, the broader community. According to a senior researcher of BTFs in three Free State universities at the time, university managements in the province did not take these forums seriously and remained comfortably aloof in their position vis-à-vis the stakeholders.[45] In other cases, 'Vice-Chancellors wanted the forums removed from the governance framework of institutions', according to an activist researcher who worked with the student movements to advance their case for the adoption of BTFs in the face of resistance.[46]

Most analyses of this earlier period of shared decision-making in South African universities failed to grapple with the actual effect of this new and unlegislated intervention, the BTFs, on governance in and beyond the transition. In fact, there were two very important consequences. First, it introduced into university governance a flat structure of decision-making, in which every stakeholder had an equal say in the decisions made. This flattened notion of democracy was, again, a retort to hierarchy and to top-down decision-making in universities emerging from the apartheid past.

Second, it instituted an inevitably conflictual relationship between management and stakeholders, and among the stakeholders themselves.

What had been a pattern of oppositional activism in the anti-apartheid struggle now became part and parcel of the negotiations in everyday decision-making on campuses. Ordinary academic decisions became politicised in the process. As Magda Fourie-Malherbe observed at the time, 'Because of the context within which transformation forums originated, their meetings often degenerated into political power struggles between the representatives of the various constituencies. Staff not only found it frustrating to spend long hours in meetings without apparently achieving anything, but also had to adapt to a style of negoti-ation according to which decisions arrived at one day would be revisited the next.'[47]

The argument advanced here is that while the subsequent govern-ance arrangements to some extent dealt with the first problem, the par-allel model of democratic decision-making, it did not resolve the second problem – the intense politicisation of ordinary decision-making. What happened next?

Slowly, white university vice-chancellors and senior executive teams would be replaced by black leaders in the years after 1994. Now, manage-ment could not so readily be dismissed as the enemy; in fact, at several universities there was an undisguised attempt by political bodies to bring in as vice-chancellors the politically connected rather than outstanding scholar-leaders from the academy. In the course of time, even these pol-itical credentials did not protect VCs from being targeted as the problem by students or workers. The idea of management as the enemy, regardless of their struggle credentials, would be sustained across the transition and entrenched in institutional cultures.

In the meantime, there was new legislation on the table that would seek to alter the interim governance arrangements for universities during the transition. The new government instituted a National Commission on Higher Education (NCHE) in 1996, whose main recommendations were responded to by the minister in a consultative Green Paper in December 1996, were then taken up in a White Paper on higher education in 1997, and were codified in the new Higher Education Act in the same year. The passage of the idea of BTFs across these four documents in a relatively short period of time is, in itself, a fascinating study in the politics of policymaking. In short, what the early documents hailed as a fighting role for BTFs in the democratisation of institutions gradually fizzled out in favour of a replacement concept called institutional forums (IFs) with the role of advising councils.

Where the BTFs were unwieldly democratic structures that acted in parallel with and in opposition to the inherited governance arrangements of universities, the IFs would effectively de-fang their political activism. True, the IFs were composed of all the university stakeholders, including students, management, workers and staff, but their role had changed from negotiating partners pressing for urgent institution-wide outcomes to an advisory body that would merely advise the council on major policy changes or new senior appointments. Not only were the IFs restricted to providing advice to councils, but 'the Act ... does not specify either that council must seek or heed the Institutional Forum's advice'.[48]

Even though IFs were part of 'cooperative governance' in official policy, the reality was that the BTF had lost its political sting. In interviews and documents, a dental metaphor was often invoked among stakeholders to describe the IF: 'toothless'. Cooperative governance was supposed to mean that the government was not the only decision-maker, but acted in concert with all other stakeholders in a transparent manner. And yet, cooperative governance ought to balance political demands and managerial imperatives, as the NCHE would concede: 'the co-operative governance model ... is an attempt to combine, in a particularly South African way, more democracy with more modern management'.[49]

For the new government, managing this political hot potato of transitional governance was not easy, and it shows in the ambivalence of official thinking, as expressed in this extract from the 1997 White Paper on forums: 'The Ministry continues to support strongly the establishment and operations of Broad Transformation Forums. At their best, they have emerged as structures in and through which institutional stakeholders can unite to determine collectively the agenda, timetable and strategies of transformation, to prepare codes of conduct, agree and implement dispute resolution procedures, and draft new legislation.'[50] But the Higher Education Act which followed shortly thereafter stated that it 'reaffirms the position of the White Paper towards the role of the Institutional Forum as *a statutory advisory committee* to the Council' (emphasis in the original).[51] Clearly, both positions could not be true – a BTF that drafts new legislation coexisting with an IF that merely advises council.

For one set of observers, the Act did the political dirty work: 'Despite the rhetoric of the National Commission Report and the 1997 White Paper, Institutional Forums do not have decision-making powers, and cannot override the decisions made by Senates and Councils. While they can – and are expected to – have a major influence on transformation, this must be achieved through an advisory role.'[52] Nevertheless, the doublespeak on such a critical governance issue simply indicates the political tightrope on which the new democratic government was walking during the difficult period of transition.

What were the advisory functions of the 'permanent institutional forums' supposed to be? The multi-stakeholder body would, according to White Paper 3:

- Interpret the new national policy framework
- Identify and agree on problem areas to be resolved
- Participate in selecting candidates for top management positions
- Set the change agenda, including race and gender equity plans
- Improve institutional cultures
- Provide a forum for mediating interests and settling disputes
- Participate in reforming governance structures
- Develop and negotiate a code of conduct
- Monitor and assess change.

Some of these functions would be refined in the legislation that followed. In short, through a quick succession of documents (NCHE, White Paper and Higher Education Act) and an ambiguous but later clear redirection of wording, the BTF as an activist forum was displaced by the IF as an advisory body that was 'permanent' in its governance duration, 'statutory' in its legal status, and 'advisory' in its political influence.

How did this all work in practice? One example must suffice. When a new VC was being considered for appointment, the IF would meet, examine the documentation, and advise the council on whether the person was appointable. Sometimes, that advice would emerge from consensus among the stakeholders; at other times, there would be a majority and minority view, with both being relayed to council.

Giving the IF only an advisory role caused three things to happen. First, the IF in most universities became both ineffectual and unattractive for stakeholders wanting more power and influence in policy or appointment outcomes. More than one study has reported on the disaffection of constituencies with the forum.[53] Second, the activist organisations on campus unmoored themselves from the IF as a self-contained, representative body of stakeholders. The students, workers and staff would continue to protest and make demands, whether on matters of policy broadly, or the lack of transformation specifically, or the usual range of concerns about material conditions (fees, accommodation and so forth), outside this advisory body. In other words, it was activism as usual – external to the ordered and controlled environment required of institutional forums.

Third, the more formal and organised contestation shifted elsewhere – from the IF as an advisory body to the council, where the important decisions were actually made. In other words, since important stakeholders were also represented on councils, this would be the preferred site of negotiation, conflict, contestation and, sometimes, as we shall see, collapse.

By the end of the 1990s, many of the interim arrangements had fallen away as institutions themselves changed.[54] Councils were increasingly transformed from being all-white institutions. Senior management collectives were much more diverse. Student bodies on former whites-only campuses became significantly, if not majority, black. Slower to change were the senates, where the professoriate was for a long time majority white and male, owing to the fact that such appointments depend largely, if not exclusively, on scholarly standing. Senate, however, was less of a target for power-brokers on campus, because their remit was to deal with academic matters. The place where the big resource decisions were being made was council.

THE POLITICS OF INSTITUTIONAL FORUMS INTO THE 2000S

As most universities settled into some form of governance stability after the transitional contests of the mid-1990s, the IFs would gradually lose their power, and even relevance, in most institutions. Some patterns were discernible. Where IFs still functioned as if they were BTFs, contesting institutional decisions as stakeholder groupings, there was chaos. In fact, the NCHE had already warned that 'At certain institutions transform-ation forums attempted to be the highest decision-making bodies'.[55]

One authoritative study on higher education governance saw the following correlation: 'The Institutional Forums that most resemble the earlier Broad Transformation Forums – and are consequently only com-pliant with the 1997 policy and legislation in the most general of ways – were at those institutions where governance was in endemic crisis.'[56] In other words, under the new IF legislation these BTFs had not changed their political DNA as activist organisations challenging and under-mining the authority of university management. This was done by one set of stakeholders colluding against another set for political advantage. The IF idea of cooperative governance and decision-making was not at all the modus operandi of these groups. In one case, it was in fact 'the Institutional Forum [that] played a central role in a crisis that had led to the suspension of normal governance arrangements'.[57]

But there were cases in which the IF slotted perfectly into the role envisaged for it in law and policy. The example of the Durban University of Technology (DUT) under the chairmanship of Dr Lavern Samuels is probably the best case available. At the point of merger, the IF of the new institution first struggled to establish its voice in governance, since the university management, remarkably, decided to chair the new body itself. Eventually, the VC handed over the leadership of the IF to a staff member, who chaired the advisory body for a stable and consistent 14 years. The chair was clear about the role and significance of the IF in the life of a higher education institution. Stakeholders were told over and over again that they should work together 'in the best interest of the university'. Meetings were well attended, issues were vigorously debated, and positions were clearly articulated for the agenda of council.

I saw the workings of the IF at DUT first-hand. It was the first stake-holder group that insisted I meet them at the start of my administratorship as a 'one-man council', so to speak. I was fully briefed by the various con-stituencies in a highly professional manner, with documentation in hand. After that, I made no major institutional decision without consulting the IF, through its leader and at full meetings of the body. I cannot remember once making key decisions that ran counter to the advice of the IF. I understood already then that the vitality and the integrity of the IF at any higher education institution depend critically on how seriously it is taken by the university council.

In most other universities, the IF was neither a well-functioning com-ponent of university governance, as at DUT, nor a completely chaotic political device for destabilising the institution. For the most part, the IF was simply a regular structure of the university that, when it met at all, and was quorate, dutifully went through the motions of considering pol-icies or appointments and advising council in the process. The political action lay elsewhere.

THE LONG SHADOW OF HISTORY IN CAMPUS POLITICS

Try as they might, the ministry of higher education, the department and university management struggled to imprint on the minds of council members who were elected on a stakeholder ticket a fundamental prin-ciple drawn from higher education law and policy – that they must par-ticipate in the deliberations of council in the best interests of the public higher education institution concerned. In the routinely dysfunctional universities, the failure to live up to this founding principle of councils in the post-apartheid era explains much of their troubles.

To act 'in the best interests' of the university required suspending their primary political identities as representatives of students or workers on institutional councils. At chronically unstable universities, this was difficult to ask of these stakeholder groups, but it remained essential for good governance. Activist groups, especially students, knew no other ideas or methods for participating in institutional governance. Over decades, student and workers organisations came into existence through oppositional politics. For students, as we have seen, repertoires of protest after apartheid were shaped by repertoires of resistance under apartheid. Whereas the apartheid state and universities were the target in the past, it was these same higher education institutions that became the target in the present. 'Best interests' was nearly impossible to attain, as the NCHE, to its credit, had already foreseen: 'The pent-up demands for equity after half a century of apartheid make it very difficult for organized constituencies to develop self-binding (to prioritize common interests over own interests) behaviour for the common good.'[58]

It did not matter that universities themselves had opened up access to students and become majority black in their student demographic or senior leadership. It did not even matter when poor, working-class students and even middle-class students could eventually obtain higher education virtually free. The routines of protest, both in prevailing tactics and targets, were essentially uninterrupted from the past and organised around sectional interests as students, workers and so on.

Therefore, the expectation that campus-based activist groups would participate in deliberative forums in the best interests of the university was contrary to their socialisation as activists inside organisations (like SRCs and unions) with a rich history of oppositional politics. Deliberation leads to specific outcomes, mostly reached on the basis of consensus among cooperative governors under the banner of the institutional forum. The point of politics, however, is to keep the goalposts moving; this was as true of the BTFs in the 1990s[59] as it is of campus politics in the 2000s.[60]

This logic of opposition, especially demonstrative antagonism against management or council, comes with its own rewards. The more outlandish their demands, and the more remonstrative the spectacle, the more respected are the student leaders and the more likely their own political ambitions will be advanced after graduation. The poo flinging, the burning tyres, the defaced artworks, are the performative points of the disruptive politics of campus protest whose origins lie in past struggles.

The establishment of IFs certainly was not intended to disestablish student representative councils or worker organisations on campuses. It did, however, imply that students and workers would do their bargaining around important issues inside structures such as the IF and university council. However, what has happened in practice is that unabated and often intense student and worker politics have continued outside these statutory arrangements, but nevertheless bring those contentious issues to the council table. This is the modus operandi of campus politics under the new order.

As our case studies will show, when students or workers could not bend management to their political demands in the day-to-day struggles on campus, they would bring those issues to the council table for contestation, with two vastly different outcomes. In the stable, functioning universities those concerns would be processed through deliberation, and either consensus or a majority position would be reached in accordance with established procedure.

It was a completely different matter in the chronically dysfunctional universities. There, students and workers would begin by haranguing council about an unresolved concern, such as the behaviour of the vice-chancellor, or the state of the residences, or an allegation of corruption. In such contexts, the council is often already split into factions that align on both sides of the issue. Long before the council meeting, the well-established tactic of caucusing is employed, except now the caucus is not against apartheid bureaucrats or politicians, but rather an opposing faction, management or the council leadership. In caucusing, a position is taken, brought to the council meeting, and fought over there.

With this heavy politicisation of councils, meetings would be extended as single items became political sparring points that occupied hours of time. The point was to break down resolve, exhaust councillors, and frustrate procedure to the point that the caucused position would eventually triumph. Inevitably, the good people on council leave, turning a barely functional council into a completely dysfunctional one.

How does this happen? In every instance studied in this book, what made a difference was the strength and resolve of the council leadership. Where council leadership was weak and ineffectual (the chair and executive committee of council, in particular), the opportunities to scupper the agenda as well as the operations of institutional governance were many. Where a university council leadership itself was fractious and unruly, out-of-control student or worker politics could easily break the institutional rules. Conversely, where there was strong and resolute council leadership, the opportunity to challenge and collapse governance procedures was almost nonexistent.

This analysis of the long shadow cast by oppositional politics of the past on the contested governance arrangements of the present raises one more critical and unstudied issue in higher education. Forms of democratic protests are generally conceived of as something good: ways of expressing the will of the people or the desires of the stakeholder group. Because of its rich history of oppositional politics, the corpus of research and writing in South Africa generally upholds the sanctity of protest and the dignity of revolt – as it should. That body of work is, however, less likely to examine the corrosive effects of past politics on contemporary governance, where the legitimacy of anti-apartheid resistance shades into the ruinousness of anti-institutional protests. That distinction is what this book sets out to engage with.

6

The University as a Concentrated and Exploitable Resource

When Sibongile Mani woke up on the morning of 1 June 2017, the undergraduate accounting student from Walter Sisulu University must have thought that all her prayers had been answered. There, popping up in her bank account, was no less than R14 million, rather than the measly R1 400 monthly transfer for meals and books that she received from the state-funded National Student Financial Aid Scheme (NSFAS).

Instead of reporting the erroneous transfer to her university or the scheme, Mani decided instead to go shopping, spending R820 000 in 73 days on everything from Peruvian wigs to expensive smartphones. The Queenstown grandmother who raised Mani lives in a dilapidated structure and felt that the money could have been better spent: 'She should have built me a house instead of buying hair and such nonsense.'[1]

To those outside South African universities, several questions must have been raised by the Mani debacle. One had to be the vulnerability of systems that could allow what officials called 'a technical glitch' to transfer

R14 million of state funding to a student's personal account; indeed, NSFAS only discovered the error more than two months later, on 13 August 2017. Then there is the question of accountability. NSFAS officials said no one was to blame, as the prosecuting authority pondered whether it should make a criminal or civil case. Mani would eventually be found guilty and sentenced to five years' imprisonment for theft.[2] An astute observer of South African society would no doubt consider some pertinent behavioural questions: How many students would have reported the unexpected windfall? How many people in the broader community would be troubled by Mani's behaviour? Her grandmother certainly had other concerns – how to spend the money properly!

The corruptibility of NSFAS as a multibillion-rand resource would surely have exercised the public mind. The diversion of the R14 million to student Mani was no technical glitch, a senior administrator at NSFAS assured me; 'they made the mistake of diverting it to the wrong account'. Evidence at hand shows how NSFAS funds, distributed through a private company called Intellimali, could be hacked, as a note sent by them to the authorities made clear: 'This is evidence that students intelli account are [sic] are being hacked. Student from unisa [University of South Africa] details have been changed into wsu [Walter Sisulu University] students. And the money was taken off. Kindly look at that. Those details apearing [sic] there. Are for sm1 who is changing the account not the rightfully owner.'[3]

The Mani case would surely raise questions in the taxpayer's mind about the sheer magnitude of government funding for student financial aid: the NSFAS funding for 2022/2023 was projected to be more than R29.4 billion – a huge amount of public money flowing into universities. Even so, small as Mani's regular monthly allocation may have been, NSFAS funding is a vital resource for the poorest students in their daily struggles for survival on campuses.

For both criminals and the law-abiding, the South African university emerges as a concentrated reserve of billions of rands whose role as an accumulator and generator of resources certainly demands closer examination.

THE UNIVERSITY AS A RESOURCE ACCUMULATOR

The twenty-first-century South African university is indeed a massive aggregation of public and private resources. The total income of all 26 public universities in 2020 stood at just below R86.8 billion (see Appendix D).[4] The total state budget for the university sector in 2022/2023 was a staggering R76.7 billion.[5]

State funding comes to universities in the form of block grants and earmarked grants. Block grants, which form about 84 per cent of the total state budget for universities (excluding the allocation for NSFAS), are meant to be used for operations (for instance, personnel and maintenance costs) and they fall under the discretion of the council and management of each institution. Earmarked grants, on the other hand, are not under the control of council and are meant to be used for specific purposes, such as building new infrastructure on campuses.

The established universities also boast a significant private revenue stream. For example, the University of Cape Town (UCT), whose total revenue stands at R6 billion, brought in more than R734 million in donations and gifts,[6] raised almost R167 million in endowments and related income, and secured R222 million from corporate sponsorships. UCT's research contracts and grants, a mix of private and public funding, broke the R1 billion ceiling in 2020, as reported in its annual financial statements.

Of course, the ability to raise private income differs greatly across the university sector (see Figure 6.1 and Table 6.1). At one end is Wits University, with more than R4.4 billion in third-stream income, and at the other end is the University of Fort Hare (UFH), with a mere R138 000.

What does this mean? In the first place, these figures demonstrate the enormous inequalities between the established, former white universities in the major cities and the black, former bantustan universities in the rural areas. Such colossal differences in the third-stream income (that is, revenue from neither subsidies nor fees) are, in part, a reflection of historical disadvantage, but they are also partly a function of the incapacity of some universities to make themselves credible and attractive as recipients of private investment. For example, South Africa's oldest university, Unisa, which receives the largest allocation of state funding (R4.5 billion) as well as the biggest share of NSFAS funding (R1.65 billion), in 2020 raised a meager R560 878 in third-stream income[7] – a result, no doubt, of the institution's public image as a place of severe and ongoing dysfunction, with corruption on an industrial scale.[8]

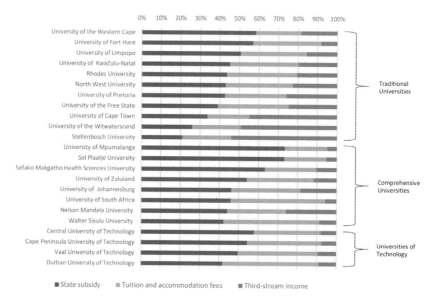

Figure 6.1: Income streams by institutional type, 2020 (%)

Table 6.1: Income streams for Wits, Free State and Fort Hare, 2020

	Total income	Government subsidy	Tuition and accommodation	Third-stream income
Wits	R9.010bn	R2.335bn	R2.246bn	R4.430bn
UFS	R3.995bn	R1.599bn	R1.448bn	R988m
UFH	R1.690bn	R960.977m	R590.768m	R138 222

What is not visible in the statistical tables as they are typically presented is the inverse relationship between the amount of a university's public or private income and the degree of corruption or dysfunctionality within it. That is, the established residential universities with significant revenue streams are more stable and less corrupt than those with less overall income, regardless of the source of income. In other words, it is the institutions with fewer resources in the aggregate that are more likely to be the focus of government intervention to resolve their problems of chronic dysfunction.

This does not mean that the less well-endowed universities do not receive significant levels of state subsidy. With the exception of the newest universities, Sol Plaatje University (SPU) and the University of Mpumalanga (UMP), all of the historically disadvantaged institutions earn revenues in excess of R1 billion per annum; in the case of Walter Sisulu University, more than R2.5 billion.[9] Put differently, the problem of the routinely dysfunctional universities is not simply explained by their relative funding levels, but by problems of institutional capacity and institutional integrity acting in concert to maintain instabilities (see chapter 9).

In sum, public universities are huge receptacles for external revenues from subsidies, fees and private income, which they put to use in the delivery of higher education and economic development.

THE UNIVERSITY AS A RESOURCE DISTRIBUTOR

A university does not merely contribute to the national economy through human capital development in the form of skilled graduates; it also makes an outsized contribution to the local economy. This is especially evident in small 'college towns', where universities such as Rhodes, in Makhanda (formerly Grahamstown); Fort Hare, in Alice; and North West, in Potchefstroom, are major contributors to the municipal economy. In small rural towns like Thohoyandou (home of the University of Venda), and even urban townships like Mamelodi (home to a University of Pretoria campus), the university is often the major employer in the area.

There are, however, very few studies in South Africa that measure the economic impact of a university on the local economy.[10] And, as the research for this book found, universities are reluctant to participate in impact assessments, even when offered without charge and despite the marketing benefits that come with this knowledge. The one major economic impact assessment (EIA) ever carried out was by the Bureau for Economic Research (BER), which measured the contribution of Stellenbosch University (SU) to its municipal area in 2018, using data from 2016.[11] That study merits a closer look, merely to illustrate the often unseen value of a university as a generator of resources for the local community.

How much, and in what ways, does a university with 32 255 students and more than 4 706 staff (1 408 academic staff; 3 298 support staff)[12] contribute to its local economy? We answer the question through the comprehensive BER study. First, through student expenditure in the area: for those residing in Stellenbosch, student spend in the local area is a whopping R1.665 billion, with the big-ticket items going towards monthly rent (31 per cent), food (12.7 per cent) and accommodation on campus (12.6 per cent). For students living outside of Stellenbosch, expenditure amounts to R201 million.

Therefore, when the students leave for vacation, or the campus closes unexpectedly (as a result of the pandemic lockdown, for example), the vendors in the area immediately feel the economic pinch of a significant loss in revenue from the student base. In fact, the economy-wide impact of student spending on local employment in this small town is estimated to sustain 3 535 jobs.

In addition to student spend, there is also the contribution of university staff to the economy of the Stellenbosch municipality. Staff spend is estimated at R541 million for those residing in Stellenbosch and R98 million for those living outside the municipal area. The major categories of expenditure are groceries (R103 million), bond repayments (R87.2 million), rent (R79.4 million) and utilities (R48.1 million). Since students come and go, this huge contribution by staff to the local economy is more stable and enduring, with important contributions made to school fees (R20.4 million), doctors and pharmacies (R25 million) and petrol/fuel (R34.3 million). In this way, an entire local economy is kept afloat.

But the financial impact of the university as a major contributor to the local economy (at R319 million) is even greater outside the Stellenbosch municipality (amounting to R1.355 billion). As a good citizen, SU contributes more than R117 million to the municipality itself, mainly through rates and taxes. The main sectors benefiting from overall SU expenditure are businesses (12.1 per cent), wholesale and retail trade (11.1 per cent), construction (10.8 per cent), and even transport and storage (7.2 per cent).

Then there is the small matter of visitor spending in the Stellenbosch area, which offers enviable attractions for tourists, parents of students, academic visitors from South Africa and abroad, families of employees, and so on. The attractive environment is ideal for big events such as the Woordfees (the Afrikaans Word Festival), whose ticket sales alone exceeded R7 million in 2017; by 2020 the total spend by visitors was around R62.8 million. One study put the overall economic impact at close to R250 million. Visitors buy arts and crafts, stay in hotels, eat and drink in street-side restaurants, fill up with fuel: all of these outlays represent sizeable injections of money into the local economy. This is apart from the steady stream of international academics in university centres like the Stellenbosch Institute for Advanced Study (STIAS); those using the world-class sporting facilities; and, of course, the economic value of spin-off companies and the licence and patent income generated by the business incubators and laboratories on and around the campus.

In sum, the university directly and indirectly makes a massive con-tribution to the local economy, accounting for more than 15 per cent of output and 18 per cent of gross value added in the municipality.[13] More than 13 000 jobs are sustained by SU, which, according to the BER study, constituted 17 per cent of local employment in 2016.

While SU, as a well-endowed university in a prosperous vineyard economy, has a very significant impact on its well-functioning muni-cipality, all universities make a major contribution to the surrounding community. In less well-endowed universities surrounded by dysfunc-tional municipalities, the stakes are high for those dependent on the institution for their livelihoods. As there are few options for employment, unions become a powerful force on these campuses and, unsurprisingly, salaries and conditions of employment are recurrent themes in shutdown protests. And, with municipalities broken, the universities can run out of basic services such as water, as at Rhodes,[14] or must take over services like the sewerage from the local government, as at Fort Hare.

Under such conditions, the hiring of large numbers of unskilled or semi-skilled workers invariably leads to 'overemployment' of staff and heavily contested retrenchments. The university as a resource generator takes immense strain, and invariably the institution is prone to high levels of criminality in the management and administration.

To understand what happens when the resource generation capacity of a university is undermined by incompetence and corruption, consider what happened at Rhodes University when its water supply dried up. The vice-chancellor did something that few university leaders would venture to do, given the potential political backlash: he marched with the campus community and penned an open letter to the municipal authorities that contained this revealing quotation: 'We are again on the brink of having to close the university. Despite the valiant efforts of our staff and the great fortitude of our students we cannot cope any longer. Can you at all imagine the chaos that will occur if the university has to close its doors? Or the economic impact that this will have on the town, which is highly reliant for its economic well-being on the university operating?'[15]

Resources, large and small, play a major role in institutional instabilities, as can be seen in four significant revenue streams: NSFAS, council remuneration, research funding, and the market for student accommodation.

NSFAS AS AN EXPLOITABLE RESOURCE

In 2020–2021, NSFAS was granted a state subsidy of R28.2 billion[16] to fund 755 116 students[17] in colleges and universities – a growth of 67.06 per cent in funded student numbers since 2016. As indicated, the amount of funding varies across institutions, from as little as R400 000 on a small campus to well over R1 billion in 7 of the 26 public universities. 'In most countries, defence contracting is where corruption is located,' said a senior member of South Africa's science councils, who added, 'but in South Africa, it is in all sectors of the public economy.'[18] With this concentration of resources for higher education, NSFAS was always going to be a target for corruption.

Things came to a head in 2017–2018, when 'irregular expenditure' of R7.5 billion was recorded alongside more than 440 000 'irregular records' of students generated at about the same time. NSFAS was put under administration in 2018, which was extended to 2020, and the administrator's handover report to the responsible minister contained this chilling paragraph: 'In August 2018 NSFAS teetered on the verge of institutional collapse threatening the stability of the entire HE system. Unable to respond to its mandate of supporting the poor and vulnerable to achieve higher education, more than 650,000 students were faced with hardship and deprivation jeopardizing [their] academic years.'

At the very time when there was an explosion in applications, the systems were coming apart at the seams. By 2020, 'half of the more than 600,000 first-time applicants came from households receiving grants from the South African Social Security Agency (SASSA), a doubling from the prior year'. But in 2018 NSFAS dysfunctionality led to 'delays in disbursements to students of up to 8 months [which] triggered student protests on a national scale'.[19]

Here, too, is a chicken-or-egg conundrum. What came first: the archaic IT infrastructure and cybersecurity vulnerabilities, or the widespread corruption embedded within and around the organisation? What is clear in the voluminous documentation on the crisis at NSFAS is that criminal elements fed off the broken systems. This raises a question about the extent to which manufactured incapacities in NSFAS systems have enabled crime and corruption in this billion-rand industry in higher education. How exactly did this happen?

When it became clear that several universities did not have the capacity to manage the large volume of NSFAS funding or to efficiently distribute those funds to students, two intermediary companies were contracted for this purpose. The distributive facility of choice was the voucher system. The company would issue vouchers to the students that could be spent only at designated stores. However, 'what the voucher arrangements instead opened up', said the administrator at the time, 'was a whole sub-economy in which criminals came to thrive'.[20]

Vouchers went to the accounts of criminals or to those of non-NSFAS-qualifying students. They were also exchanged for cash. A chain of operators was in place to exploit the voucher system. There was only one obvious solution, and that was to eliminate the third-party system, end the voucher mechanism and pay students directly. That decision instantly removed an opportunity for fraud, but the backlash by criminal elements was immediate and intense. New security arrangements had to be put in place, including 24/7 protection for the administrator.

Another form of corruption involved so-called travelling students. Students who failed repeatedly, and therefore fell foul of the N+2 years of qualification for NSFAS funding,[21] would simply move from one university to the next and start afresh as new applicants for state financial aid. The 'system' as it existed at the time did not discover the fraud, and it was during the period under administration that 6 000 students had to be 'unfunded' for fleecing the scheme in this way.

This problem of poor controls at NSFAS was also manifested in other ways. For example, fictitious landlords would be loaded onto the system and benefit in this way from NSFAS-funded students. NSFAS staff and university staff in some places would collude to defraud the fund through the creation of ghost students as beneficiaries. Sometimes, alternative criteria were created in institutions, thereby allowing non-qualifying students to benefit from the fund. Dead fathers were in fact alive, false commissioners of oaths attest to false documentation, and so on.

Nothing, however, was as disturbing as the corruption that enveloped the distribution of laptops when the country entered the pandemic lockdown in the months following March 2020. What was frightening in this case was how high up in the political system the rot of alleged corruption would reach – all the way to the chair of the parliamentary portfolio for higher education.

When the lockdown began, universities, like other institutions, closed their doors. The intention was that students would have uninterrupted access to emergency remote teaching in these crisis conditions. This was nearly impossible in a deeply divided country where the shift from face-to-face instruction, to emergency remote teaching, and then to fully online learning happened seamlessly for the middle classes but severely disrupted the education of everyone else. Poor and working-class students simply did not have devices or data credits for uninterrupted teaching and continued learning. With the prospect of extended lockdowns, given the course of infection and disease, this kind of interruption could be particularly catastrophic for university students.

The answer from government was to provide laptops loaded with data for all students in need. By one estimate, the total costs for the NSFAS population would have been in the region of R3.6 billion, of which about R1.1 billion was allocated to the technical colleges. Most of the distribution of laptops was carried out through university procurement systems and the rest through service providers appointed by NSFAS.[22]

At an earlier moment, there was the possibility of the distribution being managed by the Department of Higher Education and Training (DHET) itself – an unprecedented move that was more than a signal of misplaced interests in government circles. Common sense prevailed, and it was left to NSFAS to oversee the procurement processes for the speedy delivery of the laptops so that tertiary students could continue their learning without too much disruption. However, even in a pandemic crisis that carried severe repercussions for the teaching and learning of poor and working-class students, corruption would ensure a maddeningly delayed process.

The internal mechanism for allocating laptops was administratively simple. There was an existing book allowance available to students, which was already designated as a 'teaching aid allowance'; thus, this facility could be the vehicle for purchasing IT devices like computers. With accumulated reserves of about R3.66 billion, there was confidence at NSFAS that the laptop project was feasible, while the minister himself expressed enthusiasm for this Covid relief plan.

When the DHET first wanted to look after the procurement itself, the chair of the portfolio committee on higher education rejected the idea, saying it was properly an NSFAS function. NSFAS took charge but insisted that it would work under the oversight of National Treasury and the Attorney General's Office, with the DHET as observer in the form of a ministerial adviser.

A problem arose when the team adjudicating the tender bids split its vote. There was a bitter confrontation between those pushing for one preferred bidder and those opposed to this choice. At this point, the administrator realised that the adjudication committee was compromised, so he scrapped the tender and restarted the bidding process. That brought swift condemnation from the chair of the portfolio committee, and harassment commenced against the administrator, whose armed security was placed on high alert. The administrator fired the adjudication committee and the bidding was reopened with firm criteria: local content (that is, not computers from China, for example); down-streaming capacity; and a record of having previously successfully provided more than 30 000 laptops. The last-mentioned requirement was relaxed somewhat, since few black suppliers would have built up that kind of track record. In the end, four suppliers were appointed. The chair of the portfolio committee was livid: 'The portfolio chairperson went ballistic when I announced the cancellation of the first tender to the extent that on the Monday morning he went onto television. He demanded that I award the tender to the one favoured supplier.'[23]

What followed was continued harassment and bullying; false accusations that the administrator was tipping the tender scales in favour of other interested parties; and a nine-hour interrogation in Parliament of the administrator and his staff. Internal NSFAS reviews, including those by the audit and risk functionaries, revealed a fair and just process. NSFAS would, for the first time in years, receive an unqualified audit opinion.

The political pressure to exploit the heavily funded laptop resource was unrelenting. What happened in the tussle between NSFAS and the portfolio committee found parallels within some universities themselves, in particular the Sefako Makgatho Health Sciences University (SMU) and the Vaal University of Technology (VUT). At VUT, the laptop tender process was abandoned on grounds that the bidders could not meet the targets for the R20 million contract. An 'independent procurement process' was followed instead, and two companies rather than one were appointed, to minimise the risk of non-delivery of laptops to 4 102 students.[24] At SMU, the costly delay in the delivery of laptops to the health sciences students was attributed to ongoing feuds between two senior managers within the university, as was revealed in a leaked forensic report into the R17 million tender. Incensed students took to the streets in protest against the delays in obtaining these devices vital for learning remotely in a lockdown. Two months of academic time was lost waiting for laptops. Eventually, two companies were appointed to buy 2 850 laptops for students and an additional 100 staff members.[25]

The laptop procurement saga at the two universities demonstrates how, even in a pandemic that threatened a serious loss of learning time, the constraints of capacity and the conflicts of management combined to ensure that students were left further behind than their counterparts in functional institutions. Whether there is corruption in the two institutional cases is not clear from the evidence available; but what cannot be contested is the debilitating consequences of the incapacity to manage vital resources under crisis conditions.

COUNCIL REMUNERATION AS AN EXPLOITABLE RESOURCE

For decades, the more established universities in South Africa did not remunerate council members for attending governance meetings. The men and women who served on council regarded their appointments as a privilege and a duty. To be associated in this way with an institution of higher learning was something to be proud of, even an honour. It was, moreover, an opportunity for doing public service at the highest level of the education system. Skills could be shared, networks built, and funds raised, all for a worthy cause. The idea of receiving money for civic duty or privilege bestowed was beyond the pale.

Admittedly, these councillors did not need the money. By and large, council members were wealthy industrialists or successful professionals in the fields of law, accounting, management consulting and business. They were more likely to donate money to the university than take money from it. In addition, they were often locals from the surrounding community, and even when they were from further afield, universities like UCT expected councillors to pay their own way to and from council meetings.

All of that changed as the dominant demographics of council members changed. Council members were no longer solely wealthy businessmen, though some still were. Representatives from the municipalities or the mayor's office did not have the same kind of disposable income as their predecessors. The small business entrepreneurs that emerged in the wake of apartheid were often struggling in difficult economic times. Some members of council were unemployed. Today, every external council member is reimbursed for travelling costs to meetings, and for overnight accommodation when necessitated by travel or the extension of meetings beyond a single day.

Until recently, there were a handful of universities that still did not pay council fees to attend meetings. These were a mix of established, well-endowed universities and less wealthy ones: UCT, Wits, the University of the Western Cape (UWC) and the University of the Free State (UFS). At the time of writing, the UFS was contemplating basic remuneration for members. Other than these four institutions, council members are paid to attend meetings. The total sum of such fees, using 2020 data, amounts to R2.1 million in the case of the University of South Africa (Unisa) and R1.3 million in the case of the deeply rural institution of the University of Venda (see Appendix C).

It is in the breakdown of compensation that the meaning of these fees at the individual level takes on some significance. In 2020, the chair of council at Unisa earned R3 500 for attending a meeting, and an additional R750 for chairing the meeting; when the chairperson of council attended a separate meeting for university business, a further R2 800 was paid. When there were four meetings of council per annum, plus one or more special meetings and, say, three to five external meetings for university business, the amounts could quickly add up to a significant source of income. At one university, the chairperson also receives R5 622 annually as a cellphone allowance.

Compared to the billions of NSFAS funding and the millions set aside for laptops, council remuneration may seem like a drop in the ocean when it comes to exploitable resources. But the value and significance of this income depends very much on who receives it. When council members are unemployed, or their business is struggling, or they have low-paying jobs, fee remuneration makes a significant difference to personal income. The question becomes: how can such remuneration be optimised for individual council members in need? This is where the chair of council plays a critical role in the manipulation of fee income as part of the exercise of power. Throughout this book, there are examples of council chairs extending meetings beyond one day or calling for special meetings on a whim. Those additional council meeting hours are, to put it crassly, billable hours. With every meeting, income accumulates for the individual.

Council chairs also have a say in the deployment of members on subcommittees, which earn additional income over and above attendance at the regular or scheduled meetings of the governing body. Therefore, skilfully allocating members to subcommittee duty is a way of securing and maintaining loyalties when important decisions have to be made – such as support for one or other preferred bidder.

An unscrupulous chairperson can exploit the added material benefits that come from being a council member. A disgraced council chairperson of a university spent days holed up in a five-star hotel long after the day-long council meeting had ended. In a story heard often during this research, the chair of a university council in KwaZulu-Natal was asked to attend a meeting with the minister's assessors. He told them to meet him at the classy Intercontinental Hotel at the Johannesburg Airport. To their surprise, they found the chairman on the same flight as theirs from

Durban going to Johannesburg, sitting in business class. They had their meeting at the airport, whereupon the chairman took his return flight to Durban – all at university expense.

In a most unusual move, a council chairman at a Western Cape university demanded university funds for meetings and events that he arranged and attended on campus. Management realised the mistake, but it was too late. The chairman would for years cross the line between governance and management, leading to a confrontation with the executive, and the vice-chancellor in particular, which is still in the courts long after the VC retired. However slim, the funding enabled the chair, a skilled political operator, to continue to wield influence among stakeholders on the campus. When further funding was not made available, conflict ensued between the chairman and management.

In sum, council funding can leverage political influence over council members who might be included or excluded from these compensatory benefits, depending on whether they are prepared to play along with the schemes of the chairman. Being a member of council, and especially the chair, also extends access to and control over other resources of the university. Small as it may be, the remuneration is intertwined with other resources and opportunities, and therein lies the real value of council compensation.

To be clear, merely receiving council remuneration does not make a governing authority corrupt; fees for members attending board meetings are certainly commonplace in the private sector. What this inquiry into council remuneration does reveal, however, is how a completely legitimate line item in the annual budget of a university can become a major headache when that expense shades into corrupt activity, as happens with another form of compensation – research income.

RESEARCH FUNDING AS AN EXPLOITABLE RESOURCE

According to 2021/2022 data,[26] the research industry in South African universities is a R5.26 billion enterprise in public funds alone.[27] Public funding comes through the science councils as well as directly from government in the form of state subsidies. State subsidies are based on the research generated per annum as quantified in terms of publications in recognised scholarly outlets (books, journals, conference proceedings, and chapters in books) and postgraduate students (at master's and doctorate level) graduating in the reporting year.

But universities also generate research funds through private sources, such as the mining and banking sectors, foundations and philanthropies. Take UCT as an example. In its 2020 annual financial statements, the university reported contract income exceeding R1 billion, which constituted 36 per cent of research income. In fact, the research-related donations of R734.9 million far exceeded government grants of R479.4 million, which made up only 17 per cent of research revenue.[28] The major non-state funders included the Bill and Melinda Gates Foundation, the United States National Institutes of Health, and the Wellcome Trust, while the state-funded National Research Foundation (NRF) contributed 22 per cent of total research revenue.

At the other end of the spectrum, the research income from private sources at historically disadvantaged universities is close to zero, and these institutions rely almost entirely on state funding. Since their publication outputs are relatively low, NRF bursaries account for much of that income, which in 2021/2022 amounted to about R6 million at the Mangosuthu University of Technology (MUT), R17 million at Walter Sisulu University (WSU), and R32 million at the Vaal University of Technology (VUT). These also happen to be universities prone to routine corruption and dysfunction, where there can be enormous pressure on this very limited research revenue to be diverted towards other ends. As a senior official at the NRF revealed:

> University X was going through financial troubles and used the grant deposit given to universities to pay salaries. So, that was a drastic thing that happened and the ultimatum we gave them is that if the money isn't put back into the system where it is

supposed to be, there would be no future funding for your university from the NRF and of course they put this thing right quickly. There is another university with THRIP [Technology and Human Resources for Industry Programme][29] funding where the business was set up falsely and we had to get a forensic audit to sort this out, the university was in denial and we brought forth the evidence and then they put it right.[30]

The constant pressure for irregular access to NRF resources by those working in universities led this official to brief the incoming CEO in 2021 about 'the rent seeking behaviours of staff in higher education institutions'.

A more recent and lucrative means by which universities exploit subsidy income from research funding involves the subterranean academic economy of predatory journals. On the surface, the activity appears to be legitimate, but it does not take much investigation to discover an academically corrupt practice of enormous proportions. Predatory journals are for-profit outlets that offer researchers publication through a quick turnaround process, often without peer review or editorial oversight on open-access platforms, and for a fee.[31]

What explains the explosion in predatory publication over the past few years? It is the high incentive value that comes with subsidisation. In 2021, the unit value for a research output such as a single journal article was R123 635;[32] this was a drop from the previous year's R130 000 because of across-the-board cost cutting in government departments as state resources shifted towards Covid-19 priorities.[33] Nevertheless, the growth in subsidy value per publication has increased by 64.9 per cent since 2006, when it stood at R75 000. This is what makes the scramble for subsidy research income so intense in the 26 public universities, some of which instruct their academics to publish articles based on their master's and doctoral students' work. Under this kind of pressure, predatory journals are the low-hanging fruit of the publication industry.

The highest share of predatory publications within an institution measured over a nine-year period (2005–2014) occurred in our sample of dysfunctional universities, including MUT (at 16.3 per cent), WSU (at 16 per cent), Univen (at 14.9 per cent), and UFH (at 14.7 per cent).[34] The reason is simple: with low institutional capacity for producing quality research in significant volume, and with low institutional integrity for screening out bogus journals, academics take shortcuts to publication to enhance both the status of the individual and the standing of the university. The institutional interest in sustaining such exploitative practices among individual academics will be considered shortly.

It would, however, be a mistake to assume that publication in predatory journals happens only at the smaller, less stable, and poorly endowed teaching universities. It is as much a phenomenon in the larger and wealthier research universities. In sheer numbers, in fact, most of the articles in predatory journals come from the more established universities, such as Unisa (with 546), North West University (with 357), University of KwaZulu-Natal (with 269) and University of Johannesburg (with 224). And the picture looks a lot worse when one focuses on particular disciplines, as a study found in the field of economics: 'Eighteen percent of academics in South African economics departments publish in one of the five predatory journals … This is a very high number. It indicates that a significant part of South African academic economics research is of extremely low quality and potentially that fraud or incompetence is possibly prevalent in many departments.'[35]

There is, however, another way to game the system and optimise subsidy income, and that is through the mass publication of journal articles. Typically, an academic regarded as highly productive would – setting aside scholarly books for the moment – produce at most five to seven articles a year in competitive journals; that number would, of course, differ by discipline (fewer in mathematics and more in sociology) and by the ranking of the journal. One academic, however, found it possible to produce 132 articles in a single year. To be sure, most of the articles were co-authored, but in my view this kind of output is clearly impossible in legitimate academic work, no matter how smart, energetic or well-funded the individual might be.

The University of Johannesburg (UJ) as an institution has done little to stem the tide of this dubious kind of academic activity, even as it has benefited handsomely from the massive subsidy income that results. One example concerns UJ's participation in an international conference on industrial engineering and operations management in Rabat, Morocco, in 2017. At this three-day conference:

- Forty-four unique papers were 'presented' by UJ staff and submitted for the subsidy. One of these papers was not approved for subsidy. A total of 50.46 subsidy units were awarded for these. This translates into an amount earned, for participation at one conference, of R6.15 million.
- These papers were authored or co-authored by 34 individual staff members or students from UJ. Because of multiple authorship, a total of 106 authorships resulted.
- One academic (who was on the advisory committee of the conference) co-authored 29 of these 44 papers.
- In their submissions to the DHET, these papers were submitted under two names which refer to the same conference: the 'International Conference' and 'International Symposium' on 'Industrial Engineering and Operations Management'.[36]

What the responsible government department, the DHET, has done is to incentivise academics to conduct and publish research. That is a good thing. However, in some universities and for many academics, this has been turned into a perverse incentive, with damaging consequences for both the quality of scholarship and the reputations of academic departments and universities as a whole.

Sometimes, incentive-driven policies in disadvantaged universities have emerged from the familiar struggle to reward academic staff working under difficult conditions like salary freezes and limited income options. The UFH is a case in point. When in dire financial straits in the 1990s, its VC would have to go begging to the government for a bailout so that the institution could meet its payroll for the month. And UFH was certainly not alone among the disadvantaged universities in this respect.

What was not possible in those times was to raise salary levels through the annual raises for which most universities make provision. Under such constraints, the UFH did something else to sweeten the difficult situation with staff. It established a scheme whereby staff could hire a car and reimburse the university for the costs without having to pay insurance and other added expenses; this was certainly much cheaper than buying a car on your own.

In addition, staff were encouraged to generate their own income in lieu of salary increments. But unlike at other universities, that extra income was not subject to cost recovery, whereby a percentage of the funds raised goes back to the institutional coffers, especially in cases where campus resources – material and intellectual – were used. Some staff went even further and created their own companies, which then proceeded to do business with the university, for example, a catering company serving the campus.

The UFH even provided incentives for research outputs whereby the subsidy from a publication or a master's or PhD graduate went straight into the pocket of the industrious academic rather than the institution. Most universities would not tolerate such a scheme, on the grounds that it was academic work for which the academic was hired, and that it was done using university time and facilities. Indeed, in some universities, the entire research-generated subsidy goes back to the institution's coffers.

In other universities, a portion of the subsidy earned from research goes into the research account of the academic, to support his or her research activities, and the rest goes to the university administration, which manages research across the institution, such as research training for young academics or the preparation of academics for making grant applications. Few universities provide cash incentives from the subsidy.

At the UFH, however, all income from research was paid out as cash. The inevitable happened. A few academics would graduate several doctoral students in one year, generating huge personal income for themselves, while at the same time inviting sharp questions about the quality of those graduates produced in even less time than the minimum allowed by serious research universities.

In short, what started as an understandable strategy for academics and management 'to meet each other halfway' became a gross exploitation of subsidy income, which would prove very difficult to change. But the demands on universities as an exploitable resource also reside off campus, in a corrupt relationship between the university and the community.

THE STUDENT RESIDENCE MARKET AS AN EXPLOITABLE RESOURCE

Universities were caught off guard when huge amounts of funding first arrived for long-postponed infrastructure development on campuses, including the provision of residence buildings for the growing numbers of students. In the Ministerial Statement on University Funding (2021/2022 and 2022/2023), universities were projected to receive more than R3 billion through the infrastructure and efficiency grant.[37]

What was not foreseen was how the arrival of new infrastructure funds for student accommodation would destabilise a fragile but established residential economy that relied on the steady flow of institutional resources in the form of payment for student housing. The disruption of this cosy economy would cause conflict with all the elements of a sensitive township ecosystem comprising landlords, taxi operators and food vendors.

It is not the case that provision of housing in the community was always of an acceptable standard. Students often complained about discovering, for example, that their rooms would be shared with the owner's young children, which meant that it was lights out when they needed to study. Others lived in outbuildings in backyards. Women students found that the landlord had keys to their rooms and would enter without warning. There were even rooms that became part of a tavern on weekends. Altogether, the physical state of rented facilities was often dismal.

However, armed with state resources, universities marched in and installed their own residential arrangements for students. The problem was that these were often NSFAS-funded students, and therefore they could take up residence only in accredited facilities, that is, residences and rooms that complied with minimum standards for student occupation. Most landlords could not meet those standards, such as the requirement that the property be rezoned as a business for accommodation purposes; that there was an approved building plan; and that rooms had to meet spatial requirements to avoid overcrowding. Landlords literally saw their resources walking out of the door.

To make matters worse, large property developers would muscle in and build multi-storeyed properties to draw students to facilities that met the accreditation standards, but at a steep cost. Students would often have to augment the NSFAS funding out of their own pockets. If, for example, the company charged R40 000, but NSFAS provided only R30 000 for accommodation, the student would have to pay the R10 000 difference. Some university authorities would then negotiate with the company for the student to pay off that debt through monthly deductions. As one vice-chancellor summarised the situation: 'The community around the university was revolting also because the new accredited residences provided the transport. Next thing, the taxi association says they are being robbed of an income and that we've robbed the gogos [old women or grandmothers] of an income. These were the unintended consequences for the township economy.'[38]

It was not simply a case of the landlords being victims of competitors in the residency business; they all too often were also aggressors in the student accommodation market. Nowhere was this clearer than in East London in the Eastern Cape. It has no independent university, but there are thousands of university students connected to WSU to the north and UFH to the west; for example, WSU has about 8 276 students on its Buffalo City campus (about 25 per cent of total student enrolment in 2019), while UFH has 6 805 students on its East London campus (42 per cent of total registrations in 2020).[39] These more than 14 000 students attend the satellite campuses of their respective institutions, neither of which provides its own residential accommodation in East London. In other words, there is a happy market for landlords.

The problems started with UFH leasing buildings and equipping them with security, Wi-Fi and the other basic facilities that students need. Local operators, recognising the need for student accommodation, would find some money, purchase a building, lease it to the university, and then 'sit back, relax, and watch the money flow in for five years, easy money', as a university leader mused. As student numbers grew, operators would again take old hotels, old-age homes, and 'anything that has multiple beds and rooms, and they will buy and refurbish them'. The new landlords would then entice the students to view one or two of the rooms in the spruced-up buildings. Students would then confront the university about the quality of its own leased residences and demand to move. This situation made East London 'a hotbed of mischief and corruption' when it came to accommodation.[40]

Then, of course, there was the downright thieving that came with residence accommodation. At the VUT, the government had provided the university with so many rands per residence bed that could be built or procured. The university management then decided to test the market and see whether it would cost more, or less, if they could find a private provider willing to sell an established facility. So, a tender was advertised and the recommendation was that the bid go to a company that would actually build fewer beds than what the allotted rands would allow.

Council was divided on this recommendation. Some felt the university could build the residence accommodation at R60 000–R80 000 less than the tender amount, a major saving for the institution. Others on the governing body insisted that external providers be contracted. There were suspicions of corruption involving a senior person in procurement, who was placed on suspension. The battle was fierce, and the council collapsed. Soon afterwards, an administrator was appointed. The spark was residence accommodation, the loser was the institution, and the delays meant that beds for students would not be built anytime soon.

CONCLUSION

As a highly visible concentration of resources in unequal and under-developed communities, the university offers two immediate possibilities. First, it can be a formidable resource for education that contributes significantly to the development of the community. Second, the university can simply be a resource up for grabs by those who would exploit its assets for nefarious ends.

In highly functional universities, the institutional effort can be focused on optimising resources to advance teaching, research, service and innovation in defence of the academic project. In dysfunctional universities, by contrast, much of the institutional energy is absorbed in making the most of limited funds, on the one hand, and fending off the relentless claims on scarce resources, on the other.

To therefore grasp both function and dysfunction in universities, it is important to understand the centrality of, and the struggle over, resources in the life of the institution – a struggle that sometimes descends into sheer criminality.

7

The University as a Criminal Enterprise

There aren't a lot of ways out of poverty and universities provide one of those ways.[1]

At around five fifteen on 22 May 2018, Professor Gregory Kamwendo parked his car outside a flat in Empangeni, a beautifully situated town overlooking the Indian Ocean in the north-eastern part of KwaZulu-Natal. Malawian-born, he was an accomplished scholar in the field of sociolinguistics and dean of the faculty of arts at the University of Zululand (UZ). The man who pumped bullets into Kamwendo's upper body as he sat in the parked car on that fateful Tuesday evening was an *inkabi* (assassin). He had been hired by a taxi owner, Oscar Mthiyane, who himself had been called out of the blue to arrange the murder. The caller was Selby Nkuna, a one-time lecturer at the University of Zululand. The 53-year-old professor died bleeding in his car as the two men sped away in a getaway car driven by Mthiyane. On 29 November 2018 detectives arrested Mthiyane and Nkuna, and in October 2020 the two killers were sentenced to life in prison.

Why would a university lecturer murder an academic dean? Quite simply, because the dean was disrupting a revenue stream that enriched the lecturer. Kamwendo had exposed a fraudulent PhD operation in which the university allegedly sold poorly printed doctoral diplomas. It did not help that there was already bad blood between the two men because Kamwendo had testified in an arbitration case against Nkuna for physically assaulting a student. Nkuna had threatened to send Kamwendo 'back to Malawi in a coffin'.[2] The murder took place in the context of institutional dysfunction, as one statement so poignantly captured: 'In grieving the loss of a man of such principle and integrity, we call for justice, not just in prosecuting his murderers but in addressing the institutional and system-level dynamics that his murder draws attention to'.[3]

INSTITUTIONALISED CORRUPTION OF THE ACADEMIC ENTERPRISE

The PhD scandal was matched by a much bigger case of certificate fraud at UZ in 2016. An investigation there showed that as many as 4 000 people might have paid for their degrees over a period of twenty years. Between 400 and 500 of those certificates appeared to involve teaching qualifications. In one instance, five staff members made R260 000 selling 15 fake degrees. About 80 students were deregistered after it was found they did not even have matric (school-leaving) certificates. A student tutor confessed that he had doctored the results of more than a thousand failing students. Probes, suspensions and firings became a regular part of the administrative procedures at this university for years.[4]

When Professor Chris de Beer, one in a long line of government administrators, came to UZ in April 2011, he found continuing chaos and fraud around academic certification. A highly skilled university administrator, De Beer literally took things into his own hands. As it is important to grasp the kind of rescue operation required under conditions of serious dysfunction, his recollections of the lengths to which he went to protect the integrity of the university's certificates are worth quoting in full:

I will tell you what I did with regard to the certificates. I had a search and seizure operation done, with the forensic officers and the police, of all the offices. I found more than 750 blank degree certificates in the offices. I then destroyed all graduation certificates that they had anywhere, and I designed a new one that was delivered to me personally.

I was the only one with a key to the safe and there was a register so not even the registrar could get access to that. I went down to that petty level of carrying the key of the safe with me and controlling how the new design of the certificate goes out of that safe.

Then there was an external audit done to verify the names of those who had actually completed [their studies]. Verifying if they were actually enrolled and whether they attended the programme. *My way of doing things may have created some respect but it was a lot of danger for me as a person* [emphasis added].[5]

De Beer's courageous attempts to get a grip on academic fraud delivered results during his tenure as administrator. But those who study institutions will know that where corruption of this kind is ingrained in the culture and operations of a university, the behaviour is likely to recur when such tight controls are released. It is fair to ask, therefore, whether the administrator's intervention would outlast his term of appointment.

There is always great risk associated with the disruption of a corrupted revenue stream. As in the case of Kamwendo, there is the threat of bodily harm. Chris de Beer was not allowed to drive his own car, and armed personnel accompanied him to and from his university office. He was also escorted to the toilet with armed bodyguards. The case of UZ underlines the difficulty of institutionalising honest practices in contexts where there is no agreement in the university's value system about right and wrong when it comes to public resources. But it is not only within institutions that the struggle for power and resources is constantly fought. People outside the university also participate.

So, who are the criminal actors inside and outside universities that target institutional resources? The analysis that follows is limited to the workings of four powerful agents.

ROGUE TAXI OPERATORS

The students at the University of Fort Hare's Alice campus were excited as they prepared for a choir competition in Port Elizabeth (since renamed Gqeberha), about 230 kilometres away. Several buses had been hired to transport the choir members to the venue. The local taxi organisations were very upset when they learned of this. Why hire buses when you have taxis available? A stalemate ensued, and a compromise was reached. The buses would take the students to Port Elizabeth and, once there, the taxis from Alice would ferry the choir members to and from the local venue. It was a strange sight: full buses and empty taxis travelling from Alice to Port Elizabeth and back, simply to ensure that the taxi owners shared in the spoils. From the perspective of university management, a serious crisis was averted. From that of the taxi operators, their threats had worked. For the bus company, all was well as long as they were paid the contracted fee, regardless of the additional transport arranged. In the end, a rural university whose finances were precarious had to pay twice for what should have been a straightforward service to students.

Taxis form an integral, if often corrupt, part of a university's business arrangements. Threats of violence are a key component of the strategy of taxi bosses to gain a hold on university resources. One Fort Hare vice-chancellor vividly recalls his boardroom being packed with taxi owners one day. The men were from the local taxi association, and the message they conveyed was crystal clear: 'We have reached the end of our tolerance with the university. The university goes to Port Elizabeth to come and load students [in buses], and go to Cape Town, but in the meantime we are here. We are not going to allow that. The next time PE comes around here we are going to show them, and you'll see your students might be hurt.'[6] And then, as if to make the logical link between external power and institutional resources as transparent as possible, a taxi boss stood up and offered this lesson in candour, which the vice-chancellor recalled as follows: 'VC, I want to tell you something. To us here in this region, Fort Hare is a goldmine. We don't have any other goldmine, like Gauteng. Fort Hare is our goldmine. You must understand that. So now, when you are bringing someone from outside in here, you are basically bringing a stranger to take the gold from our mouths.'

There is obviously nothing wrong when a local entrepreneur seeks a partnership with the local university for purposes of mutual benefit; those kinds of transactions happen in any business context all over the world. What is different here is the insistence that the partner must have exclusive access to 'the goldmine'. Nor does one need to read between the lines to detect the threat ('You must understand that …') or discover that outsiders to the local community had been declared a potential enemy ('a stranger').

In 2021 the taxi association in Mpumalanga province showed exactly what penalty would be paid when the local university did not 'play ball' with the self-appointed transport authority. The University of Mpumalanga (UMP) is one of two new universities in South Africa, launched in 2013 with 169 enrolments and growing to more than 4 000 students by 2020. As at many universities, UMP students would often use private accommodation within range of the campus, especially when on-campus residences were oversubscribed. Sometimes, the university would have formal, accrediting arrangements with private providers to ensure certain standards for accommodation; at other times, students made their own arrangements with owners of private residences.

In 2021, something unusual happened at the Mbombela campus of UMP. Taxi operators blockaded routes to the university to protest against students making their own arrangements for travel or doing so through agreements with their private accommodation providers. They demanded that the university put a stop to the exercise of choice and free will. In the words of the dean of students, 'They told us they wanted to transport students who are staying in accredited private accommodation facilities to and from the university, and that the university must pay them for the service.[7] Several unsuccessful meetings were held between the taxi operators and the UMP management. The university was clear that in this specific case, the agreement with private providers required that they organise student transfers to and from the Mbombela campus. This arrangement might even have been funded, sources claimed, by the government's National Student Financial Aid Scheme (NSFAS), which offers generous study benefits to students. The taximen provided a novel counter-argument, to the effect that private transport of students constituted 'illegal acts' on a public road for which they had public permits from the National Public Transport Regulator.[8] In the end, they made the simpler admission that 'we also want to benefit from the university'.[9] 'We appreciate the work of the university in providing education as well as creating job opportunities in the area; we also want to be counted in.'[10]

In sum, universities in South Africa walk a tightrope in balancing the needs of students and the demands of the taxi industry. What on the face of it appears to be a legitimate expression of the needs of local businesses can cross the thin line that separates the quest for income from outright criminality. 'I have seen it with my own eyes,' says a chair of council of one of the country's rural universities. 'The taxis line up at the gates of the university, and heaven help you if you offer a student a lift and they see you.'[11] It is not, however, only rural universities that suffer the sting of competition for resources from taxi drivers. In the past the University of Cape Town, too, came under threat from operators if its Jammie Shuttle transport system used routes that local taxis saw as their own.[12] It was at the historically disadvantaged institutions (HDIs), however, that the most intense demands on institutional resources were experienced – sometimes with the university leadership at the head of the criminal enterprise.

ROGUE VICE-CHANCELLORS

It should have been hard to find a case to match that of the rogue vice-chancellor at the Mangosuthu University of Technology (MUT) (see chapter 4), but then one reads investigatory reports on a man famously dubbed 'the Jesus of the Vaal,' the head of the Vaal University of Technology (VUT). Aubrey Mokadi emerged from the once politically volatile PWV (Pretoria, Witwatersrand, Vaal Triangle) region in which this institution is located. With rich social networks in the political and church organisations of the surrounding area, Mokadi came to power not by progressing through the academic ranks but through the machinations of members of council. He had been an external member of council, then became the chair of council and finally made himself available for the position of vice-chancellor. But he did not choose himself. Mokadi would, for a number of years, maintain his position through the well-oiled machinery of the politics of the region, even after he was suspended, and then reinstated, as leader one of the most dysfunctional universities in the history of South African higher education.

Starting off as a College for Advanced Technical Education in 1966, the institution became the Vaal Triangle Technikon in 1979, and eventually gained university status as the Vaal University of Technology in 2004. Both before and after that change in status, as technikon and university, the institution was subjected to ministerial intervention in the form of no fewer than three administrators, owing to the constant turbulence in the institution and the regular turnover of vice-chancellors. However, the roots of VUT's dysfunction can be traced to Aubrey Mokadi. How did such a man rise to leadership of a South African university?

At the time of writing, the VUT administrator was Professor Ihron Rensburg, the former vice-chancellor of the University of Johannesburg. Rensburg, a thoughtful person trained in education and the social sciences, with a record of astute leadership of a major Johannesburg university, situates the problem and the personality of the VC in the context of the surrounding region.

On the one hand, the university is located in an area with a violent history of repression and a record of fierce resistance. The Vanderbijlpark campus is located near the site of the Boipatong Massacre of 1992, where 45 township dwellers, perceived as belonging to the ANC, were massacred by hostel dwellers associated with the Inkatha Freedom Party (IFP) at the high point of negotiations for a democratic South Africa.[13] The campus is also close to the historic town of Sharpeville, where in 1960 apartheid police shot and killed 69 pass law protesters. In other words, the university is situated in a place of high politics and deep trauma that have left their mark on the collective memory of the people of the region.

It is, however, also an institution that, by virtue of its geography, is dislocated from the major economic hubs of South Africa. As surrounding municipalities crumbled,[14] and the local economy stagnated, this isolated university loomed large as a tempting target for criminal designs. In the words of the administrator, the attention of stakeholders turned inwards on a university that was socially, economically, politically and intellectually isolated from other institutions. 'It is in this context that the cult of the individual leader emerges,'[15] with the big man flaunting his power over institutional resources, which he opened up to anyone on campus or in the community with a transactional interest in this public university's assets.

The allegations against the rector detailed in the more than 400 pages of the report of a commission of inquiry, the Jansen Report (after the commission's chair, Judge Mabel Jansen), are quite simply staggering.[16] According to this report, the big man in question suffered from delusions of grandeur. Staff had to stand up out of respect for the VC when he entered his office, and those working there had to wear special uniforms. Men coming to his office without a jacket and tie would be berated. Everyone was instructed to purchase a photograph of the VC with university funds and hang it in their offices. His CV had to be read out at length by staff members at every function where he spoke. If the function had already started, proceedings had to be stopped for his introduction. The great leader would be accompanied by an entourage of bodyguards.

The VC built a chapel on campus and appointed 12 disciples from among the staff to pray for him. The vestry was for the exclusive use of the VC and contained the sacraments as well as an elaborate golden robe. When the big man faced suspension, the 12 disciples were asked to pray for a favourable outcome to an urgent council meeting convened that day. When the Commission for Conciliation, Mediation and Arbitration (CCMA) ruled against his suspension, Mokadi wrote of his return: 'The one moment I shall never forget was when throngs of students and staff supporters, acting on the spur of the moment, stripped garments from their backs and laid them on the ground for me to walk on. I hesitated for a moment, images of Christ on his triumphant return to Jerusalem flashing through my mind.'[17]

Two days were set aside in the VUT calendar to honour the rector, including 'the Day of the Rector' and the rector's birthday. A concert and sporting tournament were named after him. Official campus magazines had 'to contain a photograph of him on each and every page'. The commission of inquiry called his monograph *A Portrait of Governance* nothing more than 'a book of self-glorification [that] has nothing to do with governance in higher education'.[18]

Whereas the VC at MUT hid behind steel doors, Mokadi at VUT was 'out there', on a never-ending quest for self-promotion and personal aggrandisement. But what they had in common was the ability to use their positions as VCs to create a climate in which criminality could flourish under their authority. How did Mokadi create such microclimates of corruption?

First, he completely flouted the institutional rules for good management and governance. It is not that there were no rules (the policy vacuum argument) or that he did not understand them (the capacity argument); it was that the rules did not matter. 'I told him, VC, you cannot do that,' said one of his deputies when the leader wanted to raise his own salary or increase his personal benefits. 'He completely ignored me, claiming that as CEO he had unlimited authority to do as he pleases.'[19]

If the tone is set at the top, in the words of the corporate governance authority Judge Mervyn King, then Aubrey Mokadi did his best to create a climate for criminal dysfunctionality. This was his modus operandi, as detailed in the report of the commission of inquiry.

Mokadi's first step was to centre all authority for decision-making in his person as 'CEO' of the university, a title seldom used in the leadership of South African universities. It was meant to signal the kind of executive authority invested in the heads of private companies. In this case, it also meant, for him, the power to ignore the institutional rules, such as accounting to the council for decisions that lay well beyond the purview of a university VC, like matters of personal compensation.

Mokadi was no doubt aware that he was acting beyond the scope of his authority. So, what he did on a routine basis was to have his underlings commit unethical and illegal acts on his instruction but without his signature. This meant that when the wrongful act was discovered, he could claim innocence and lay the blame at the feet of the person following his orders. As one of his staff observed in testimony to the Jansen Commission: 'Professor Mokadi will not put his thing on the paper, he will just tell you to go and do it, and you go and do it. He will never write it down, *never* he will *never*. He will tell you and you will have to do it' (emphasis in the original).[20]

The next thing the VC did was to build alliances on campus and secure allies in the surrounding community. Student leaders would be given money for nonexistent events or lavish allowances for parties. By keeping students under his influence, he could rely on these important stakeholders to advance his own interests, including his reappointment, or to create havoc when necessary. It turns out that the churches in the community, particularly those of the evangelical variety, enjoyed privileged access to the VC and his chapel, as well as to university funds. The resources of the university were therefore carefully wielded to both project and secure the power of the VC on his campus. This act of using money to buy the support of students will feature again in a more fine-grained analysis of the micropolitics of institutions (see chapter 8).

However, it is not enough to incentivise your supporters; it is equally important to punish your critics. Those who did not energetically support the VC or obey his instructions would face reprimand, removal or the 'restructuring' of their existing posts. The use of disciplinary letters to deal with perceived enemies was standard operating procedure at VUT. A direct apology to the boss man could gain reprieve for a wayward staff member. The slightest hint of dissent could end in dismissal. The Jansen Report gives ample examples of 'the abuse of power'. A wave of punitive actions rocked the institution after the CCMA ruled in favour of the suspended VC; some staff resigned, others fell ill with depression, and at least one staff member committed suicide following Mokadi's return to office.[21]

The combination of penalties and rewards kept staff and students in their place for the next step in the process of criminalisation – the wholesale abuse of institutional resources. Secretaries and other staff were used to look after Mokadi's children at home and help them with their homework. Official photographers were hired for private events with university funds. University vehicles were commandeered for family purposes, even though the VC received a generous car allowance. Furniture purchased for the university would be sent to his home.[22] Private telephone lines were installed at his house on the university budget. The Jansen Report is scathing in comparing the behaviour of the VC to that of politicians: 'in the academic environment no one expects a "wolf in sheep's clothing", someone who comes in and proceeds systematically to steal from the institution; indulge in corrupt activities; plot and plan fraud; sexually abuse staff, and so forth.'[23] In the case of Mokadi, the Jansen Report linked his misdeeds not to ethical lapses or the lack of managerial oversight but to criminality itself: 'what is completely inexcusable is Professor Mokadi's ever-increasing greed for money and his lack of qualms to obtain it by whatever means necessary. The cases of outright corruption and fraud delineated above per se constitute criminal conduct which warrants the summary dismissal of Professor Mokadi by Council.'[24]

What is intriguing about the Mokadi case is, on the one hand, the longevity of his rule at the VUT and, on the other, the institutionalised corruption that continues to leave its mark on the university long after his sacking. Why is this important in the present and for the future prospects of VUT as an institution?

In the first place, Mokadi was kept in power by networks of influence that enabled a corrupt and incompetent leader to reign and even to return to office after being suspended. In other words, it would be an error to dismiss the problem as a case of personal pathology in a rogue vice-chancellor, and to ignore the social and institutional forces that made possible his grip on power. An institutional culture that was shaped by established routines of corruption was left largely undisturbed in the transition to the replacement leader. Not surprisingly, yet another administrator would be appointed in 2020 to deal with undisturbed corruption and criminality at the VUT.[25]

ROGUE CHAIRS OF COUNCILS

Rogue chairs of council present yet another potential challenge to university governance. Few universities had a more traumatic experience with a rogue chair of council than the University of South Africa (Unisa) in the early years of South Africa's democracy. Catapulted straight into the most senior position in governance at a higher education institution in 1999, McCaps Motimele was a lawyer without experience in university leadership. As a senior member of the Unisa council reflected, 'Normally, people go through a number of steps to be on council, where one would be deputy chair and then chair, so that one can have a long period and evaluate how things are handled, the philosophy and approach to governance.'[26] The vital experience of induction did not happen in this case. Among the senior members of council who knew the candidate, there was some anxiety because of rumours of corruption associated with Motimele from his work in the North West province. 'This was the wrong person to head up council,' said a senior member of the governance body on her way out of Unisa.[27] His appointment as council chair would soon cost Unisa dearly, in public reputation and in the loss of expertise in both governance and management. More importantly, it would entrench a legacy of dysfunction that remains to this day. How did this happen?

The first action taken by the chair of council was to establish absolute control over the governance function of the university. He would chair like 'a judge in the courts': his rule was absolute and his rulings final. Those who dissented were taken down in public and challenged with inappropriate responses, such as 'Are you for me, or against me?' What in normal council meetings would be the development of consensus through skilful chairing on a complex matter became a matter of agreeing with the chairman of council. Another measure of control was the manipulation of the minutes of meetings, as a veteran council member recalls: 'You had to read every set of minutes in minuscule detail because he would have changed them.'[28]

It did not help that these were the early days of democracy in the country. The chair had no qualms about using 'the race card' to attack contrarian voices belonging to white members of council. Unisa was, at that time, still a largely untransformed, former white university as far as its governance, management and administration were concerned, and this applied to the composition of council as well. For the unscrupulous, 'the race card' was a blunt instrument that could be recklessly used when wayward black authority was being challenged.

Council meetings became the playground for Motimele's particular brand of power politics, a stage on which he could assert autocratic rule through his domineering presence. For that, he needed an office where he could 'hang his coat', a most unusual request in contemporary South African universities.[29] It was in this office that Motimele worked, and from which he interfered in the daily business of the university.

Furthermore, allegations of sexual harassment were made against Motimele by members of staff, notably Professor Margaret Orr.[30] When a labour union reported this case and demanded action, a train of events followed that at once demonstrated the weakness of the university management in its failure to take firm action and the deftness of the accused in avoiding accountability. The union threatened court action. The university management, through its vice-chancellor, sought an apology from Motimele as a way of putting the matter to rest. A council committee set up to investigate the matter could not meet with the chair for months, as he evaded any attempt to start the inquiry. Eventually, an out-of-court settlement was reached, but with the errant council chairman still firmly in place.[31]

Apart from sexual indulgence, there was an indulgent use of university resources for personal ends. Meetings would be held in hotels, and the chairman and his friends would arrive the night before and wine would flow: 'petty things', recalled senior people, but consequential for good governance and management at Unisa. Between council meetings, the principal's dining room, with a small bar, would be occupied for lunch, and then far beyond the two o'clock closing time. When the rector decided to close the bar, the council chair instructed the waiter to remove the whisky for later consumption. In the bigger scheme of things, these everyday malpractices were extremely petty; as one senior deputy vice-chancellor (DVC), a whistleblower at his university, reflected: 'What appalls me about these corruption stories is how low the aspirations [of the corrupt] are.' While trivial, such corrupt behaviour 'created the kind of atmosphere that was destructive to the university'.[32]

The university was a resource to be exploited, and this continued to be demonstrated in the small things that played out on the council stage. Meetings became a source of revenue for individual members, and while the amounts earned were not excessive, they were much needed by failing businessmen or junior members of council. A senior member of council recalls of that time: 'The big issue was money. He wanted to be remunerated like an Anglo American board member. He would quote that board members on these firms get this and that [and] they have these advantages and perks, etc. So, he wanted the whole array of things which you know in the university world is not normal.'[33]

The obvious way to optimise meeting income was to set more meetings, and Motimele paid council members for each meeting attended. For a cash-strapped member, this was an easy way to make money. As one remembers: 'We would pay council members per meeting at that stage and then he would set additional meetings. And the meetings would start at nine and then at twelve we would stop for lunch with all the trimmings and alcohol, etc., and we would not be able to continue after lunch because we were tired, and then would continue the next day and then you would get another payment.'[34] The pettiness of these operations was troubling not only for the sheer waste of institutional resources, but for what it allowed – a degree of manipulation and control over dependent council members that would secure the position of the leader from whose hands these material benefits flowed (see chapter 8).

But not everything was petty. Sometimes the rogue council leader would directly threaten the university VC with personal consequences if things did not go his way, as in his attempts to quash the sexual harassment investigation. At a meeting in Midrand, the rogue leader promised the VC, as the latter recalled in an interview, that he would 'ignite a bomb under Unisa. He would blow the place up in the air. He would blow me up in the process and destroy my career ... One thing I could be certain of is that I would not be reappointed because he was going to destroy Unisa and me with it.'[35] Whether the threat was meant to be taken seriously or not is hard to gauge.

But what did happen was that the rogue leader descended into a period of highly destructive behaviour. All senior appointments already approved by council were blocked, including one which involved another woman who had accused the chair of sexual harassment. This meant that the workload of the VC's office multiplied in the absence of senior appointments at this large institution. The VC at the time remembers that 'besides doing the VC's job I was doing three others. I was just working night and day trying to keep the ship afloat while all this was going on. It was a terrible period.'[36]

Since he had access to institutional resources, the rogue chair would use the newspapers to inveigh against the university management and those who opposed him. He bought a double-page spread in the newspaper to complain about the racism against him, saying that all complaints were racial attacks meant to discredit his person. At a *bosberaad*[37] of council, he gleefully presented copies of the newspaper to council members; they had, by this time, lost faith in the chairman as his power started to wane.

The minister of education then decided to recall his ministerial appointees on the Unisa council and to replace them with a mix of persons who included hardened struggle activists and accomplished executives in their respective fields. Until then, Motimele could sway council members in his favour through a combination of material incentives and veiled threats. Now the tables were turned. At a crucial meeting to eject him from council, the rogue leader decided to sit in on the proceedings deciding his fate. The goal was clear: to intimidate those of his allies who might have second thoughts about continuing their support. As a senior member of the council remembers:

> McCaps went to sit in the back of the room because he knew that there were lots of people who owed him stuff in the room, and he wanted to see if they would continue to support him as they had done earlier and when we had then lost the initial vote … The swing in the vote was extraordinary because it was the same people who had voted in one direction when McCaps was sitting in or casting a vote himself in a matter that referred to him.[38]

After a fiery clash with one of the new ministerial appointees – the general secretary of the Communist Party who would later become minister of education himself – Motimele was forced to leave the room. At that point his fate was sealed.

The finer details of the leadership behaviour of a rogue council chairperson are once again less interesting than what such conduct allowed, its consequences for the institutional environment and the possibilities of change. Perhaps the most important consequence of the Motimele council was the effects this systematic and sustained attack had on the executive management at Unisa. Those attacks, spearheaded by the chairperson of council, substantially weakened executive authority at the university, thereby enabling other actors to take centre stage in decision-making at the continent's largest distance-education institution.

Chief among those actors was the largest staff union on South African campuses, the National Education, Health and Allied Workers' Union (Nehawu). On several campuses, such as Unisa and VUT, the union would come to completely dominate not only administrative but also academic decision-making. It would be a root cause of institutional dysfunction. What was common to all affected universities was a seriously weakened executive authority in campus leadership. For Unisa, that was a direct consequence of the devastating years of the Motimele council.

ROGUE EXTERNAL MEMBERS OF COUNCIL

Finally, we turn to rogue external members of university councils. Here the University of Fort Hare (UFH) provides an illuminating case study. UFH did more than most universities in the post-apartheid era to honour the flat stakeholder model of democracy in which every constituency would be represented at the governance table. This was particularly true when it came to representatives of Eastern Cape municipalities on the UFH council. The 2010 institutional statute loaded the council with municipal and local government officials: one member designated by the Nkonkobe municipality (Alice); one member designated by the Buffalo City municipality (East London); one member designated by the Amathole district municipality; and two members appointed by the provincial government.

The dominating presence of local politicians on the council, representing in the main the ruling party at the provincial and municipal levels, was a recipe for disaster. These leaders came from municipalities that were seriously dysfunctional, receiving qualified audits, and worse, for reasons including poor governance in areas such as risk management and internal auditing.[39] If competence and good track records were supposed to be factors in selection for council membership, these officials represented the exact opposite – thereby posing a further risk to good governance in the university. As the vice-chancellor explained: 'The turbulence is caused by their business interests. I have seen them destroy government departments, they have destroyed SOEs [state-owned enterprises], they sucked up all the juice in municipalities and government departments and the only institution that remains where there is massive flow of money because of infrastructure [funds] and other things is the universities.'[40]

The institutional risk to council and the university was immense because 'the impulse to interfere was in the room' from the very people who had run down local government in the municipality where the university was located: 'The municipality is totally dysfunctional, and the university does the whole issue of waterworks and sewerage disposal for the town of Alice because, without that, Alice is not functional at all.'[41] Here, the interdependence between the campus and the city was exemplified in a salvage operation led by a fragile university to rescue a broken-down municipality. It is precisely this fragility that made the university vulnerable to 'rogues' on council who saw an opportunity to loot.

This flat model of stakeholder democracy would be costly for an already vulnerable university like the UFH. In its revised statute of ten years later, municipal representation on council was dropped in favour of a lean structure with only two government-related appointees: one nominated by the Eastern Cape provincial government and one by the Eastern Cape executive committee of the South African Local Government Association. The trimmed-down membership arrangements did not, however, stop a continued run on institutional resources from those on and off the council not only of Fort Hare but of other dysfunctional universities as well. University leaders found themselves fighting on two fronts: 'the rogues that were embedded in the structures' and 'those forces standing at the gates wanting a piece of the action'.[42] How did the internal and external interests vying for university resources interact to gain access to them?

First, they used the students. In every one of the dysfunctional universities we studied, there were reports of students being paid to influence council and management decisions and, if they failed, to create havoc on campus and pile pressure on decision-makers to facilitate access to vital resources. Student leaders would ally with unions and form a powerful bloc within council that would influence important outcomes, such as the ejection of a vice-chancellor who had closed the taps on corruption (see chapter 8). Student leaders would receive extraordinary benefits from rogue leaders, such as a registrar at one university (who was later fired) and the VC at another (who was also fired). These benefits included cash payments, travel to local and international conferences, access to rental or university cars, and ample funding for a student 'bash' that went by various names on the different campuses (for example, the Freshers Ball). In short, in the dysfunctional universities, students could be bought by internal or external agencies to influence the distribution of resources.

Second, these outside agencies used proxies. What this means is that while a council member might declare on the record that they had no interests in the business of the university, in reality there were indirect circuits for the command and flow of institutional resources. One vice-chancellor observed: 'Those people [external council members] were sitting in the boardroom and they were being proxies. Some of them would sit and they would WhatsApp throughout the meeting … because the taps are running dry every day.'[43] Another vice-chancellor remembers that he could never figure out why certain bidders for university business would quote charges that came in exactly on or around budget when no one outside these meetings supposedly had knowledge of the planned allocation of resources. The proxies on council would, of course, receive kickbacks on tenders awarded to the front companies. One DVC in charge of catering contracts was approached to consider awarding a tender to a company that promised to give R1 million (in 1980s rands) to the university if it became the successful bidder. The person making the suggestion was her VC.[44]

One of the most egregious of these internal-external corruption incidents involved a UFH professor who irregularly registered the premier of the Eastern Cape for master's studies and the provincial health MEC for an honours degree. The university later laid charges against the professor for defrauding it of about R5 million for 'unauthorised academic work and programmes for the Eastern Cape legislature and municipal authorities without the knowledge and consent of the university'.[45] Given the openly anti-corruption stance of the VC, it came as no surprise that the same premier would do something highly unusual for a political head of a province: launch frontal attacks on the university's vice-chancellor over issues like violence against students off campus or student suicides.[46]

Beyond using students and proxies, councillors would present themselves as legitimate members of the external community who could not, therefore, be conflicted in doing business with the university. 'I had to insist that the chair of the council could not be the chair of the tender committee,' said one of the most experienced managers of higher education in the country.[47] There was no pretence here of fairness in the process or any hint that conscience might give cause for withdrawal.

In these intertwined ways, corrupt council members placed a grip on governance at universities in order to secure their own interests in accessing institutional resources. This also meant that any threat to those material interests would be met with force, and in every dysfunctional university there are horror stories of how efforts to bring stability could turn deadly.

WHAT HAPPENS WHEN A UNIVERSITY'S TAPS ARE CLOSED?

Peter Mbati was the new vice-chancellor at the rural University of Venda (Univen) in the northern province of Limpopo. One of his first tasks was to root out corruption in the university by taking specific steps to close the taps on resources. He established a strong internal audit function, which was outsourced to a major accounting firm in order to secure its integrity. Procurement processes and reports were tightly managed, and documents were passed through the audit and finance committee of council so that 'if anything was picked up we could deal with it'. A whistleblowing facility was created whereby staff and students could report incidents of corruption for investigation. The legal department would scrutinise any significant expenditures and ensure that the supply chain processes were all above board. These tight controls over university resources resulted in decisive managerial action and the dismissal of junior and senior people alike: 'I even had some members of council who appeared to have [an] interest in procurement at the university and it was clear that about 10 per cent of council would have liked to see the back of Mbati as soon as possible because of restrictions placed on the tender processes.'[48]

It did not take long before the closing of the taps had near-fatal consequences for Peter Mbati. During the week he would work at Univen in Thohoyandou, but he had a home in Pretoria to which he would return at weekends. On one of those visits to his home, Mbati had a visit from strangers. The full story is best related by his own account:

> When I was busy cleaning up Univen, the stories that never appear in the media, despite the fact that I tell people. People had come to my house when I had come to Pretoria one weekend very smartly dressed in ties, suits, and a brand new white bakkie. And that morning I had just left Pretoria to go back to Venda because I had surgery to my eyes.
>
> They come with flowers and the housekeeper texted that they bought flowers for me and the lady says I had gone back to Venda and they ask if they can't just give it to her. And the lady says, let me call Mrs Mbati because my wife was working and when she was making the call, they lift my gate and these gates have a way where they can just literally lift from the rail, reversed and suddenly there are people in my house. They are armed, they ask if she is sure I went to Venda, so they made it look like a robbery, took a few things and left. In my house in Venda I had, one evening, because I travel back home every weekend, people got into my official residence, the alarm went off and the armed response company called to ask if everything is okay because they can see movement in my house. I said no I am away.
>
> There is another day that they came because my housekeeper used to stay outside my official residence, in the servant quarter, went into the room, took the keys to the house and she was terrified after that because the door was open. Luckily, they didn't get into my house that day but they had managed to get into the official

residence and then, of course, after that I added cameras and have dogs because before that I didn't have those kinds of things. When I used to have meetings from Pretoria to Venda, I had a driver and we would be trailed by unknown vehicles to the extent where we had to get my driver trained for defensive driving and we got him armed because it was obvious that I was being trailed. We reported that to the police and, of course, nothing happened, I have had people come and throw dead animals in my yard, I think just to scare me.

I have received hundreds of threatening SMSs sent to me, reported it to the police. I have had people do caricatures of myself in very compromising positions, sending them to the university community, so I have gone through, like I said it is a story not told when media is reporting other issues. But it has been a nightmare, people have called my wife and told her they will deal with me, people have written emails to my wife, saying all sorts of things and basically threatening her and the family. So, it is the horror side of my time at Venda, just for cleaning up the system and preventing corruption. And I have even told this to the portfolio committee, the kind of things that they are beginning to do, they have to be careful that people that are corrupt don't get and are defended by the portfolio committee, they must allow university processes to happen, we have courts of law in this country, there are places where people who were accused could get support from them.

But to the extent that a portfolio committee starts to intimidate VCs by saying that they have this complaint against you by somebody who was dismissed from the university. Basically, what we are going to do and it is a warning that you gave us years back when you were VC, that if we are not careful, our universities are going to go to the dogs because suddenly the whole accountability system is going to be broken. The portfolio committee that goes past the minister, council, VC and management and deals directly with things that students and staff have presented to them. But I have a horror side of my story when I was VC that is horrible, my wife even wonders how I managed to survive at that time, I think I was very lucky that I wasn't taken out.

But we had instances where we would be driving to Venda from what you call the Punda Maria Road from the N1 and you would get a car that would block the road and my driver would have to find a way to get around the vehicle. We had situations where we were driving from the university with my driver because I used to chair one of the committees of the Premier in the province and somewhere along the way we had stopped at a garage or a hotel, my laptop gets stolen. And these things happen one after the other, my official car gets stolen and then a week later they attempt to steal my private car, so the level of intimidation was impossible and then you still have to run a university.[49]

This detailed first-person account of retaliation against a university vice-chancellor for closing the taps on corruption is not at all unusual in contemporary South Africa. In several dysfunctional universities there were reports of assassination in which implicated people were killed. One senior manager at a troubled university recalls that 'there was a lot of skulduggery and people lost their lives in the process and every time someone lost their life, a story would come out as to their probable involvement'.[50]

At this same university, students and unions were represented on the tender committees, and 'government oversight bordered on interference when it came to tenders'.[51] In the process, the necessary boundary between governance and management was often breached. In one case, an external member of council 'would go past the vice-chancellor and speak to middle managers in the finance department and, late on a Friday, would demand to look at the contracts'.[52] In another instance, a member of council who had a security business competed for the security tender and won it.

Under these conditions, at almost every one of the dysfunctional universities, the vice-chancellors, and sometimes also their deputies and other senior executives, all travel with armed security. The administrators who come into these institutions are also required to have security and not to travel without guards. This is the real 'securitisation' that has crept up on universities, leading to a dramatic shift in campus life largely invisible to those living in the urban centres of South Africa. Ironically, it was the securitisation of universities that would spawn another source of corruption – tenders for security services.

Turning off the taps faced another formidable obstacle in post-apartheid universities – the direct involvement of the political classes. As a senior member of the University of the North (now the University of Limpopo) recalls, 'Politicians were in universities hands and feet, seeing the students as votes.'[53] More recently, the administrator of UFH was called to address the parliamentary portfolio committee on higher education about the situation at that beleaguered university, where issues of corruption in governance featured prominently. Unbelievably, after his presentation, 'one of the politicians came to me and offered to help with the IT contract at Fort Hare. I told him that he was not familiar with the legislation that governs a university.'[54]

It would be naive to think that the ministerial appointees to councils (up to five in number) always act in the best interests of the university. While many appointees are credible and ethical persons, there is abundant evidence in this study of individuals who themselves tried to eat into the institutional resources of some of the struggling universities. One vice-chancellor said he was shocked that a ministerial appointee had put pressure on council to remunerate members for attending meetings. Sometimes, the ministerial representatives were the backbone of strong governance in a failing institution; at other times, they were ineffective, at best, or part of the problem, at worst. From time to time, the minister would recall and replace the team of appointees out of frustration with their ineffectiveness at resolving problems in council.

Nothing draws a council and a campus into corruption quicker than well-funded projects from government. The millions at stake bring out the vultures on and around council. 'There was no interest in development,' observed a senior manager in a failing university, 'only in big projects where they can make money.'[55] And no projects were as attractive, from a looting point of view, as the hundreds of millions of rands poured into infrastructure, for everything from university residences to new academic buildings. What made matters worse is that most of the dysfunctional universities did not have the capacity to manage such large projects or the finances attached to them. The combination of institutional incapacity and availability of large-scale funding became an invitation for criminality.

CONCLUSION

What are the consequences of this embedded criminality in institutional cultures for South African higher education and, in particular, among the dysfunctional universities?

According to the research for this book, the focus of so much of the university's attention on its material resources – to grab them or to protect them from being grabbed – was essentially a massive distraction from the academic mandate. Major investments had to be made in securing those public resources, as demonstrated in the case of Univen; the financial outlay grew markedly where internal structures were ineffectual and expensive external companies had to be hired to do work in areas open to corruption, such as the audit function of the university. Significant attention had to be paid to the political actors on and off campus as they sought out the weak points in the administration and management armoury of the university.

In other words, the academic agenda of an institution became completely distorted in corrupt and dysfunctional universities because leadership attention was redirected to non-academic matters. The most powerful insights on this problem came from university leaders whose experience covered both historically white and historically black universities, as this sample of quotations reveals: 'Rhodes was a more academic-administrative institution, whereas Fort Hare was a more stakeholder-administrative institution'; 'Walter Sisulu University prides itself as a protest institution, not as an academic institution'; and 'What the top five [universities] guard religiously is the academic culture; the mistake that the HDIs made was to mess up our academic culture'.

What these insights reveal is how in both the self-presentation of a university and in its primary orientation, the academic agenda was not central to its core purpose, owing to both the shadows of the past and the preoccupations of the present. The past matters: 'Since these universities had no academic tradition, the academic project was marginal,' remarked a senior policymaker in higher education.[56] The present matters too, because the narrow focus on resources meant that academic matters remained secondary to the agendas of management, senate and council. A council member at one dysfunctional university resigned precisely because of the distortion of the academic agenda; in her words, 'an hour or two would be spent on discussing compensation for council members!'[57] These council members were simply uninterested in the academic project.

When students, staff, managers and governors come to the university primarily to gain access to its resources, it ceases to be a university. When criminals are members of councils or embedded in the administration and management of universities, then higher education institutions begin to resemble corrupt state-owned enterprises outside campus. That is why, throughout the interviews for this research, unflattering parallels were drawn by senior academic leaders between public universities and state parastatals or welfare bodies.

What happens when criminality seems to be embedded in the institutional fabric of a South African university; when senior leaders in higher education talk about universities being 'captured'? Can these universities be rescued and set on track to reclaim their academic mandate? Or were these dysfunctional institutions, in the words of one assessor, never universities to begin with?

8

The Micropolitics of Corruption in Universities

Wasteful, irregular expenditure and theft happen so often that people don't even think of it as theft.[1]

It was easily one of the most humiliating spectacles that could occur in a place of higher learning. Students stormed into the office of the university vice-chancellor, a highly respected man of letters, lifted him up by the armpits, and frog-marched the bespectacled academic to the gates of the university as an act of ejection. They had done this before. In fact, most leaders of this university were at some point ousted from their offices and taken to the campus exit, where the police would sometimes rescue the professor from the mob.

About 300 kilometres south of this northern campus, another vice-chancellor experienced something even worse. Five or six campus bullies came into one of the offices of the 'no-nonsense leader who insisted that staff and students work strictly according to the rules and regulations …

so they got fed up with him'. The invaders told the vice-chancellor that this was his last day in office and that he was leaving 'right now'. One of the deputy vice-chancellors tried to intervene, saying, 'You cannot treat our vice-chancellor like this,' but he was told to shut up and get on with this work. The VC having collected his belongings, the thugs drove him off campus in his own car. Council, his nominal boss, did nothing. The vice-chancellor was never seen on campus again.[2]

These acts of institutional thuggery targeting principled leaders are visible, in-your-face confrontations that work to undermine the managerial authority of a public university. What is much less obvious is the hundreds of smaller events that, as a senior adviser to government put it, 'silently eat away at the institutional integrity of a university'.[3]

This chapter makes visible in finer detail the micropolitics of corruption in South Africa's dysfunctional universities – how and why it happens, by and for whom, and with what consequences for higher education institutions. The chapter also gives some conceptual flesh to the myriads of corrupt activities that occur in dysfunctional institutions.

There is a broader intellectual interest in this endeavour, for we still do not have research that, in the words of education scholar Jacky Lumby, 'unravel[s] the nuances and subtleties of daily activity at the micropolitical level'.[4] As Lumby argues, 'Research on the technical aspects of HEIs [higher education institutions] remains incomplete without knowledge of the relationships and maneuvering that drive and shape such processes.'[5]

THE MICROPOLITICS OF CORRUPTION

Using an amalgam of standard definitions, micropolitics can be defined as the formal and informal activities through which individuals or groups exercise power to advance their interests and objectives within an organisation.[6] That exercise of influence and authority can be both visible and covert, and can be used in both positive and negative ways. All leaders of universities are engaged in micropolitics, using their authority to achieve particular goals. For example, a vice-chancellor who deploys a mix of persuasion, rewards and incentives to increase the production of high-quality articles in accredited journals is exercising considerable authority over the members of senate and academic departments to achieve an important organisational end – elevating the university in the international ranking systems.

This chapter is, however, concerned with the micropolitics of corruption; that is, those circumstances in which individuals or groups use their influence or authority for corrupt ends. Here, the goal is not to advance the standing or performance of the organisation but to pursue self-interests, such as personal enrichment or positional advancement, through irregular or even criminal conduct. Our context is the public universities, and therefore the almost exclusive resource in the sights of the corrupt is governmental funding in various forms, such as the money disbursed for infrastructural projects or for the operational needs of these institutions.

The micropolitics of corruption inside higher education institutions does not enjoy much attention in learned journals or scholarly books. The subject is decidedly understudied outside the thick reports by foundations or multilateral organisations on corruption in education,[7] and, even there, the focus is more likely to be on schools than universities.[8]

What happens in the day-to-day social and financial transactions of largely dysfunctional universities? How does corruption become habitual in such institutional contexts? Who benefits from ingrained corruption? In what myriad ways does corruption play out in broken universities? And what makes the micropolitics of corruption possible in the macropolitics of South African society? The normalisation of corruption within a sample of South African universities gives context to some of these questions.

In one university, an international donor gave the institution an expensive vehicle, which a dean took over for his personal use. It was never used for any other purpose than to transport the dean to and from home. The external finance expert sent in to rescue this dysfunctional university noticed a few disturbing parts to this story: for one thing, the dean was already being paid a car allowance by the university for the use of his own vehicle; for another, he never paid the obligatory taxes that come with such a donation, so the university was at risk of being investigated by the revenue authorities. Nobody seemed to care.[9]

'Wasteful, irregular expenditure and theft happen so often that people don't even think of it as theft,' said an expert sent in to rescue a university. Of the chair of council of another university, he observed: 'We speak about dysfunction, but some things have become tradition.'[10] This normalisation of corruption in plain sight has drawn a literary comparison in another reflection on the micropolitics of universities: 'As in [Edgar Allan Poe's] *The Purloined Letter*, a stolen object is left in full view and as such escapes notice, the exercise of micropolitics is both visible in almost every activity that takes place and yet also unseen.'[11]

It is evident from this study that when a critical mass of campus citizens become involved in corrupt activities, those irregular or criminal activities are viewed differently. Everybody does it, as the saying goes, and therefore not being 'in' on the corruption means not benefiting from what is available. This is the same logic that drew thousands of people to pillage stores in South Africa in July 2021: as word got out that malls were being looted, more and more people wanted some of the bounty.[12]

There is a criminal psychology at work here that explains the behaviour of large groups within organisations. A widely cited authority on the subject explains that corruption in organisations becomes normalised through three processes:

- *Institutionalisation*, whereby corrupt actions become embedded in the structures and processes of an organisation;
- *Rationalisation*, when self-serving justifications are made to defend corrupt behaviour; and
- *Socialisation*, when prevailing norms and values induce new staff to tolerate corruption and even view corrupt activities as acceptable.[13]

In these circumstances, 'As the repertoire of corrupt practices becomes embedded in the ongoing routines of the organization, a deviant culture ... tends to emerge to normalize the corruption.'[14]

The rest of this chapter is devoted to a fine-grained analysis of ten specific micro-actions that work together to normalise corruption in South African universities.

The subversion of the institutional rules

It is not that institutions lack rules that govern management and council decisions; that assumption – the absence of something – led to the capacity-building routines of the early years of South Africa's democratic transition: hire consultants to write the institutional rules and find experts to teach the meanings of those rules. One of the important observations made in the research for this book is that the path to corruption lay in consciously breaking the formal rules available to those in power. In the subversion of those formal rules, informal ones were established that became regularised within organisational functions.

Vice-chancellors who consciously take huge financial decisions without council approval were found to be common across dysfunctional universities. Those decisions included approving multimillion-rand projects that exceeded the delegated authority of the vice-chancellor, that is, the maximum amount a VC could spend without council oversight. The purchase of a car for personal use; the abuse of the limit on credit card transactions; the approval by junior staff of salary increases for senior staff (including the vice-chancellor); the refurbishment of the VC's house with university funds – all of these are examples of disregard for the institutional rules, which was rampant in dysfunctional universities.

It is, of course, not only vice-chancellors who 'flaunt the institutional rules', as a seasoned council member phrased it, but council members themselves. An assessor recalls that even when appointed to a governance position, one council member 'wanted to continue to engage in remunerative projects.'[15] Most universities have clear policies governing conflicts of interest, and several of them routinely pass around at every council meeting a form to be signed, titled 'declaration of interests'.

It is reasonable to ask, then, what the purpose is of institutional rules when they are being so flagrantly ignored. One answer is that the existence of rules and regulations gives the appearance of compliance with what is required by outside authorities, whether they be the external auditors or the government's higher education department. Signalling compliance has its own value, as evidenced by the glossy annual reports, which prompted one group of researchers to examine what they called 'institutional self-representation' in such compliance-oriented submissions.[16]

Other campus citizens quickly learn that institutional rules are flexible instruments. Students, for example, would press management to override their own rules on academic progression or financial exclusion because they have learned that these provisions are negotiable. And every time a rule is relaxed, it is recorded within institutional memory for use when the next crisis comes round. The rules are there, but what is happening is the kind of 'willful blindness' that Margaret Heffernan writes about, in which, through conforming to an organisational practice (that is, ignoring the rules), you also choose not to see the breaking of those rules.[17] Or, as Yavuz Selim Düger puts it, 'Willful blindness behavior appears as the behavior of being inactive, ignoring and eventually being silent, believing that nothing will change, similar to the learned helplessness behavior.'[18]

The abuse of the disciplinary function

In order to pursue corrupt activities, rogue leaders in a university need to keep their critics in place, through a mix of penalties for disobedience or non-conformance. A sword wielded with disturbing regularity in our sample of corrupt universities is the disciplinary function. Of course, all universities have disciplinary codes of conduct, with specific rules for how and when they apply; these are necessary measures to protect the integrity of any organisation. However, what is less well documented in the literature is how the important disciplinary function of a university can be abused in the hands of unscrupulous leaders.

At one rural university, the vice-chancellor was ruthless in his wielding of disciplinary instruments, as the appointed administrator found: 'Power would be used and abused to the extent that some [staff] felt marginalised. There was a culture of fear and victimisation where very senior people were disciplined.'[19] In these circumstances, the party being hounded goes silent, falls into line, or simply resigns out of fear of being fired, which would have negative consequences for finding another job.

Staff learn the administrative routines of institutional punishment rather quickly: offend the leader and a letter of warning follows or, worse, a letter of suspension, pending a disciplinary hearing. Suspended persons could be left waiting for months, and sometimes years, for a decision by the leader. The uncertainty is the point, loss of reputation the risk, and anxiety the cost. Sometimes an apology would be demanded, and on that condition the person charged could be reinstated.

The abuse of the disciplinary function is seldom criticised by the council, in the case of a vice-chancellor, or by the minister – except, of course, in the case of a ministerial intervention. Yet, in the day-to-day life of a dysfunctional university, such abuse of disciplinary policy is regular and routine, carrying with it little risk to the rogue leader but a high cost for the target of such mistreatment. This is precisely what drew the attention of the ministerial task team investigating Unisa in 2021–2022:

> The mechanism for lodging grievances is used as a way of threatening or stalling processes. When these are investigated and determined to be unfounded, there are no consequences for those who employ these tactics. As a result, *these behaviours have become the norm*. They frustrate the normal conduct of operations, consume time, money, and energy. Staff are offered no protection from the institution and left to incur substantial costs if they are to

defend themselves. There appears to be no discipline in practice at Unisa [emphasis added].[20]

The promise of rewards

A rogue leader at any level of a corrupt institution dangles both carrots and sticks in front of corruptible followers. The threat of punishment (for instance, the disciplinary letter) and the inducement of reward (for example, cash) work hand in hand to establish and entrench corruption in the fabric of an institution. In every dysfunctional university studied, there were countless stories of how staff and students were 'bought over' to the schemes of the corrupt leader.

One rogue council chairman was adept at keeping student leaders on his side by 'promising them jobs, small jobs that were under the radar at the university and somehow they managed to get them', recounted a long-term council member. The same observer told of fellow council members who were kept in line through membership and committee assignments that increased the remuneration of 'those from rural areas without a job in areas of high unemployment'. From the council leader's point of view, disbursing benefits kept him in the chair, 'because when you want this job so desperately, you start to buy patronage'.[21]

Rogue vice-chancellors did the same thing, using institutional resources to ensure everyone played along with their corrupt schemes. This was most clearly demonstrated in the case of the Vaal University of Technology (VUT) leader who used university funds liberally to 'bless' his base of community church leaders, maintain his home, fund students and appoint family members to the institution.[22] These are not random acts of kindness; they are calculated transactions to benefit the position and spread the influence of a rogue leader. There is a quid pro quo at work in corrupt organisations, says Sarah Meny-Gibert, an expert on homeland institutions: 'this unstable patronage politics limits the ability of people to work in organizations and creates a vicious cycle of constant instability'.[23]

Buying the loyalties of student leaders is still a common practice in dysfunctional institutions, and for a good reason. Students can create havoc at the press of a button. The puppet masters are sometimes political agencies outside the campus, as in the case of the Eastern Cape premier who chose to lambaste a sitting vice-chancellor in the provincial newspaper for student deaths on or off campus.[24] But at other times, the manipulator is a member of the senior management team. At one university, he was the registrar, and when he was fired, the protests stopped. No vice-chancellor wants his or her campus in the headlines of the local newspaper, and student protesters can provide scandal for the right price.

'It is hard to prove, but we know it happens,' said several participants in this study. Yet the cited examples of paying off students are endless: trips, both at home and abroad; university cars (that often end up wrecked); parties; clearing student debt. In one university, rogue students would be admitted to the university's administration offices and register prospective first-years, even if their matriculation marks did not qualify them for acceptance. All of this was done for a price, of course. Those staff working in administration were either complicit or scared, knowing that there could be repercussions if emboldened student leaders were denied what they wanted.

The wilful mismanagement of meeting administration

You can distinguish a functional university from a dysfunctional one simply by looking at the length of their council (or management) meetings. At one university, a council meeting would start on Friday afternoon and end on a Sunday morning. At another, nine-hour council meetings were not uncommon. Hours would be spent discussing small matters of interest, like the compensation of council members. Often, meetings would be held up by long debates over membership credentials of individuals already present at the meeting.

At a first glance, some of these extended meetings suggest a lack of capacity, at best, or gross incompetence, at worst. There were, of course, instances of such inexperience and ineptitude observed in this study – for example, the chairman of council who had never governed anything in his life but who was now in charge of overseeing an institution's multibillion-rand budget. But, digging deeper, it became clear that dysfunctional meetings, as measured by their length, were not always so innocent. Consider this fairly common practice in a highly dysfunctional and fractious council: 'It was a 50-50 split on council. They would wait for council members to leave the meeting to try and get the upper hand, and we would not leave.'[25]

The unions were particularly adept at the politics of exhaustion in council or management meetings. Peter Morris,[26] the HR rescue-man called on by administrators to salvage broken institutions, knew the labour regulations better than most, and found a way of neutralising this strategy:

> I believe in a strong union. But I worked on three principles: you share information, you consult, and you negotiate. What I found in a lot of institutions is that they allow the unions to drag them into negotiations all the time so that management loses its power. I followed the three principles, but you were not going to drag me into negotiation. If you continue, I take you to the CCMA and I have won all my cases there. Where management is weak, this happens. But I need to be squeaky clean to apply those principles and often the guys who have to apply the principles are not clean. That is where they pull people like that into constant negotiations.[27]

There are several important insights in this extended quotation. First, the leadership of a university must create the grounds for a firm approach to unions and rapport with them. Second, this must be a principled approach, based on sound knowledge of labour relations as it affects higher education. And, third, the leadership must be cognisant of the political strategy of weakening management authority through protracted negotiations, which could subvert what Morris called the academic imperatives of the university.

There is, of course, a maturity aspect to leadership that shows up as a common weakness in the administration of meetings. But when a council chairperson manages a governance meeting like an imperious judge, the chances of joint decision-making or consensus-building diminish, and contrarian views are seen as a problem. The ingredients for dysfunction are then present. Where a vice-chancellor believes that only his authority counts, and that any challenge to his position amounts to insubordination, then management meetings quickly descend into chaos.

One way in which the management of meetings can be subverted in dysfunctional institutions is by allowing stakeholders to bring their unresolved concerns with the executive to a council meeting. Inevitably, the council meeting then drags on, because it is addressing and trying to resolve day-to-day management issues, such as student protests over fees or union demands for higher salaries. A weak council chair who lacks the knowledge or authority to recognise these types of concerns as management issues would allow a governance meeting to descend into lengthy and heated fights that not only consume the agenda, but strain already fractious relationships.

This kind of micropolitics of corruption is all too common on dysfunctional campuses. When management says no to a matter under its legitimate purview, students or unions sometimes seek a second bite at the political cherry and burden council with concerns about which executive decisions have already been made. And where factions on council have been primed to engage with those issues rather than defer them to management, meeting dysfunction is inevitable.

It does not help that in many of these universities, the registrar's office is itself incompetent. In South African universities, the registrar, as the secretary of council, is responsible for the quality of council documentation. The registrar advises the chairperson on governance matters, including policy and legislation. When the registrar is incompetent in these functions, council meetings can degenerate into bedlam. Our research revealed stories of hundreds of pages of documentation – completely inappropriate for a council meeting – being placed on the meeting agenda, overwhelming the councillors. An inept council chairperson, in some institutions, would then proceed to wade through these documents page by page, thereby ensuring long meetings in a dysfunctional governance structure.

One way in which the chaos of meeting administration enables micro-corruption is revealed in an account, not at all unique, of a selection committee at the Vaal University of Technology. It is worth quoting at length for the insights it provides into the links between dysfunction, corruption and politics:

> At VUT, I was invited to be on a shortlisting committee for the DVC [deputy vice-chancellor] two years ago. They had a lot of applicants, between 16 and 20 people, and they don't send the documents ahead of time. I go to the meeting and ask why the documents weren't sent ahead of time. 'Oh no, because we feel it might leak.' How do you go through a shortlisting of 16 people and then they don't give you the documents?
>
> They give you the documents right there. There is no way you can go through all the CVs. They put it up on a screen. The VC simply does the welcome and doesn't say a word the entire meeting. Members of the university start to fight amongst themselves about why the position was advertised. The chair of the HR committee was there. Completely dysfunctional, in one meeting I could see that the university was completely dysfunctional. It was people fighting amongst themselves about why the job was advertised while doing a shortlisting. I can't even begin to tell you how shocked I was.
>
> But what shocked me is that the VC, aside from welcoming, never said one word. He was sitting there while all this commotion went on, never said a word. His chairperson of HR is in this meeting. You know what he says to me, the VC? He said, 'Will you lead the discussion?' I haven't even looked at the CVs! I was shocked out of my mind.[28]

This member of council was surprised because she came from a functional university, where council or management meetings ran for two hours, documentation was received in advance, and the chairperson was in charge of orderly meeting procedures. Nothing was decided at her selection committee meeting, and she felt that the time she spent travelling to Vereeniging had been wasted.

This same senior executive recalled another 'shock' she experienced when she did a presentation at another dysfunctional university on behalf of the government department for which she worked at the time.

> I had only been that shocked twice in my life, one was at VUT and the other was when I was at the Department [of Education]. I ran a workshop on fiduciary responsibility for council members, and I did it at Zululand and the VC came into this council meeting with a plate full of meat like I have never seen before in my life, in a council meeting! He is there with a plate of meat! And this is a meeting that he organised for his council, and I was watching that man dig into that meat in a formal meeting. That plate was in front of him and him only! And the chair of council didn't say anything.[29]

The point is not, of course, about the big man and his plate groaning with meat. It is about an organisational disposition in which decorum has no meaning. As a result, it becomes much more difficult to manage or govern in ways that convey the necessary dignity, respect and gravity.

The manipulation of meeting records

In a troubled university, those who control the minutes of a meeting control the decision-making. It should not, therefore, be surprising that rogue council or management leaders would manipulate something as apparently straightforward as the recorded minutes of a meeting to exert their influence and authority. The minutes of council and senate meetings are also powerful because they can be used to expose corrupt activities inside the day-to-day operations of a troubled institution. At one university, the minutes of a council meeting were quietly given to the minister as evidence of governance dysfunction. In submitting the minutes to the political head of higher education, a distraught vice-chancellor told the minister: 'Here is the truth in terms of what actually happened, substantiated with hard evidence from council minutes.'[30]

With access to council minutes over the period of one academic year, another study on behalf of the authorities found that 'two thirds of the council meetings are spent on arguing about a contract for air-conditioning in the library, [and yet] nobody was actually interested in the air-conditioning; it was a fight for everyone's comforts.'[31] In yet another broken university, the council minutes were used by a member in good standing to expose the pettiness of a chairman's complaints against a vice-chancellor which were based purely on hearsay; the gossip recorded in those minutes nonetheless led to the suspension of the recently appointed vice-chancellor.[32] Then again, an assessor from a highly functional university probed the minutes of a senate in a dysfunctional university and found that 'senate minutes and meetings seemed to be dominated by administrative matters and no debate, no rigorous discussion about the nature of the university or of teaching and learning within the university'.[33]

Minutes are also a rich source of data for research on public institutions, with the potential for negative exposure that comes with the terrain.[34] We should not be surprised, therefore, that in such contexts minutes of important meetings are challenged and changed.

A senior HR manager at one university was responsible for recording the minutes of a meeting for a senior appointment at the institution, but he noticed that when the record of the decision was presented to council through the vice-chancellor's office, the details had been altered. He then told the chairperson of council, who removed the item from the agenda.[35]

What was happening in incidents like these was an attempt to change the official record of decisions that had been made in order to subvert them. It is crude and elementary, yet not uncommon. One consequence of the manipulation of official documents is to add to the distrust within the organisation; another is that council members or senior executives are drawn into the tedious and time-consuming task of labouring over the minutiae of meeting records, just in case a rogue leader has decided to change, by stealth, important decisions already made.

Tripping-up tactics

One of the most disturbing accounts that emerged from this inquiry concerns the ways in which campus factions work to trip up a vice-chancellor or any other member of the executive who dares to exercise firm managerial leadership on difficult issues. An experienced leader in South African higher education was asked to take over the management of a chronically unstable institution in the position of vice-chancellor. This is his story, in short: 'I had a great time for four years until I had the audacity to suspend a key person. I had evidence and everything about this key person receiving R500 000 from service providers as a result of a tender that was won. Then I was pressurised to let this thing go. They wanted me to forget about this whole thing.' An ethical leader, the vice-chancellor refused to budge. The key players came to his house, insisting that 'we can't do this to a comrade'. The vice-chancellor showed them the evidence indicating that he had no choice but to discipline the comrade. 'Within a few days they mobilised students and staff. They wanted me off the campus and they fabricated things to help with that.'[36] From that point onwards, the university leader would suffer the angry attention of student leaders and unions, acting in concert, for any mistake or perceived lapse in judgement.

The mistake would come soon enough. The leader commissioned a re-tiling of one of the residences, and before getting his sign-off, the contractors ordered the necessary materials, to the value of R3.5 million. That amount was beyond his delegated authority, which meant that council needed to approve the expenditure. But by the time the leader noticed the error and apologised to council for the lapse, it was too late; his detractors had their man.

The facts that the vice-chancellor did not benefit at all from the transaction and that the benefit was solely directed towards renovating a student residence were irrelevant. He had been tripped up. Both the chair and deputy chair of council resigned in dismay at the pressure to eject the principled leader. His last act as vice-chancellor was to hand over the case involving the fired comrade to the public prosecution agency, so that 'a whole network of corruption' at this university could be investigated.[37]

The simplest things can trip up a university leader who refuses to play along with corruption games. At an Eastern Cape institution, something as straightforward as building a decent gate at the entrance to the university would become a snare, as an administrator from that time recalls:

> One of the things that the union was very upset [about] at the time was the fact that the VC had spent money to build this gate with a welcoming sign that you are entering the University of Transkei. They said: 'Look, this man is wasting money on gates when students are starving and sleeping outside without accommodation.' It was quite clear that they were simply mad because they as unions had not been consulted, not given their stamp of approval. In the bigger scheme of things, what it eventually turned out to be was that the management had an institution that was ungovernable.[38]

All universities rebuild and upgrade their entrances from time to time. However, here was something mundane that became the means for hounding the vice-chancellor, disabling executive authority in the process. The rhetorical tactics are familiar to those who manage dysfunctional universities – for instance, the emotive reference to starving students. The undisguised ambition of the unions to manage the university was on full display.

In yet another dysfunctional university, the outgoing chairperson of council decided to make available a bursary to a student in need. However, there was a delay in transferring the money from the chairwoman, so the student asked the vice-chancellor, a squeaky-clean administrator, to advance the R5 000 from his discretionary fund, which he agreed to do. The replacement chair of council, a rogue leader, finally found something he could use to get even with the man who had confronted him about his sexual harassment of female staff and abuse of university resources. There was little appetite in council for pursuing such pettiness, but the chair persisted until he himself was ejected from council. Only then was the objection to a student bursary advance set aside by the new council – against the backdrop of huge scandals implicating the tripper-upper at this university.[39]

A final example shows the pervasive use of tripping-up tactics in many dysfunctional institutions. A senior manager of one university spoke out against the regional chair of the ruling party coming onto campus in the evenings and speaking directly to managers in the finance department, demanding access to contracts and so on. 'I spoke out against that and I was joined by some of my fellow executives and it ended up there was only one person standing. Ten of us lost our jobs.'[40]

To dismiss someone from an institution, you need something with which to trip him up. And so, one day the fraudsters gave the senior leader documents to sign. Everything looked in order. But there was fraud in the fine print, and through an elaborate set-up, money was transferred from the university's account to the fraudsters. Even though this deputy vice-chancellor was the target of fraudsters, he was ejected from the institution for a crime that everybody knew he was neither responsible for nor benefited from. He had been tripped up badly but would find himself appointed as the vice-chancellor of another institution.

A few things are clear from the micropolitics of corruption when it comes to tripping-up tactics. They are almost always performed by aggrieved parties who have been called to account by principled men and women in university leadership. It sometimes works for the corrupt, as in the fraud example, but at other times it does not, as in the case of the bursary award. It is often a charge completely out of proportion to the real scandals besetting an institution. It can precipitate resignations and departures, even if the tripping-up action fails. And it always leaves a stain on the reputation of the target, whether innocent or not.

The well-placed rumour

Few things can more effectively paralyse the leader of any large organisation than well-timed and well-placed malicious rumours. It is a deft tool of micropolitics in universities and a powerful one in efforts to dislodge an ethical and competent leader at any level of the institution.

An Eastern Cape university's independent whistleblowing service received an SMS in 2018 charging that the vice-chancellor was in romantic relationship with his office manager; that he did not declare this conflict of interest at the point of her appointment; that the two had a child together; and that the vice-chancellor had a hand in the irregular salary increase of his lover-cum-office manager. It was a devastating set of allegations that would create considerable turbulence inside the university, scandalise the reputations of the two persons involved, consume many hours of administration time, and cost the university tens of thousands of rands.

What was the upshot of the detailed, costly and time-consuming forensic investigation that ensued? In short, the allegations were false. The vice-chancellor and the office manager had never met each other until her interview. There was obviously no child from the rumoured relationship. The salary increases were made within the HR rules, and were necessary since the appointee would have been paid less than at her previous job. In the estimation of the head of the assessor's team, 'rumour and gossip was a tactic, deliberately employed as part of the destabilisation process. Truth is not part of the game.'[41] None of this elaborate fabrication stopped the rumour-mongering from taking its course on this fractured university campus. The scandal was advertised on social media. The banners at campus protests carried the lies as fact. National media ran with the story. The destabilisation effort continued, unperturbed by the truth.

Common to all universities, but especially prevalent at dysfunctional ones, is the leaking of confidential university documents or anonymous memoranda to the media. A pernicious rumour can be whipped up overnight and appear in the headlines of the local newspaper the next morning, before staff reach their offices and students their lectures. When a reporter is told to follow the story, it could run for days, and sometimes weeks or longer. Denials by 'management' are printed as an afterthought, but the damage is done.[42]

The politics of rumour does not require an elaborate construction of lies. All it needs to fuel disfavour and besmirch a reputation is something random, even casual, about an ethical leader. Patrick Fitzgerald was one such administrator, who would bring far-reaching changes to the University of the North as he cleaned up what was then a chronically unstable university. One day he went to shop at a grocery store in Polokwane, the big city near the university campus. He had a trolley-load of food, but the shop's card machine system was down, so they could not process his payment. He then went to a nearby ATM, drew the R2 000 required, and paid for his groceries. 'The next day there was a flyer on campus saying that this administrator who earns so much money does not have enough funds in his credit card to even pay for his groceries.'[43] Childish, of course, but the intention to diminish the credibility of an authoritative leader through innuendo remains a potent weapon in the hands of the disaffected.

The threat of violence

Much of what passes as the micropolitics of corruption in universities is subtle, invisible and behind the scenes, such as the anonymous whistleblower report or the retailing of malicious rumours. But sometimes there are direct threats to life and limb. Any challenge to the organised looting of institutional resources in the form of a disruptive administrator or an ethical staff member could be cause for retaliation (see chapter 7). This threatening kind of politics is especially common in dysfunctional and corrupt universities.

A sitting vice-chancellor told of the horrors of his current job as he tried to end corruption in the procurement chain:

I have already received anonymous threats since I have started here, accusing me of all sorts of things and I reported it to the police because of the strict processes we are putting in around tenders. We bought in a contractor to help us with supply chain. Somebody was sent here and almost killed this lady with an axe, came to campus with the axe hidden in the school bag and because they put on masks, got into where this lady was and removed an axe. She was in ICU for almost six months, she is recovering but she will never be able to get back to work. Cleaning up a place is complex.[44]

The fear was palpable, as a veteran council member explained. There are democratic representatives on council in areas of high unemployment; the stakes are therefore high to get onto council and benefit from the modest income for participation. And 'when you want this position so desperately, you buy patronage and one can see in that environment how easy it is for someone who has spilt the beans to get a bullet in their back. That's what I feared for my husband [that] he would get a bullet in his back if he went to University X as administrator.'[45]

None of these acts or threats of violence are episodic or random. As Charles King notes, 'Violent episodes are, if not predictable, then certainly patterned forms of social interaction … that begin with precipitating events such as prejudices or rumors.'[46] These threats also send the message up and down institutions that anyone who disrupts the illicit flow of resources can be got rid of. This is one of the explanations for the silence, even complicity, of many staff on university campuses where such behaviour has become 'patterned forms of social interaction', grafted onto the institutional culture.

These purposes of violence are detailed in a 2021 report on corruption inside South Africa's largest university, where

those who do not 'buy' into the prevailing culture are victimised and vilified. In addition, there have been incidents where violence has been used as a method of 'keeping people in their place'. There were recently reports, in the national press, of assaults at University X involving knives by certain members of staff (including a council member). There appear to have been no consequences visited upon the attackers. It is not surprising that many staff choose simply to leave rather than take on such forces.[47]

What is particularly disturbing in this task team report is the observation that 'Council (or at least one group within Council) has created an environment where corruption appears to be commonplace, supported and sustained by a culture of fear, victimization and vilification'. The factionalism described here ('one group within Council') is key to understanding the micropolitics of institutional violence in South African universities.

Factionalisation

It is, of course, not uncommon in organisations to have colleagues who disagree on small and large things, and even to form affinity groups around contending policies, plans or programmes. However, when such divisions become organised around factional interests in gaining illicit access to institutional resources, then the institution becomes a toxic mix of competing groups that fuels further dysfunctionality.

Factions within university leadership lie at the heart of dysfunctional governance and management. The lines are typically drawn between those operating with the intent of looting institutional resources and those who wish to prevent corruption from happening. At a Western Cape university, the battle lines between two factions were strongly drawn. The chairman of council ('A') repeatedly disregarded the line separating governance from management and clashed openly with the vice-chancellor ('B'). It was a micro-conflict that continued for years, including well-publicised court appearances. For the chairman, the university was a platform for advancing his personal standing in higher education through active interference in the management of the institution and its resources. For the vice-chancellor, the defensive lines had to be secured to prevent governance encroaching on management.

Perhaps inevitably, 'little cabals were formed' around A as his group continued to 'go beyond their mandate in governance'. At the same time, B ensured that his management team acted in concert against this intrusion into the operations of the university. The see-saw battle between the factions seemed to go on forever. While A was an experienced unionist with organising skills who would 'establish alliances within council', B lacked the kinds of political instincts and experience to counter such moves and establish the authority of the academic mandate of the university.[48]

Factionalism has its own uses, as one assessor observed in a series of visits to a dysfunctional institution: 'The kind of factionalism that we saw in that institution was likely to continue because there was nothing else that people united around [but] resources, rather than uniting around a vision.' Factions form and re-form as necessary in order to gain leverage over institutional assets. When it comes to campus politics, students and unions are joint partners in dysfunctional universities. Sometimes those alliances are positive, and necessary to shore up numbers and build influence around a particular issue, such as the demand by unions for insourcing workers or the pressure from students for affordable tuition fees. At other times, factions form for purposes of leveraging resources by corrupt means. One way to do so is by agitating for the appointment of a vice-chancellor perceived as pliant, one who would work in the interests of corrupt persons or interest groups.

The capturing of a university under a corrupt vice-chancellor or a chair of council extends all the way down through the committee structures, as this former vice-chancellor and sitting administrator revealed: 'One of the things I found is that the university established in its HR division a staffing committee comprised of five Nehawu [National Education, Health and Allied Workers' Union] members and five members of NTEU [National Tertiary Education Union] and the executive director [of] HR and they sat and made appointments and promotions including academic appointments and academic promotions.'[49]

By taking over such important management functions as staffing, the unions were at the same time protecting labour. And you are especially well protected if you are a union leader since, in these political arrangements, nobody will touch you. If they did, the repercussions would be swift, as we saw earlier in the case of the departed vice-chancellor who tried to fire a corrupt comrade.

Of course, the roots of faction formation come from South Africa's long history of stakeholder politics. Caucusing is a venerable mechanism for binding factions together before, during and after meetings where critical decisions are made. Here, a group might intervene in a meeting and call for an opportunity to caucus for purposes of a joint position on a particular agenda item. Again, this is an innocent manoeuvre, except when the purpose is to gain influence or grab resources for the benefit of the faction. It has often been observed, in this context, how easily this perfectly reasonable strategy for exerting political influence becomes part of a range of corrupt activities in universities.

Sometimes, factions were formed within the executive management of the university, which immediately compromised the authority of senior leaders to execute the academic mandate of the institution. More often, those factions existed within council, thereby rendering the governance structure ineffectual. Under these conditions, as an administrator of one of the most factionalised universities observed, things fall apart: 'University Z was in a sense a very divided institution. Students and unions were pretty much in charge. Management took instructions from union leaders and student leaders on everything from who to appoint, who not to appoint, who sits in tender committees, all those kinds of things. You end up with a very divided university.'[50] In short, the factions had done their political work, and the university was now vulnerable to resource stripping.

The control of staffing resources

Staffing is the largest expenditure item in any university's budget. In fact, it is often a matter of contention in dysfunctional universities that the staffing budget in general is too high, leaving little money for basic operations like building maintenance or library subscriptions. Another typical concern in such universities is that the budget for academic staffing is much less than for administrative staffing, clearly a problem for a teaching and research institution. None of these concerns are immaterial to the micropolitics of corruption.

As already shown, an important strategy in staffing politics is to ensure that the 'right' vice-chancellor is selected. For corrupt factions, this means someone who will play ball and facilitate access to resources through, for example, favourable appointments to key decision-making structures. As a result, at every dysfunctional university the fight over who the vice-chancellor will be often turns into a very public contestation. In one case, the race card was used against a favoured white candidate, with his opponent putting openly racist placards on the lampposts leading to campus; the white professor nevertheless got the job at this overwhelmingly black institution.

Not surprisingly, the political parties outside campus work to influence the outcome of the vice-chancellor appointment, depending on whether that person is aligned with their interests or not. At one large university, there was not even an attempt to disguise political interference. Party delegates were dispatched to inform council members who the preferred candidates were. Pressure would be put on the 'comrades' on council to exercise their influence rather than their conscience. Invariably, incompetent and sometimes corruptible persons get appointed to the top job, with predictable consequences for effective management and administration of the university – Unisa is a case in point.[51]

It is not uncommon for stakeholder groupings, like unions or academic factions or student leaders, to meet with their preferred candidate the night before her interview to brief the chosen one on what to expect. The real goal is for these factions to align themselves with the candidate ahead of a decision, so that if their person wins, they can expect something in return. The politics of staffing always has a point, as this experienced incumbent administrator explains: 'How did we get to a point where malfeasance just continued? You appoint agreeable senior managers who appoint themselves agreeable managers who themselves appoint agreeable supervisors and staff. That creates its own kind of local microclimate.'[52]

The other way in which staffing becomes a contested resource is in the appointment of family and friends. Persons who would never be able to qualify for a job in university administration, or any job at all, now enjoy access to a monthly salary, with disastrous consequences for effectiveness and efficiency in the operations of the institution. And because it is hard to dismiss staff, given South Africa's pro-worker labour laws, other ways must be found to retain these persons who lack the necessary competencies for the job. One administrator decided on a retraining programme, with limited success. Another tried redeployment to basic jobs in the university. With a now bloated staff, the financial capacity to hire competent people is limited, thereby aggravating the problems of dysfunctionality. It is a vicious cycle, with nepotism often on the charge sheet of investigation teams in corrupt universities.

Once again, the instability in staffing is neither accidental nor disinterested. Instability is often manufactured precisely to create the kind of uncertainty and chaos that enables the plundering of resources. With councils responsible for appointing senior managers, one strategy in a conflicted governance structure is to delay or postpone these vital appointments, simply because it is easier for corrupt leaders to work with, or get rid of, people in acting positions. It is seldom a lack of resources for senior appointments that holds up the works; it is, rather, a preferred condition for enabling corruption. As a former vice-chancellor of a functional university found when he was called to take over a dysfunctional one: 'On arrival, I got the management of the university together, the academic deans and the [senior] administrators. Every single one of them was acting, a drama school, I joked. Decision-making had been incapacitated in this way [because] the moment you stepped out of line [the former vice-chancellor] would take the acting benefit away from you. It was a very shrewd and ruthless system for keeping people in line.'[53]

Thus, staffing as a resource remains a powerful mechanism for playing out the micropolitics of corruption inside broken universities.

CONCLUSION

Five key insights emerge from this close-up inquiry into the micropolitics of corruption in universities.

First, there is a myriad of ways in which various types of corruption operate within dysfunctional institutions. The ten categories of corrupt micro-actions discussed in this chapter are not exhaustive; discussed elsewhere are other methods, such as predatory publishing, benefits scams, the destabilisation of governance and management meeting agendas, the abuses of the council honorarium, the bugging of meeting offices, and the wanton waste of institutional resources (see chapters 6 and 7). More than a few administrators made the point that 'you will not believe the levels of corruption at this university'.

Second, it is not single acts of corruption that bring vulnerable universities to their knees, but the combination of all these corrupt acts. As we have seen, these micro-actions are ubiquitous in institutions, touching everything from the HR department to the auditing division and the councils themselves. Together, they place a heavy burden on the governors and managers trying to defend vital assets in the life of a university. The combined impact of these many attacks on institutional integrity over a span of years renders the university unstable and dysfunctional in the execution of its most basic duties.

Third, these multiple and enduring micro-actions have corrosive effects on institutional functionality. They destroy trust in the institution among stakeholders, bearing witness to rampant corruption. Illicit actions within mainstream operations encourage others to participate in corrupt activities, thereby further diminishing the ability of the university to make good its academic commitments. All three critical areas of institutional functioning are corroded in the process: governance, management and administration.

Fourth, the long duration of such a micropolitics of corruption means that crooked behaviours become entrenched in institutional practice. The corrupt activities begin to take on a life of their own and assume the status of 'normal' administrative or managerial procedures. What shocks outsiders does not disturb insiders long associated with a particular (mal) practice. Put differently, those inside the organisation are no longer able to distinguish right from wrong, and, even if they manage to do so, they just shrug their shoulders, for 'it's the way we do things around here'.

Fifth, with the entrenchment of corruption, it is easy to understand why changing wrongful practices is so difficult. It is no surprise, therefore, that several of the dysfunctional institutions studied in this book have had two or more assessors or administrators pass through them since the end of apartheid.

This chapter has shed light on the different categories of micropolitical actions that sustain the instability of institutions, and it examined why it is so difficult for external interventions to succeed. The question that remains is this: what is it about institutions that enable these micro-actions to emerge and thrive in the first place? The pursuit of that question requires an understanding of the two legs on which a highly functional institution stands: institutional capability and institutional integrity.

9

The Twin Roots of Chronic Dysfunctionality in Universities

Nthabiseng Ogude was the talented new deputy vice-chancellor of a recently merged university on the east coast of South Africa, the Nelson Mandela Metropolitan University (NMMU).[1] Its organisational core was the established white University of Port Elizabeth (UPE), which had merged with the Port Elizabeth Technikon and incorporated an urban black campus (Vista), together with a smaller campus in George about 350 kilometres away. All eyes were on this young professor of chemistry, one of the first black women to be appointed as a senior executive of a major university.

One evening, a petrol attendant put ordinary petrol in her car's diesel tank, sparking a small crisis. Ogude had to travel to George the next day to officiate at a graduation ceremony of NMMU's Southern Cape campus. She called the vice-chancellor's assistant, who hastily arranged a replacement car from the rental company used by the university for official business. The car was duly delivered, but out of an appreciation for the university's business, the rental company decided to deliver an

A-class Mercedes-Benz sedan rather than the basic Toyota-level vehicle normally used for travel – without charging for the upgrade. The vice-chancellor, a mild-mannered Christian who was ethical to a fault, was furious when he heard about this break with protocol. He confronted Ogude. Why did she take a rental car when the university gave her a generous car allowance? And why an A-class vehicle when university policy restricted staff to a smaller vehicle at the lower end of the rental car range? While the vice-chancellor had clearly not heard about Ogude's car travails, the message from the top of the university could not have been clearer: integrity mattered.[2]

INSTITUTIONAL INTEGRITY

What happens in low-trust environments when those responsible for managing universities cannot trust one another to act with integrity? The consequence, in a nutshell, is dysfunction. But what is this thing called institutional integrity?

Whereas individual integrity is the practice of honesty and doing the right thing on the part of an individual person who shows consistency in adhering to the values that connect words and actions, institutional integrity refers to 'an organization that defines and acts within a strong code of ethical conduct and positive values and that adopts no tolerance of attitudes, actions and activities by its employees or partners that deviate from that code'.[3] There are several insights that can be gleaned from this deft conception of institutional integrity. First of all, it describes the orientation of an organisation as a whole towards 'doing the right thing', not simply the well-intentioned commitment of individuals within it. It also speaks of a set of steering values, which, in the case of universities, is (or ought to be) their core academic commitments. And it implies sanctions, in that an institution of integrity would have built into its systems active procedures for disciplining those who deviate from the rules.

A broader conception of institutional integrity further suggests that institutions like universities not only make particular value claims but pursue those commitments with energy and devotion. Institutional integrity, in this view, is the 'robust disposition of a public institution to legitimately pursue its legitimate purpose, to the best of its abilities, consistent with its commitments'.[4] Whether an institution is therefore perceived as legitimate depends very much on whether it adheres to its declared public values.

This is not easy, since there are both internal and external threats to institutional integrity. Gordon Davies calls such threats 'intrusion', by which he means 'ideological pressure on the curriculum, interference in staff appointments, and favoritism in awarding contracts'.[5] Some of those threats to institutional integrity are less obvious and may find their origins in the very founding and funding of universities. It may be, for example, that the underfunding of an already disadvantaged higher education institution renders it vulnerable to breaches of the thin membrane of institutional integrity.

In this regard, integrity has another and, for social scientists, less obvious meaning, one drawn from the construction sciences, as when they refer to the 'integrity' of a concrete bridge or building. For engineers, 'the structural integrity [of a building] does not turn upon whether it stands, but whether it is easily vulnerable to collapse in adverse environmental conditions'.[6] This is an important insight, in that it distinguishes the mere existence of a structure from its soundness in the face of challenging circumstances. And one of the factors that engineers regard as a problem in the potential collapse of a building is what they call a foundation failure, which weakens the visible structure.

It is clear from the evidence in this study that several of the dysfunctional universities suffer from what can be called foundation failure. To extend this handy metaphor to the social sciences, this means that in their very founding these institutions were compromised, and are therefore vulnerable to weaknesses in their institutional integrity – the ability to withstand adverse environmental conditions.

The point was made earlier that the historically black universities of South Africa were not established with academic excellence in mind.

Whether in the bantustan universities or the urban black universities, the official intention of apartheid authorities was decidedly not to create outstanding centres of excellence in research and development. Narrowly conceived, these post-school institutions were intended to create a trained labour force to serve the bureaucracies of the racially and ethnically divided communities from which students came and where they would be employed. It is not surprising, therefore, that the government bursaries made available at the time were not for those studying medicine and engineering, but for librarians, teachers and other civil servants in the state machinery. Some individual universities offered one of the highly prized disciplines, such as dentistry at the University of the Western Cape, medicine at Walter Sisulu University and engineering at the University of Durban-Westville, but even these were underfunded by the state.

Some leaders of universities have therefore argued that since the black universities were not intended to be academic centres of high repute, the post-apartheid expectation that they should behave as such was unreasonable. To extend the metaphor, it was like building an impressive structure on shaky foundations and expecting it to stand strong. A senior university administrator who worked at all levels of functional and dysfunctional universities, as well as in the role of assessor, put it this way:

> This is the fundamental question, whether these institutions were universities. They never were. They were established initially as some kind of apartheid project, and they were a place where the apartheid regime dumped their excess non-intellectuals [white Afrikaners] to teach, and many of them couldn't even speak English. And they were just dumped there, you know.
>
> The aim was not to establish a university persona with academic freedom, autonomy, and so forth. In fact, they were far from autonomous. The vice-chancellor was appointed by the state, because he reported to the state. So those institutions were despised by everybody.

The academic mission has never been the main objective of this institution, and so I maintain that they have never been able to out-live that. Learning and teaching and research are not important. They don't even think about it.[7]

When such institutions started to wobble on their weak foundations, the more courageous in the post-apartheid government came to the realisation that it was time to close down some of them, since there was no way they could become centres of academic distinction under extremely adverse conditions. Worse, the wobbly universities would offer a second-rate education to the children of the black poor, the very same criticism that had energised the struggle against apartheid education.

No university was more prone to continuous collapse than the University of Transkei (Unitra), a veritable 'basket case' in the estimation of scholars and administrators alike. A senior bureaucrat in higher education who served as deputy director-general in the department as well as adviser to the minister recalls the turn in the government's thinking about what to do with this university: 'There were governance problems, systems problems, declining enrolments, financial difficulties, [and] this was the moment where many of us in the department thought we had to radically rethink the future of this institution. Is a university viable in Umtata? We wrote submission after submission to make the case for a radical rethink. We did not feel that Unitra in that form was viable.'[8]

All sorts of options were on the table: make the university a vocational college; close it and give its more viable medical school to a custodian university, such as the University of Cape Town (UCT), the University of KwaZulu-Natal (UKZN) or nearby Rhodes University. Closure of the main campus was firmly on the table. What gave this pending decision some chance of success was that the minister at the time, Professor Kader Asmal, was a senior and influential figure in both the cabinet and the ruling party.

What happened next would become a familiar tale when any radical changes to universities were proposed in the post-apartheid period.

While the proposals on the table were rational to the core, there was the small matter of politics, and no one was more resistant to closing Unitra than the founding father of democratic South Africa, Nelson Mandela. When the minister gave the university an instruction not to take in a new first-year cohort, the first step towards closure, Mandela stepped in and demanded a reversal of the decision, as a former director of university planning recalled: 'Mandela said, "If you don't reverse the decision, I will personally lead a march in Umtata." Asmal reversed the decision the next morning. We were hammered, we were hammered. I was personally hammered. Nelson Mandela was lobbied, and he made it clear that Unitra would not close. Stofile[9] was premier [of the province] at the time and he took it right to Luthuli House [the headquarters of the ruling party].'[10] Even a figure as charismatic, knowledgeable and powerful as Minister Asmal could not steer the decision through the choppy political waters of the time. 'You can give all the technical advice, but if the political will and the political authority is not there to take those hard decisions, it was not going to happen,' reflected the official then in charge.

This applied not only to Unitra in Mthatha, the capital of the former Transkei homeland. The same logic extended to an even more desperate situation at what was then the Border Technikon in Butterworth, about 120 kilometres south-east of Mthatha along the major N2 highway. 'There was nothing there,' notes a senior official, 'no industry, something vital for a Technikon's mandate to deliver "workplace-based education and training".'[11] The staff lived far from their place of employment, in cities like East London, more than 100 kilometres away; they drove in and out every day. The only signs of life in Butterworth were spaza shops, a taxi rank and a bus terminal. That was all. But instead of closing this isolated rural technikon campus with its constant and often violent protests in an economic desert far from any industrial hub, the government then did something even more risky: it merged the technikon with Unitra to form Walter Sisulu University in 2005. In other words, two dysfunctional campuses were merged into one, in a move that now placed the structural integrity of the new institution on even shakier foundations.

The medical school of Unitra was not predestined to remain in Mthatha, recounts the director of higher education planning at the time.[12] In fact, a major study on where to place the medical school in the Eastern Cape pointed to East London as the preferred location. That city had a functioning hospital with the kind of infrastructure and facilities that could easily be expanded into a teaching hospital at minimal costs.

Most of the required political support for the East London location of the medical school was in place, including that of Minister Asmal, based on an expert study prepared for another interested party, the Department of Health. The Treasury, reporting to the minister, was also in agreement, because properly developing the medical school in Mthatha would require a staggering R100 million, whereas using the existing facilities in East London would have been much more affordable.

But when the proposal went to cabinet, the minister of health pushed for maintaining the Mthatha location. The costs did not matter, and the logic even less. It was the troubled politics of the region, where the ruling party was already being criticised for moving the administrative centre from Mthatha to Bhisho. Taking the medical school out of Mthatha would have added to the mounting political costs for the ruling party.

What followed was a complete breakdown in the capacity of the university, the medical school and the local hospital to deliver quality education and training to future doctors. 'The conditions inside that medical faculty were absolutely appalling,' remembers a senior official from the department, following a walk through the facility. 'I felt like crying the day we went to that old Umtata hospital; no patient should experience that kind of environment, which itself needed critical care.'[13]

This situation at Unitra and its medical school was not simply an apartheid legacy, but a crisis manufactured by the post-apartheid government in defiance of evidence that an East London location would have delivered a more efficient and affordable health facility to serve the people of the Eastern Cape.

Despite their troubled histories, unsteady institutions are subjected to the same policy pressures as highly functional institutions – to deliver quality education, graduate students on time, generate more black professors, compete for limited research funds, and so forth. However, in the comparative metrics released by governments and science councils on institutional performance, these faltering institutions rank consistently at the lower end of the scales, as if their relative showing was self-explanatory. 'You cannot transform a dysfunctional and confused organisation,' says a senior administrator of universities and corporate executive; 'you make it worse.'[14]

COLLECTIVE INTEGRITY AND FUNCTIONALITY

There is something that lies between the individual integrity of the individual person and the institutional integrity of the whole organisation, and that is the critical mass of people who are involved in, dedicated to and responsible for the institution's state of functionality. This construct of collective integrity foregrounds the behaviour of individuals, but it only exists when the vast majority of the staff, students and council members are committed in word and action to good management and governance. The evidence of collective integrity is strong when there are limited cases of corruption or malfeasance in an environment where deviance from the institutional rules is quickly detected and resolved through effective monitoring and compliance enforcement. Conversely, where collective integrity is absent, institutional integrity is regularly breached by individuals inside and outside. The sense of the collapse of collective integrity was often described in the interviews conducted for this study as 'the rot running deep'.

Importantly, to acknowledge the problem of structural integrity, where universities are founded on weak foundations, does not in any way excuse corruption among those who work there. This is for two principal reasons. First, the people who work in dysfunctional universities are not machines, but conscious agents with the moral capacity for choosing whether to do the right thing or not. Second, there are examples of historically disadvantaged institutions, both urban like the University of the Western Cape and rural like the University of Venda, that demonstrate the possibility of overcoming legacy conditions when ethical leadership diffuses its influence throughout the university.

Nor does the notion of collective integrity ignore the fact that there are often good people and departments of high integrity in corrupt institutions, or that there are sometimes corrupt people and departments in otherwise highly regarded universities. What the construct points to, rather, is contexts in which corruption is so routine that it occupies a significant amount of the governance or management agenda. This raises the question of how integrity is built and sustained in functional institutions. What, in other words, holds highly functional universities together?

ACADEMIC VALUES AT THE CORE OF INSTITUTIONAL INTEGRITY

As argued earlier, successful institutions pursue and deliver on their core mandate, which in higher education is the promotion of academic values. This is the glue that holds functional universities together and that gives focus to their operations. Importantly, those academic values also serve as rudders that steady the institution in turbulent times. Such values are primarily concerned with the delivery of high-quality teaching, the enablement of higher learning and the commitment to cutting-edge research, which, together, advance social and human development. They enjoy prominence on the agendas of management in their weekly meetings, of senate in their term meetings, and of council in their quarterly meetings. Everything revolves around the academic project.

In this regard, the older and more established universities have enjoyed a long tradition of embedding those academic values in all aspects of their work. One of the longest-serving senior executives at UCT says those values are 'the DNA of the institution', and that their roots lie in the British, and especially Scottish, origins of the curriculum and culture of South Africa's English universities (see chapter 2). Those academic values include standards set for the professoriate, which, though tested from time to time, still form part of the mandate of such institutions: 'There is still a very strong sense of the academic project [including] the research project and you still cannot be appointed as a full professor at UCT on teaching excellence alone. You have to have a research profile and that is [also] strongly supported by black staff.'[15] Academic robustness is a two-edged sword, UCT executives argue. It means that everything becomes a matter of debate in a highly decentralised structure, making speedy academic decisions difficult to achieve; however, under adverse conditions, the academic character of the university 'also builds in some kind of safety net for functionality'.

For somewhat different reasons, the former white Afrikaans universities also hold a strong sense of academic values as central to their mission. However, the academic identity of the Afrikaans institutions is maintained in a much more centralised authority (even if there are, on paper, devolved faculty and department structures), where firm decisions can be made without rancour or resistance. Despite the contrast with the seeming unwieldiness of academic debate in the English universities, the command-and-control culture of the Afrikaans universities achieves the same outcome, guided by a strong sense of academic values at the core of their institutional identity.[16]

One of the most important functions of academic values is to hold the institution together in times of challenge. For example, when the integrity of the academic degree is at risk through prolonged shutdown, every resource is thrown at the problem to prevent an extended break from teaching and learning. This was most obvious in the student protests of 2015–2016, when the established universities quickly moved to emergency remote teaching to ensure that the academic year was not lost. By contrast, in 2021 a dysfunctional university specialising in the health sciences was shut down amid routine protests for months on end, and yet the students received their degrees as if nothing had happened.[17] The academic project was seriously compromised, but there was no institutional panic about the integrity of the degrees.

In one investigatory analysis after another, the issue of the academic integrity of the university looms large as an explanation for both the cause and consequences of dysfunction. For example, at the University of South Africa (Unisa) it was found that institutional integrity collapsed as a result of a systematic and, indeed, criminal campaign to undermine the development of the technological infrastructure that held the institution together. Here, 'the failure to ensure a robust, modern and secure ICT infrastructure has not only been damaging to Unisa's reputation with respect to administrative competence but also to its academic standing. Academics have been hampered in their efforts to improve the student support they are able to provide and their ability to engage with what it means to be an online university.'[18]

This damning conclusion linked the effectiveness of the academic project directly to corruption in the supply of IT infrastructure needed to make teaching, learning and research possible in the first place. It is an observation also made in an earlier crisis, at the University of Venda (Univen), when the experienced academic leader and vice-chancellor James Leatt was sent to rescue this institution in the Limpopo province. Here he would discover an answer to the question I had posed earlier in my academic career when invited to speak at a rural, former bantustan university. The place was in a mess, academically as well as physically, with little in the infrastructure to suggest a modern university. I changed the title of my talk on the spot to reflect the question that grabbed my imagination at the time: When does a university cease to exist? After one month at a dilapidated Univen, Leatt claimed that he had found the answer: 'A university ceases to be a university when the infrastructure can no longer support its core business of teaching and research.'[19]

There is an important observation to be made in this regard from the earlier discussion of institutional integrity. It is quite possible see a structure or an organisation and to misrecognise it as an institution of higher learning. As I put it in my paper on the question, 'It would be easy to be fooled by the symbolic functions and routines of university life, and mistake this for a university.' I went on to argue that 'a university ceases to exist when the intellectual project no longer defines its identity, infuses its curriculum, energizes its scholars, and inspires its students.'[20] Such a university clearly has no institutional integrity at all.

In the absence of academic values, what takes their place in the everyday dynamics of institutional life? This study finds that it is the preoccupation with getting their hands on the university's resources that instead focuses the attention and absorbs the energies of those who manage and govern a corrupted institution. The consequences of such a relentless clamour for institutional resources are devastating, for, as the literature shows, 'corruption is one of the most significant risks for institutional integrity.'[21]

HOW INSTITUTIONAL INTEGRITY IS BREACHED IN DYSFUNCTIONAL INSTITUTIONS

The integrity of institutions starts with the personal and academic integrity of the people chosen to the lead them. More often than not, dysfunctional universities do not hire the best vice-chancellors, with the combined traits of scholarly achievement in their fields and management expertise in higher education. In one of the universities under serial administration, the assessor's report found that 'Professor M is a very talented person who, by his own admission, does not have an aptitude for hands-on management in administration. He states himself that he does not like to sit behind a desk "shuffling papers" and that he is not interested in financial management. As such, he is more suited to an academic post than a managerial one.'[22]

The question, of course, is how such a person, an eminent professor of literature, even came to be appointed to lead a university that, at the time, was in deep financial trouble? Outside the established universities, politics played a massive role in the appointment of vice-chancellors. Closeness to the ruling party helped. Lobbying on the part of stakeholders was commonplace. At the largest South African university, 'Luthuli House was directly involved,' reported senior council members. The ANC Women's League would, in one instance, put up advertisements on lampposts in favour of their preferred candidate.

At the university where Professor M's contract was not renewed, none of the previous vice-chancellors were academics who had progressed through the ranks as scholars or administrators. They were all political placemen linked to the ruling party. One of them crossed the street, almost literally, from running a party-linked government entity to leading a university. The title of professor was liberally awarded to people who had no scholarly credentials whatsoever. This was a political move that several of the dysfunctional universities would make, with often disastrous consequences. Institutional integrity thus took a blow, both in executive appointments and in the professoriate as a whole.

The scramble for vice-chancellor positions sometimes meant a complete disregard for academic credentials. In one institution, there was a prolonged struggle for the position because an appointed vice-chancellor was found to have a fraudulent doctorate from a dubious institution called the St George's University International in the Bahamas. The council defended the appointment, even though the advertisement for the job stated that a doctoral qualification was a prerequisite. Higher Education South Africa (HESA) released a statement expressing concern about how this appointment reflected on the academic reputation and integrity of the university.

Institutional integrity is breached when political appointees become vice-chancellors, as demonstrated in the case of dysfunctional institutions like the Vaal University of Technology (VUT) and Mangosuthu University of Technology (MUT) discussed earlier. The costs of malfunction were high not only in financial terms, but also in human terms. In these universities, a vice-chancellor's appointment was treated no differently from the ruling party's cadre deployment policy. In the historically white, established universities, such political intrusion had little to no influence, but in the more vulnerable and dysfunctional institutions, institutional integrity was regularly breached through external interference in appointments.

A further cause of weakness in the institutional integrity of vulnerable institutions was decisions made about appointments and promotions at the middle and lower ranks of the staff. Here, managerial functions were compromised through populating crucial positions in administration with friends and family members. A whistleblower at a serially dysfunctional university gave the new administrator 'a list of all the family members appointed by the vice-chancellor'. Action was promised, but none taken.[23]

The integrity of the academy is further undermined by promoting to senior academic positions, in the name of transformation, persons who would not enjoy such elevation at an established university.[24] And the governance of an institution is placed at serious risk by the appointment to council of junior members who have never governed anything in their lives. This 'juniorisation' of council membership remains a particularly dangerous trend among the dysfunctional institutions. At a university that had more than one government intervention – two administrators and a high turnover of vice-chancellors – the situation was particularly dire, as an acting vice-chancellor described: 'You have individuals in council who are fairly junior and could not have imagined that a vice-chancellor would report to them. Even in their workplaces they are fairly junior, and they do not have experience. For some of them their positions [on council] go to their heads. You have a junior person having to hold a VC accountable. What they then do is act to prove a point, that they are more important than the VC.'[25] Again, a senior academic from a different university, invited to form part of a dysfunctional university's interview committee, recalled: 'I was shocked to see the youngsters on council, many of them political appointments.'[26]

These were not just problems of foundational failure, but conscious decisions taken by human actors without regard to consequences. Put differently, universities with weak foundations were rendered even more unstable by irresponsible and unethical staffing decisions. The foundational failure lies in the fact that rural universities with low academic reputations find it hard to attract talented academics and administrators. The present-day failure is that universities make poor staffing decisions that aggravate foundational weaknesses, increasing the risk of chronic dysfunction. That is how historical origins and contemporary decision-making come together to explain institutional dysfunction – integrity was breached and capacity was undermined.

INSTITUTIONAL CAPACITY

On a visit to South Africa, Richard Elmore, professor of education at Harvard University, once spoke of the dump truck notion of capacity building. You identify the problem as capacity. Then you fill a truck with what capacity is needed and pour it out at the point of need. It is an apt metaphor that describes the dominant approach to capacity building in both schools and universities in South Africa.

At the moment of the country's transition to democracy, major external funders identified the problem of higher education in South Africa as a deficit in capacity that needed to be filled. Launched in 2002, the Higher Education Leadership and Management (HELM) programme was specifically designed to provide capacity building for university vice-chancellors and other academic leaders. At the start, the Atlantic Philanthropies gave HELM R2 million for two years and the Andrew Mellon Foundation offered a quarter of a million dollars for a period of three years. Now funded by the Department of Higher Education and Training, the HELM initiative still describes its objective as 'to assist individuals and organizations to identify their capacity needs within their specific context and align individual leadership development pathways with organizational objectives'.[27]

The identification of the problem of governance and management as one of 'capacity' brought in overseas leaders in higher education to work alongside South African academics and vice-chancellors to provide systematic training focused on filling the development needs of senior leaders of universities, including registrars and deans. In addition, the Council Capacity Development Project of a prominent non-governmental organisation, the Council for Higher Education Transformation (CHET), oversaw the publication of *Effective Governance*, which was offered as 'a guide for council members of universities and technikons'. Topics covered included how to avoid conflicts of interests (for instance, appointments of family members), the need to evaluate and support the vice-chancellor, the desired personal qualities of council members, and the importance of protecting the university's integrity at all times.

The millions spent on building the capacity of councils and managements came not only through external foundation funds but also through university investments in the training of council members. This approach to capacity building – filling the gaps in knowledge and skills – worked on the assumption that this information, systematically provided, would improve governance in higher education.

There is no doubt that the 'filling-the-gap' approach to capacity building provided important information for academic leaders at all levels of their institutions, especially in regard to the new legislation on higher education in the post-apartheid period. It was necessary, but also inadequate, as a senior adviser to ministers of education reflected on her work with dysfunctional universities: 'I think some of us were naive at the time to think you could put these institutions right only by the building of systems and human capacity. Alone, these governance building initiatives would not give us functional institutions … despite years of council training manuals.'[28]

Why did such massive investments in capacity building fail so spectacularly? An obvious reason is that the 'fill-in-the-gaps' conception of capacity building was deficient from the start. A cursory review of the literature on the subject would have exposed the limitations of that barebones understanding of the concept, as these contending conceptions of organisational capacity show:

- The ability to perform work;
- The enabling factors that allow an organisation to perform its functions and achieve its goals;
- The ability of government to marshal, develop, direct and control its financial, human, physical and information resources;
- The set of processes, management practices or attributes that assist an organisation in fulfilling its mission.[29]

One of the first insights to be gleaned from these formulations is the distinction between individual and organisational capacity – which was not made during the years when the focus of HELM was on individual capacity building. The problem was that when those empowered individuals returned to their universities, they entered rigid and sometimes dysfunctional institutional spaces that rendered their fresh training more or less useless for pursuing change. Nothing in the South African approach to capacity building, particularly as it relates to HELM, has cracked the code of organisational change, beyond talk of reaching a critical mass of individuals.

Another insight from these definitions of capacity building has to do with the ability to manage a complex of resources. This shifts the focus from capacity as a set of individual inputs to capacity defined as management capability. In this understanding of capacity, an organisation has authority and control over public resources.

And yet a third insight relates capacity to the achievement of institutional mission and objectives. Pouring capacity into ready receptacles is not only poor pedagogy (the blank slate or tabula rasa theory of education); it is also poor politics. To successfully link organisational capacity to desired organisational outcomes requires the capability to deliver that turns on both technical expertise and political craft.[30]

None of these complexities of capacity, whether in concept or practice, informed the early and naive understandings of how change happens inside established, let alone dysfunctional, institutions. In short, there was no theory of change except the resolve to 'do something' in the heady days of the transition from apartheid to democracy. And, as the long-serving HELM leader acknowledged of those times, 'when there's nothing, something will always work.'[31] It did not work, for the focus was not the organisation, but the individual sent for the personal benefits of capacity enhancement.

THE POLITICAL UTILITY OF INCAPACITY, THE OTHER SIDE OF THE CAPACITY COIN

Perhaps the single most important insight gained from this study was the revelation that incapacity was not, in fact, simply a technical problem that needed to be solved but, for those intending to fleece a university of its vital resources, a necessary state to be maintained. What was the political value of incapacity, and how did it actually work?

This study showed that the role of politics on and off campus was to undermine the authority and effectiveness of management. In this regard, two stakeholders loomed large: the National Education, Health and Allied Workers' Union (Nehawu), the majority union, acting in concert with the local student representative council (SRC) or with factions within it. There was a constant assault on management – whether the vice-chancellor and his or her team – or the administrator brought in to stabilise the institution. If the management function could be disrupted, then the systems required to protect institutional integrity – from the audit function to the tendering process – could be compromised, to the benefit of the disruptors. Nowhere was this calculated undermining of management and oversight systems more clearly in evidence than at Unisa.

For much of the 2000s, this large distance-education university was in the news for the collapse of its administrative systems, including over-enrolments, registrations, the distribution of learning materials, and examinations. The popular narrative was that the collapse of Unisa was due to the sharp increase in enrolments (from 263 955 in 2009 to more than 400 000 in 2020) with no corresponding increase in staffing or the requisite technological infrastructure to support this massive expansion.[32] What was less visible to the outside (or even inside) world was the systematic undermining of management capacity, or, in the terms of this study, the deliberate actions taken to produce and sustain incapacity within the university.

The mechanisms for inducing instability included the following actions, as reported by a ministerial task team investigating Unisa:

- Council deliberately reduced the delegation of authority to management, thus undermining management.
- Infrastructure projects were formulated and even approved but not implemented. This can only be conceived as intentional.

- Each and every procurement process, although previously approved by council, has met with resistance by staff – often very junior staff – within supply change management or by Mancom or by council.
- The method of lodging grievances is used as a way of stalling processes. They frustrate the normal conduct of operations and consume time and energy.
- Council has largely incapacitated management and rendered them powerless.
- Council has deliberately blocked implementation when it suited their purposes. This not only undermines management but positively removes authority from the vice-chancellor and the vice-chancellor's teams.[33]

There is much to unpack here regarding the manufacture of incapacity as a political end in dysfunctional universities. First, the diminution of management capacity occurs on a wide range of fronts, from the council to staff in the supply chain process. Through undermining management in procurement, for example, preferred bidders can be brought in, rather than those who compete through the formal process. By undercutting management's authority to manage through delegated powers, council can gain the upper hand in appointing staff and awarding contracts. In the case of Unisa, the vital and already approved IT infrastructure investments were held back, and the systems function collapsed. In other words, what happened at Unisa was not a question of incompetence or the lack of capacity; it was a systematic, deliberate and intentional process of undermining management processes in order to trigger institutional instability, thereby shifting authority to other powers in the university.

The union Nehawu continues to play a critical role in maintaining the weakened management structures at several universities. As the administrator at the University of Zululand, a veteran of higher education management and leadership, recalls of that institution: 'Certain stakeholders are so powerful that they trump legal, institutional processes; the unions play a critical role in this regard. The impasse at some universities means that nothing is going to happen to reclaim management and government spaces. Because once you have lost the management space, it is extremely difficult to take it back.'[34]

The story of dysfunction is, therefore, a story of the active incapacitation of management. When this 'paralysis of management' occurs, one of two things happens: either the vice-chancellor fights to reclaim management authority and is then aggressively worked out of his or her position (as at Sefako Makgatho University), or the vice-chancellor, while continuing to formally occupy the senior management position, allows the stakeholders to take over the running of the institution (as at the Vaal University of Technology).

The most direct method for incapacitating management is when the council, and particularly the chair of council, crosses that sacred line that separates governance and management. In all universities that experience the threat of dysfunction, this inability to have councillors govern and executives manage their institutions is the single most important cause of institutional breakdown.

A rogue chair of council will argue that management is not doing its job, and therefore he needs to intervene, for example, when management fails to implement the policy decisions made at council level. However, the proper response to managerial inaction is not to take over management functions, but to hold management to account, even by making changes to the management team, if necessary. More often than not, the excuse for council to interfere in, or take over, management functions carried more dubious intent.

When an ethical and knowledgeable chair comes under unrelenting pressure from self-interested stakeholders to 'deal with' management – for instance, by dismissing a vice-chancellor – then disaster strikes: she departs. In one case, an eminent chairman at a health sciences university, a legal person, came under such pressure from rogue stakeholders that 'the judge took his briefcase and resigned there and then'.[35]

It is not only council chairpersons who yield in the face of rogue behaviour. Good, ethical council members tend to leave as well, for the sake of their individual reputations. But the institutional consequences are severe. It is in referring to these contexts that battered councillors and managers use the expression 'institutional capture' to explain the handing over of the university and its resources to rogue elements.

As argued so far, dysfunction is the whole point of institutional capture. It is not that the students, staff or unions in these universities do not understand the regulations or the rules governing institutions. It is that they consciously bend the formal rules to reassign power and authority according to a different, informal, set of rules. As one University of Fort Hare administrator said, 'They [the unions] started to see themselves as a structure that senate would account to.'[36]

Not surprisingly, the authority of senate also comes under threat at dysfunctional universities. In every institution studied, the senate loses its visibility and authority in its statutory mandate, that is, scholarly matters such as academic appointments and promotions. At places like Unisa, the unions drove a process of lowering the academic standards for promotion, despite resistance from management and, of course, senior academics. As a result, the institution was significantly weakened as a site for higher education.

The manufacture of incapacity is not, however, solely a one-way process. The discussion has so far examined cases in which executive management is incapacitated by council, unions, students and other political operators. It is also the case, ironically, that the vice-chancellor himself or herself can lead the charge to disable the managerial functions of the university. Why is this? As the cases of MUT and VUT show, a rogue vice-chancellor's efforts to undermine his university's managerial operations enable him to gain access to resources to enrich himself despite the rules. Common among such disabling activities is neglect of the internal audit function, the approval of personal compensation (which is normally the preserve of council), and instructions to staff to implement irregular decisions that favour the vice-chancellor. In the process, the management structure of the university is incapacitated from within the executive function.

When management is incapacitated by both stakeholders and the executive of a university itself, what results is a form of 'skilled incompetence', as Jim Leatt observed of his efforts at turning around Univen.

WHAT AN INCAPACITATED UNIVERSITY LOOKS LIKE, AND HOW IT BEHAVES

When the management function of a university has been disabled, it shows up most visibly in the physical appearance of a campus. Time and again, assessors, administrators or parliamentarians visiting one of these dysfunctional universities would find situations like the following, which were reported by three different observers at three different institutions:

> I mean you had 4 000–5 000 students in a residence system that could take 1 500. There wasn't a single dining facility in any of these university residences, so students were cooking in their rooms on two plates and all their wet waste got rid of in the ablution block. So, the place was permanently stopped up, there was excrement everywhere, the residences were in an absolutely disgusting state.[37]
>
> The campus is dirty, unkempt, and unsafe. One of our more disturbing experiences was going into one of the residences. There we found filthy, cockroach-infested rooms occupied by people who were very likely not students. Some were simply squatting there. Other occupants were clearly running businesses – spaza shops and others – from their rooms. And this was before the term had even started. The squatting in residences appeared to be protected by some of the staff, who possibly took bribes for turning a blind eye.[38]
>
> The institutional culture seems to include a high tolerance for rubbish. When the assessment team visited, it was the most slovenly campus I have ever seen. Both in Alice and in East London, the overall impression of the campus is of neglect and decay. The campus is littered with old and broken pieces of furniture (chairs, beds, mattresses) which have clearly been standing or lying around

gathering dust for years. Especially in Alice, there is litter all over the campus but no rubbish bins. Some of the toilets and ablution facilities we saw are so bad that conditions are degrading and might constitute a health risk. The toilet designated for persons with disabilities was used for storage of cleaning materials, with its washbasin blocked and half-full of dirty water. Nobody can be bothered to keep the campus clean and tidy.[39]

In this putrid situation there is no shortage of managers; in fact, one report on the situation at Fort Hare observed 'a surfeit of managers but an absence of management'. Of the same institution, a vice-chancellor shared a popular story of the campus having 'one tractor and 25 tractor drivers'.[40] Exaggeration, perhaps, but the over-employment of staff as labourers and lower-level administrators is at the root of the financial crises of dysfunctional institutions. As elsewhere, there was a very high ratio of non-academic to academic staff in these universities. In terms of sheer numbers, there appeared to be capacity, but using the university as a place of employment regardless of higher-level skill sets worked to produce incapacities in the effective management of the institution.

At the same time, what is often less visible is the reactive behaviour of over-managing small things. Amid wholesale corruption, where millions of rands are at stake, there is an almost comical complexification of what in functional institutions would be routine administrative processes. One of the Fort Hare assessors wrote:

The university could quite literally not make a cup of tea. Instead of putting the kettle on and dropping a teabag into a mug, caterers had to be contacted. The caterers, who would invariably arrive late, would bring their own crockery, cutlery, tea, coffee, milk and sugar and usually a large tray of cream cakes. They would then set up all of these paraphernalia as though for a formal event to produce the few cups of tea or coffee that had been asked for. Afterwards, everything had to be packed up again and taken away. The next day the entire process would be repeated.[41]

What is going on here? On the one hand, even the making of a cup of tea becomes an employment opportunity for people outside, regardless of the inefficiencies or cost. On the other hand, a simple process becomes complex, as further illustrated in this vice-chancellor's story of his experiences on a dysfunctional campus:

> When I arrived, I said I want a big coffee machine in the office, you know a self-service thing. The next thing they say is we have to go to procurement, to supply chain, and I had to say a coffee machine. In Cape Town in my [UCT] office, I just said please get a coffee machine here and it will be self-service for myself, yourself, and visitors, and the coffee machine was there two days later. Here, we had to go to procurement, to supply chain management, and it would have taken at least two months to get that coffee machine, two months.[42]

In an incapacitated institution, the levels of trust are low. The simplest things become complex, almost as a way of demonstrating that the rules are being followed to a tee. In the meantime, audit functions are compromised, delegatory powers are nonexistent, regulations are ignored, appointments criteria are overlooked, tender specifications are leaked, and council decisions are not implemented. To be sure, some of this breakdown is the result of a lack of capacity, but much of it is also the result of a cultivated incapacity that shreds the integrity of an institution.

THE RELATIONSHIP BETWEEN INSTITUTIONAL INTEGRITY AND INSTITUTIONAL CAPACITY

In simple terms, integrity is the ability 'to do the right thing' and capacity the capability to do so. As we have seen, institutional integrity is maintained on the basis of a set of steering values, which in universities are the academic values at the core of their mandate. But declaring a commitment to acting with integrity, whether at an individual or institutional level, depends on the capacity to deliver on that promise. And that is why sound business principles on their own cannot guarantee the maintenance of institutional integrity in a university.

At a fundamental level, institutional integrity is breached when those steering values do not exist or are compromised. Those values exist at both the personal and collective levels because they reside in people, the human actors that give life and meaning to institutions. There is no institutional integrity without campus citizens.

The steering values of an institution are, however, not only academic values (the heart and mission of a university) but moral values. By moral values I mean holding a basic sense of right and wrong, such as recognising the difference between your money and other people's money, or a respect for public property. Such basic moral values come with an understanding that in working as a paid employee at a university (or anywhere else), you are there to deliver a service to others based on some contractual agreement. When those orienting values do not exist or are seriously compromised, there follow some of the puzzling behaviours described in broken institutions.

Why would a vice-chancellor oversee a university campus that has deteriorated into a state of filth? How can the senior executives of a university not take charge and intervene in residences infested with cockroaches and crowded with non-residents who lease their rooms to other students? When toilets are permanently clogged up and students have to live with dirty water in residence pipes, why is there not an instinctive desire to fix such things in the interest of students?

The problem here is not one of capacity but of a particular way of thinking that leads to social and emotional detachment from the plight of students. This mindset has its roots in a lack of moral commitment to both students as valued persons and the property as public assets. In other words, there are no steering values that compel leaders to act on the grounds that such a situation is completely unacceptable. A campus leader or set of leaders with strong moral values would regard the safety and security of students (and staff) in such dire circumstances to merit the same urgency and attention as if they were their own children. Put differently, it would be difficult to return to your own safe and secure home without a troubled conscience that your personal well-being depends on the well-being of those stuck without options inside dilapidated residences on your campus.

The argument here is that the connection between professing to do the right thing – claiming integrity – and actually doing the right thing – exercising capacity – is the sense of binding values to make real the institutional commitment to students. Where this connection short-circuits in the minds and values of campus administrators, then it is possible to understand how infrastructure funds meant for building new lecture halls or accommodation facilities can be stolen for personal enrichment. When there is no respect for human life, then it is possible to grasp why the physical assault on staff, and even the murder of colleagues, can proceed without consideration of the consequences. The problem remains a values question.

Why would collectives of corrupt staff not value the university as a prized academic asset or a shared social space or an escape route out of poverty? One reason lies in how a beleaguered university is seen in terms of the values of campus citizens. For a staff member at such an institution, the university is simply a place of employment, from which to draw a salary, the amount of which is contested on a regular basis through powerful union politics. The physical state of the campus matters not a jot; it is personal compensation that matters.

For an academic, it is a place for advancement, both financial and professional. Salaries are contested all the time, and promotion criteria are regular targets of union politics. Campuses might be shut down for long periods, but no concern is felt about the impact of this on the quality of education or the validity of degrees. Unsurprisingly, such agendas hardly concern the academic staff of the established universities, where values such as academic autonomy and academic freedom preoccupy senates and academic boards whenever the state overreaches or a controversial speaker is disinvited.

And for a student, it is a place to get a certificate that allows an escape from poverty. The intellectual value of a book, the rival arguments around a public controversy or the puzzle of breakthrough infections in vaccinated people seldom enjoy deep deliberation. Anything that stands in the way of a quick and efficient passage through the university brings major upheavals. The sparks that light protest fires are things like academic exclusion when a student repeatedly fails the same courses, or financial exclusion when there is no funding for continued studies.

In other words, there is no ownership of the university as one's own. There is, therefore, no value attached to the university except as an instrumental means to an end (a job, salary, promotion or certificate). From this vantage point, the residence is simply a space that provides accommodation, not a hallowed place that holds memories, honours traditions, and invokes loyalties, as at the established universities – and especially the former white, Afrikaans institutions like the University of Pretoria. To be sure, that sense of detachment derives from the history of these institutions as apartheid 'bush colleges' or 'bantustan universities'. Reclaiming ownership of the apartheid-era universities never took place, and, as a result, these institutions are still held at a distance by many staff and students.

It is not, however, simply the apartheid history of these institutions that created this sense of distance and devaluation by campus citizens, but also the fact that institutional leadership often failed to develop a sense of academic enterprise and excellence out of the ashes of the past.

CONCLUSION

Fortunately, there are exceptions, such as the University of the Western Cape (UWC), which can quickly point to its massive, visible and expensive Life Sciences Building as a metaphor for defying its apartheid origins and as concrete evidence of academic excellence in an institution that enjoys rankings above those of some former white universities. As leaders of UWC explain, 'Symbolically, the Life Sciences Building was the first to be clearly visible from the street, and it has come to represent the coming of age of the "Bush College".'[43]

Universities like UWC, and now Univen, have carefully cultivated an academic culture that places scholastic values at the centre of institutional life. Students and staff from these campuses begin to talk more positively about their institutions, and to claim the university as their own. In such institutions there is a growing bond between integrity promised and capabilities delivered.

Yet in most of the dysfunctional universities, institutional integrity is constantly breached, and institutional capacity to deliver on the values promised remains weak. Is such a state of dysfunction salvageable? Answering that is the task of the final chapter.

10

Rethinking and Rebuilding Dysfunctional South African Universities

In the early months of South Africa's democracy, there was a significant confrontation between the nascent ministry of education,[1] which sets policy, and the government department that executes it. The word in the air was 'bailout'. It was painfully obvious that there were well-endowed white universities with world-class infrastructures, highly rated scientists and impressive financial reserves accumulated in the apartheid period; at the same time, there were under-resourced black universities with crumbling buildings, mediocre scholars and parlous finances. What made matters worse was that, as the white universities gradually opened up their racially exclusive admissions before the end of apartheid, the top black students deserted their racially designated institutions.[2] This unexpected migration immediately plunged already vulnerable institutions into a major crisis of plummeting student numbers. With a government funding formula that allocated state subsidies largely on the basis of student enrolments, an already precarious situation became depressingly grim.

The minister of education (and his advisers) held the political position that there should be a major bailout of the historically disadvantaged universities to establish some degree of parity with the white institutions advantaged by a century of racial privilege in state funding. A massive bailout would not make all universities equal, by whatever definition, but it would at least provide a solid platform for the rebuilding of black institutions, in keeping with all the promises of reconstruction and development offered by President Nelson Mandela's new government.

The vice-chancellors of the black universities certainly thought a bailout was coming, a massive infusion of redress funding to correct the imbalances and injustices of the past. Banking on relief, university leaders opened access to all students, regardless of race or ethnicity, in the spirit of the new democracy. In a short period of time, the University of Durban-Westville would lose its majority Indian enrolments, and the University of the Western Cape its 'coloured' designation, as black African students took their rightful places in these public institutions. Modest-to-significant reserves were spent as bursaries on the tens of thousands of poorer students who started to press through the newly opened 'doors of learning and culture', so poetically described in the ruling party's Freedom Charter.[3] There was no institutional risk anticipated for the black institutions. The new government would surely bail them out.

If the first post-apartheid minister of education was in favour of a historic, one-off bailout of black universities, he was about to experience very quickly the limits of executive authority in organisational governance. The bureaucracy was conflicted. There were those in the Education Department who were in favour, but the majority of officials were concerned about, if not dead set against, any form of bailout. A senior official summarised the tensions and the dominant position at the time:

> The minister wanted to see more institutional redress and a shifting of resources to the HDIs [historically disadvantaged institutions]. My concern was to do no harm. Don't damage the parts of the system that are working well; [rather] make those parts of the

system more broadly available. I was very reluctant to shift funding away from institutions that were delivering on their teaching and learning and research mandates. It got me into difficulty because there was pressure for the shifting of resources.[4]

What was much more acceptable to the anti-bailout lobby was the notion of individual redress, which meant directing funding to poor and black students through the available bursary scheme of the time.[5] The students would then be able to study at any institution to which they were admitted. This does not mean that institutional redress did not happen in smaller doses over time (see chapters 2 and 3), but it was certainly not on the scale of what had been envisaged as a multibillion-rand bailout of the disadvantaged universities.

With the bailout of the HDIs off the table, it was only a matter of months before several black universities could not meet payroll. Staff were laid off. Urgent deputations were made to the Department of Education for funding to pay staff salaries. Banks were begged to extend already risky overdrafts; they might – if there was a letter of guarantee from government. University leaders scrambled. 'That', mused a now retired official in the department from that period, 'was the tipping point in the demise of some universities', and they would soon find themselves under administration.[6]

It was also a powerful inflection point in the political economy of universities in that it made visible the importance of resources in the travails and trajectories of higher education institutions in the democratic era.

THE CENTRALITY OF RESOURCES

The research for this book has underlined the significance of resources in explanations for dysfunction in the routinely unstable universities of South Africa. In highly functional universities, resources are also vital but, in these contexts, they are deployed to sustain and extend the academic project. In dysfunctional universities, on the other hand, resources are at the centre of a never-ending competition for their redirection to nefarious ends.

As we have seen, this fight for institutional resources is not the usual competition within institutions (for instance, deans vying for a bigger slice of the budget) or between institutions (for instance, university leaders competing for a larger cut of the state subsidy for publications). That kind of competition is perhaps predictable in the higher education marketplace shaped by the performance logic of neoliberal economics.[7] What was found in this study is that the competition for resources is not only driven by widespread corruption, but that its consequences can also be violent and, on occasion, deadly.

There is no systematic body of knowledge available in higher education studies generally or in the political economy of universities that explains this ruthless kind of negative competition for institutional resources. Why would campus citizens steal the very resources required to build, sustain and extend their own universities? The obvious reasons bear mentioning, before we dig deeper in search of more powerful explanations. The inequalities between white and black institutions no doubt play a role. The failure to bail out HDIs in the early years of democracy may have contributed to the ongoing dysfunction. The lack of reliable systems, from human resources to internal audit, are factors worth considering. The fact that highly competent staff are not attracted to, or retained in, rural universities no doubt explains part of the routines of dysfunction. But these are symptoms of a deeper malaise, surface-level observations of the kind that appear in hastily produced assessor reports which dutifully document the dire situations in dysfunctional institutions.

SEEKING DEEPER EXPLANATIONS FOR CHRONICALLY DYSFUNCTIONAL UNIVERSITIES

From this study seven interrelated reasons emerge for chronic dysfunction in the universities studied.

The imprint of history

We tend to underestimate the impact of history on the political economy of present-day universities (see chapters 2 and 5). The long shadow of the past shows in particularly pernicious ways in the historically black universities. As we have illustrated, the rural homeland universities under bantustan administration were, by definition, part of a corrupt and corrupted system. Sadly, there has not been as much research on the transitional university inside the former homelands as there has been for bantu administration generally,[8] or school education in particular.[9] Suffice it to say that the finances, human resources, academic organisation and institutional cultures of homeland universities were not dismantled as part of the project of transformation.

Rather, transformation took on important but narrow foci, such as student and staff equity as measured by racial representivity, but the culture and organisation of these universities were left largely unquestioned and unchallenged in policy and planning. Institutional culture was considered to be a racial problem in white universities, a frequent topic of research and writing spanning at least two decades.[10] The inherited organisational cultures and practices of the black universities never became the subject of investigation, research and publication. That was a strategic error, for such inattention left a gaping hole in the knowledge base for informed action to transform the organisation and culture of these universities.

The ingrained culture of disruptive conflict

This work has demonstrated the long and embedded history of conflict in black universities that stretches back to their inception in the wake of colonialism and under apartheid. The university was an opportunistic site for black resistance against white authorities over the course of a century. Two vital factors came together to make this possible. The relative independence of the university from the state, compared to other social institutions, meant that protests and resistance could flourish, even as they were repressed. And the mass aggregation of oppressed youth in a single place at the very point when many people gain, and can express, political consciousness made possible the ready mobilisation of students on campuses.

That positive spirit of activism throughout the twentieth century meant that rhythms and routines of protest became ingrained within the social and political cultures of South African universities. Such activism was roundly lauded in a plethora of publications on the nobility and costs of youth resistance before and since the Soweto uprising of 1976 (see chapter 5). An institutionally ingrained culture of student activism, which placed itself in a position of perpetual conflict with the authorities, crossed over seamlessly from apartheid to democracy, bringing with it the performative elements that have come to characterise protest actions in South Africa.[11] The memoranda of demands, the burning tyres, the confrontations with police, the disruptions of classes, the shutdown of campuses, are still part of an inherited playbook for student protests.

There were considered efforts to constrain student activism in the early days of democracy by replacing the activist 'broad transformation forums' with a statutory authority, the institutional forum (IF). As detailed here, the IF was considered 'toothless', since its role was simply to advise university councils. Students and other stakeholders formally represented in IFs simply took the action elsewhere, with the result that disruptive protests happened outside, and despite, these formal structures (see chapter 5).

That the continuation of protest politics in the democratic period bears witness to a vibrant student activism is not contested. What has not been accounted for, however, is the absorption of student politics into the corruption schemes of dysfunctional universities. Students as a political resource could be bought. Students and unions collaborated in many of the dysfunctional universities to weaken management and enable access to tendered resources. Students, alongside other stakeholders, often played a central role in advancing preferred candidates for the position of vice-chancellor or council chairperson to support their corrupt causes.

Nor has there been any scholarly work on the role of the dominant union in higher education, the National Education, Health and Allied Workers' Union (Nehawu), in the systematic dismantling of governance and management functions. While there is some writing available on corruption and disruption on the part of the South African Democratic Teachers' Union (Sadtu) in schools,[12] very little research has been conducted on its political ally in the tertiary sector.[13] That is a vital knowledge gap, for it is impossible to understand chronic dysfunction in universities without grappling with the politics of Nehawu on campuses. Although it was a progressive union in advancing workers' rights in the early years of democracy, evidence shows that Nehawu became a rogue stakeholder on campuses. In some universities, as demonstrated, the union took over critical management functions (as at the Vaal University of Technology); played a determining role in the hiring of vice-chancellors (at Unisa) and their dismissal (as at the Sefako Makgatho Health Sciences University); and became involved in the weakening of institutional governance (as at UFH).

Putting an end to the chronic instability in universities is unlikely to succeed without dealing with these two major stakeholders – students and unions. At the same time, it has to be said that the role of student organisations and Nehawu is uneven across South Africa's 26 public universities. In some contexts, both students and unions play a critical and constructive role in institutional transformation broadly, and in the governance and management functions specifically. The criticism here concerns those unions and student bodies whose goals are disabling management, dismantling governance and destabilising administration in order to gain the kind of power that makes corruption possible and, in the process, sustains instability.

The emergence of informal institutions

What further sustains dysfunction in universities is the emergence of informal institutions. In these universities, the 'rules of the game' that organise institutional life are informal, meaning that alternative guidelines for operations exist alongside, and despite the existence of, formally approved policies. A standard conception of informal institutions renders it as 'socially shared rules, usually unwritten, that are created, communicated, and enforced outside of officially sanctioned channels'.[14]

It is an error of analysis in past assessor reports that corrupt actors within universities did not abide by the institutional rules. They did, in fact, follow institutional conventions, but these were in the form of unwritten, informal but socially shared rules. Informal institutions are powerful. They enable the corrupt to bypass the formal rules that govern access to resources. Those socially agreed upon rules elevate to positions of authority persons or groups who would otherwise not enjoy power or influence in the normal operations of a well-managed and well-governed university. Staff and students learn where to go to in a crisis or for an opportunity that would otherwise be off limits. This kind of displacement of formal or statutory authority explains why, as recounted in this research, a vice-chancellor would sit in silence through a chaotic meeting of the management appointments committee where alternative authorities, following unwritten rules, could take charge of proceedings without any consequences.

Embedded informal institutions imply that effective interventions to break the back of corruption in these universities will require more than capacity building, enlightened policies or vigilant management. It will demand a radical overhaul of a rule-bound system that has developed its own logic of operation to jealously guard the vested interests of corrupt actors inside and outside the institution.

Institutional dissociation

Why would staff and students engage in corrupt or violent activities that collapse their own universities? This is a question that has long occupied observers of crises and corruption on campuses in the post-apartheid era. The burning of a law library at the University of KwaZulu-Natal; the firebombing of an expensive computer laboratory at North West

University; the destruction of rare artworks at the University of Cape Town – the list of facilities destroyed at public universities is endless and was at one point in the 2015–2017 protests estimated to cost close to R1 billion. Again, why?

One of the main reasons is that many black students and staff experience an institutional dissociation from the university where they study or work. The university is not experienced or claimed as their own. It is something that does not belong to them now, and historically has never belonged to them anyway. In other words, the capacity to destroy your place of work or study comes from a detachment or disconnection from the place itself.

A well-travelled former vice-chancellor and administrator shared this telling comparison from a West African university. He was strolling with a colleague in the grounds of a university in Nigeria when he was politely asked by a student not to walk on the newly laid grass. 'This is a student who cares about this institution, has affection for this institution, feels like they're part of this institution, values the institution. Here [in South Africa], the students are just there for what they can get; they don't care one bit about the institution. That is the contrast and it is quite striking.'[15]

As shown earlier, universities for black South Africans were never their own. These institutions were established by whites for blacks. The fact that, in the late 1950s, university education was 'extended' to black students on ethnic or tribal grounds meant that attendance at these institutions was under protest. There was, for more than one generation, an ambivalent relationship with these 'bush colleges' or 'bantustan universities': they were necessary for advancement in the absence of anything else, but not always loved or embraced.[16]

But historical ambivalence alone cannot explain institutional dissociation towards black institutions in the present. Clearly black South Africans do not dissociate themselves from institutions only because they were not established by them. There is another factor. The experience of these institutions is, in itself, alienating. While some of the more emotive expressions of institutional disregard appear to be exaggerated, for instance the title of a book called *Corridors of Death*,[17] it is the case that poor and working-class students experience the post-apartheid university as an extension of their hardships off campus in the ongoing struggle for survival.[18]

The idealisation of university life as being an 'at home' experience has been decoded elsewhere;[19] such a notion simply does not account for familiar hardships experienced in that space between school and work that allows for criticism, dissent and protest. The university, for student survivalists, is anything but home. It is more like that other target of community alienation and anger: failed 'service delivery', which leads to destructive forms of behaviour like burning down the community library or the mayor's offices.[20]

Institutional dissociation is now complete. The historical reality of non-ownership joins the contemporary reality of unending hardship to keep the institution far from the emotions of ownership and belonging. With this kind of disconnection, urging campus visitors not to walk on the university's newly laid grass is the last thing on the mind of a detached student or worker on a South African campus.

The politicisation of the everyday

Where there is high demand and limited resources, the policy choices made are inescapably political. That is Political Science 101. On the other hand, where every decision about resources is politicised to the extent that it invites not only competition but corruption, then politics becomes debilitating for institutions. This kind of politicisation of other-wise ordinary activities in the life of a university (see chapter 6) lies at the heart of the dysfunction of the institutions studied.

In such highly politicised contexts, as demonstrated earlier, a vice-chancellor cannot be appointed without organised politics on and off campus mobilising behind a preferred candidate. An urgent tender for laptops in a pandemic lockdown cannot be executed without the process being endlessly delayed or even terminated before being re-advertised, thereby entering an endless loop of interference and obstruction. Even when a university council approves a multimillion-rand overhaul of the IT infrastructure, it is 'slow-walked' through the administrative processes of a Pretoria university, instantly collapsing the functionality of Africa's largest distance education university.[21]

It would be a mistake to think that the over-politicisation of ordinary, even simple tasks happens only among stakeholders within and around universities. It also plays out within the minister's office. In one sense, this is perhaps unavoidable. The minister is, after all, the political head of higher education, reporting to the president of the country. In another sense, though, the minister's office should be circumspect, given that he or she is responsible for intervening in, and preventing, the dysfunction of a targeted university. How could a minister's intervention (or non-intervention) actually make things worse?

First, much depends on ministerial personality. When you have an administrative minister of education, largely concerned about the academic project at a university and its continued success, his or her actions are strictly determined by the demands of the job, as in the choice of a competent and experienced administrator. When you have a highly political minister of education, then every move is calculated; thus, appointments can be both petty and partisan, as in the replacement of an administrator who does not fit a desired political profile.

Nowhere is ministerial personality more consequential than in the choice of appointees to a university council. An administrative minister of education would appoint three to five highly skilled persons in their own disciplines, such as auditing, law or finance; in other words, the kind of people who would bring real skills to a council. A political minister, on the other hand, would look for allies, such as a senior comrade in a union or political party.

Once again, there is nothing necessarily wrong in rewarding allies with high positions in public office, but this is something else: the functionality of a broken university is at stake, and in this context competence matters more than anything else. Yet a political minister might not be averse to appointing unsuitable candidates with chequered track records or questionable competence. A senior official in higher education shared this case:

> The minister really was pushing one candidate for appointment as his representative for a council. But we as officials were unsure and so we did our own investigations. We advised the minister that this would not be a good appointment because of the person's track record. It made no difference and since we can only advise, the appointment went ahead. The person did not last, did not attend meetings, and was excluded by the council from the council. It could have been avoided.[22]

When everything in the functioning of a university is compromised by political interference, from staffing appointments to tender adjudications, then dysfunctionality is not only enabled but sustained in all the key functions of the institution.

The unsettled business of student financing

It is clear from this study that the chances of continued dysfunctionality are heightened by the inability of the South African government to resolve the problem of how to fund students in higher education. There are two principal problems that spark conflict and disruption in this regard. One is adequacy, and the other efficiency.

Adequacy is a wicked problem in student finance. The 2016 Fees Must Fall movement may have been sparked by a marked increase in student fees at one university, Wits, but its roots lay much deeper. The increasing costs of tuition, accommodation and subsistence were bound at some point to shatter the relative peace enjoyed on campuses of the post-apartheid university.[23] There was certainly funding for students under the umbrella of the National Student Financial Aid Scheme (NSFAS), but it came mainly in the form of grants or loans that had to be paid back once the student had graduated and found employment.

In the first place, that funding did not cover enough students; that is, it left out those who were neither wealthy enough for their parents to wholly cover university costs nor poor enough to enjoy access to the NSFAS grants and loans. This is where 'the missing middle' concept emerged in the 2016 protests – students whose parental income was above the qualification threshold at the time but who still could not afford the rising costs of degree studies. It was students of the missing middle who created the Fees Must Fall movement and who led the charge on the university and, sometime later, on the seat of government itself, the Union Buildings in Pretoria.

The president, Jacob Zuma, relented under fire, overrode the modest increase proposed by his minister of higher education, and promised free higher education for all those whose combined parental income fell below R350 000 per annum. In addition, loans would become grants. The immediate effect was to take the sting out of the violent protests that were engulfing campuses everywhere. At that moment, many experts in higher education finance questioned the sustainability of this stop-gap arrangement.

At the point of implementation, the generous position on student funding did not address the added problem of student debt. Over the years of disjointed funding, students had, between 2010 and 2020, accumulated debt of more than R10.4 billion in uncollected student fees. At an institutional level, outstanding historical debt ranged from R14.1 million at UCT to R4.4 billion at the Tshwane University of Technology.[24] Buckling under a steady decrease in state funding (in real terms) and uncertain about the impacts of the new funding regime, no university leader was about to abandon debt recovery. That meant only one thing for students financially excluded from further participation in higher education: a return to the barricades.

Apart from excluding the missing middle, student funding did not cover all the needs of a poor student entering university. It is now well established that students send remittances back home to support their poor and unemployed families. That leaves less money for essential costs, especially after NSFAS decided to disburse funds directly into students' personal accounts. Even with full funding, the rising costs of living, including private accommodation, made it difficult to survive without the subvention of NSFAS funding. Nevertheless, most students, especially at the historically black universities, found the new funding arrangements sufficient to cover their basic needs, except for one other problem – efficiency.

Whether institutions managed their own NSFAS funds or whether the scheme did it on their behalf, there were problems of delivery. And every time numbers of students, large or small, did not receive their funding on time, campuses would erupt in violence. Disbursements arrived late or not at all. In some universities, administrative systems did not capture student data accurately, or students had not submitted financial information timeously, or there was some communication breakdown between NSFAS and the individual institutions.

Whatever the reason, or combination of reasons, the inefficiencies of NSFAS led to the scheme being placed under administration. It was only in 2021 that it received its first unqualified audit in years. Still, for institutions, there are predictable problems at the start of every academic year that spark crises and conflicts; these disrupt university functions and shut down campuses for days, weeks or longer. Such inefficiencies contribute directly to instability in vulnerable institutions, thereby exacerbating dysfunction.

Until the unsettled business of adequacy and efficiency in student finance is resolved, instability will continue to be the lot of the historically black universities. This raises the question: how do former white universities with growing numbers of black students manage to circumvent these annual rituals of conflict and disruption? First, the black students at universities like UCT are more likely to come from middle-class and upper-middle-class families who can afford the high fees of these institutions. Second, universities like UCT have substantial scholarships and bursaries available from private, international and internal resources to comfortably fund their own students. In the words of one of the senior academic leaders at UCT, 'we are able to buy our way out of trouble'.[25] The crisis of student funding therefore disproportionately affects the historically disadvantaged universities, among which the subgroup of dysfunctional institutions is to be found.

Chronic instability also opens the door to the corruption of academic processes. What often triggers new rounds of instability is that student protesters refuse to accept the academic rules and want them replaced by alternative rules. For example, students are academically excluded when they fail a course or module two or more times. In most universities throughout the world, students accept their fates and register elsewhere for outstanding courses or change their degrees or simply depart. Not in South Africa.

Under the guise of free and unlimited education, the fight against academic exclusion is taken to the barricades at the start of every year. Often, the rules governing academic exclusions and financial exclusions are interlinked. NSFAS stops funding after repeated failures of courses or degrees. But the public would not know this, because the fights at the barricades cloud the issues, with the result that what is presented as unfairness and inequity is, in fact, the quest for continued enrolment regardless of the rules. The real unfairness is that other students cannot take up the limited places available because of the multiple opportunities afforded to veteran students who refuse to accept the rules.

In functional universities, such revolt is contained by strong managerial cultures lodged within strong academic cultures. In dysfunctional universities, their organisational vulnerabilities open them up to constant challenge and the further erosion of academic authority.

The demise of the academic project

Perhaps the most important reason for chronic dysfunctionality has to do with the demise of the academic project. In broken institutions, the collapse of the academic project is both the cause and the consequence of dysfunctionality. As argued before, the academic project and its associated academic values serve as a powerful steering mechanism in a crisis. When the academic project is central to the agendas of management, senate and council, the vision for action in times of crisis is all about maintaining the values of the academy.

In his book *Vice-Chancellor on a Tightrope*, documenting his life as a university leader in turbulent times, the late Professor Stuart Saunders shares an intriguing account of UCT's institutional understanding of what was at stake in one of its most defining crises. The political science department had invited the Irish academic and politician Conor Cruise O'Brien to deliver a series of lectures on siege societies. This came at the time of the academic boycott, which was one of the arrows in the quiver of the anti-apartheid movement. Student activists objected to the foreign visitor's presence on campus, an objection that gained momentum after Dr O'Brien referred to the boycott as 'a mickey-mouse affair'. In response, many of UCT's academics made arguments in favour of academic freedom. The senate was split, voting by 85 votes to 47 in favour of academic freedom, against the academic boycott, and censure for the disruption of lectures on campus. Regardless of one's position on this vexed debate, then and now,[26] Stuart Saunders offered a powerful reflection on the academic stakes in question: 'The senate had been concerned with the fundamental values of freedom of thought, of speech and conscience, values crucial to a university and the vocation of an academic but recognized that these values and academic freedoms did not simply come to be. Values had to be recognized and upheld.'[27]

You would be hard pressed to find debates on academic values at any of the dysfunctional universities. The academic project has long been abandoned in the never-ending pursuit of resources, for both survival and corruption. Micro-conflicts, as demonstrated throughout this book, dominate administrative, managerial and governance decisions up and down the institution (see chapter 8). As a result, there is no steering force in their state of perpetual crisis that could bring the dysfunctional university back to its founding mandate as an academic institution. That is why the institutional audits of dysfunctional universities foreground academic failings: the marginalisation of the senate, the poor academic credentials of the staff, the low throughput rates of students, and the lack of relevance in the curriculum.

Neglect of the academic project was also evident in the student protests of 2015–2016. For functional universities, the mobilising concern among students was primarily an intellectual one – decolonisation. For dysfunctional universities, it was mainly about material needs and financial resources. This distinction is not intended to elevate the one cause over the other. It is, rather, to indicate the low levels of attention given to the academic project in dysfunctional universities as the mandate of an institution of higher learning.

This lack of academic values that steer an organisation through crises does not mean that routines of academic administration do not continue. There are cycles of application, registration, admission, instruction, examinations and graduation. But these processes in dysfunctional institutions are mechanical, with a narrow focus on certification rather than education – an outcome that must be attained within the shortest time possible.

As recorded earlier, in chronically dysfunctional institutions months are lost through protest, disruption and campus shutdowns. Academics fret about the impossibility of making up lost time, given an already crowded curriculum and the need for adequate time in classes and in laboratories. Students demand that they pass, regardless of academic time lost. To avoid even further cataclysmic shutdowns, the management relents. The academic project is not only invisible; it is actively undermined, leaving the academic institution rudderless in its perpetual crises.

These seven explanations for chronic dysfunction demand a reassessment of the value and limits of the political economy perspective on troubled universities.

WHAT DID WE LEARN ABOUT THE RELATIONS BETWEEN POWER AND RESOURCES?

The first insight gained about the nexus of politics and resources is the intensification of that relationship in the context of dysfunctional universities. In broken institutions where informal rules dominate, the levels of political energy and attention trained on the exploitation of public resources are both fierce and constant. When large deposits of government funding are made into a university's accounts, a veritable feeding frenzy ensues. The intensity of that run on institutional resources absorbs all the energies of management and council, to the point that some leave, others become part of the schemes, and not a few exercise what has been called wilful blindness.[28]

This intensification of the relationship between politics and resources carries enormous institutional costs. Meetings are longer. Documents are altered. External consultants are contracted. Critical processes like pro-curement are delayed. Engagements of stakeholders, between themselves and with managements and councils, are emotionally exhausting and sometimes physically threatening. Meetings are constantly reconvened. All of this costs time and money, which eats into already strained institutional resources. In the process, staff and students lose faith in their university and its leaders as morale sinks and frustration boils over.

The second insight drawn from the power–resources question is the interconnection between what happens inside universities and what happens in the broader society. In other words, the micropolitics of university corruption not only reflects but finds its logic in the macropolitics of the broader society. Several university leaders as well as department officials reported a spike in campus corruption that corresponded to the period of state capture under President Jacob Zuma. This was also when millions of rands were given to universities for infrastructural costs that were contested through all kinds of corrupt schemes.

One way in which this happens is through the human traffic that flows from communities onto campuses, and from campuses back into com-munities. External members of councils serve in governance functions. Staff and students have connections with social, economic and political entrepreneurs in the areas where they live. In ways like these, campus–community partnerships in corruption are forged.

It was not the intention of this study to examine in depth the ways in which the political culture outside the university and, specifically, within the state influences what happens within public universities. Yet, there is little question that cultures of corruption within the state do have an influence on the behaviours, expectations, desires and values of those dealing with the public resources that flow to universities through the state subsidy. There is much more at stake than individuals who are corrupt. It is, more seriously, about the regnant norms and values in government, in public service and among public officials that imprint themselves on institutional behaviours, including those of public universities.

The third insight about political economy that comes from this study is the role of incapacitation in enabling power and influence over institutional resources. As argued earlier (see chapter 9), the incapacitation of governance, management and administration in dysfunctional universities is not simply the result of the absence of training but the outcome of a conscious scheme or plan for disabling capacity in these three critical functions. The systematic attacks on executive authority, for example, are not simply about the failure of management to yield to stakeholder demands, from unions, students or even council. The intent is to weaken senior management and, in the process, render it incapable of making executive decisions.

This is why senior management appointments are delayed for months, even years. It enables acting personnel to enter top positions under the political control of a powerful stakeholder. Compromised personnel at senior levels are then able to give access to resources that would not have been possible under a strong and ethical management team. Similarly, the constant challenge to even the smallest and inconsequential decisions, such as repairing or replacing the entrance gate, is not about the task itself; it is about eroding the confidence of management to make *any* decision without the approval of non-management actors like unions. No doubt, there are weaknesses in the capacity to deliver on mega-projects, such as residence infrastructure. But as this study has shown, the lack of capacity exists alongside the quest for incapacity, and together these two factors effectively paralyse already vulnerable institutions.

The chaos in university administration similarly enables corrupt elements in the personnel of a university to exploit resources, through a broken procurement system or a compromised senior appointments committee. Corrupted power feeds off weak and compromised administrative systems. So, too, with the governance functions in a university. At a first glance, it would appear that interminably long meetings simply reveal that the chairperson lacks the confidence or the competence to manage board functions. A closer examination reveals dysfunctionality and its perverse purposes. Long board meetings are in fact the result of crooked members contesting every item on the agenda, especially where self-interest is in play. Hours can be spent on whether and what to pay council members for attending meetings. When one faction senses it might lose a crucial vote for a compromised appointment, it seeks to extend the meeting until busy people leave and a decision can be made by those who remain. Consider the astounding action by council members in redefining meeting procedure to effectively incapacitate the university leadership:

> On 12 April 2019, there was a meeting of nine members (out of a possible thirty-one) of the Council of the University of Fort Hare: four employees of the University, two students, the President of Convocation, the Chair of the Audit and Risk Committee of Council, and a new external member appointed by one of the local municipalities. They declared themselves duly constituted as a meeting of Council, elected the new member as 'Interim Chairperson of Council', and proceeded to take a number of decisions. The main outcome of the meeting was that the 'Interim Chairperson of Council' issued a notice informing the campus community that the Vice-Chancellor had been suspended.[29]

In politics, this is called a coup. The minister had no choice but to intervene in the illegal process and reinstate the 'suspended' vice-chancellor.

In sum, this study revealed how the corrupted relationship between power and resources is greatly intensified in dysfunctional universities; that it is strongly interconnected across the imaginary lines that separate campus and community; and that it requires institutional incapacitation for its optimal functioning.

WHAT IS TO BE DONE?

The book now concludes with some pointed proposals for policy and practice that emerge from the substantive findings in this inquiry. The important question is this: can routinely dysfunctional universities in the social context of South Africa be salvaged? Put differently, can dysfunction be disrupted?

The most important conclusion from this study is that dysfunctionality requires a complete overhaul of the composition of councils. As apartheid came to an end, the founding logic of transformed councils was democratic representivity. Given the racially exclusive character of governance under apartheid, there was a popular politics as well as a pent-up emotion that demanded a flat model of democracy. That is, every constituency should have a seat at the table. In South Africa, this meant students, workers, academics, managers, local leaders, alumni, donors, political representatives and so forth.

No doubt, the flat model of democracy satisfied an urgent and palpable need for joint decision-making in higher education policy after a century of white, (mainly) male and authoritarian governance. However, in the democratic era it created an unwieldly structure of around 30 councillors that has become very difficult to manage, especially in the case of dysfunctional universities. In faltering institutions, the mere size of councils made them susceptible to corruption from all quarters.

This study proposes that reconstituted university councils should consist of no more than 15 members, composed in ways that meet the goals of both political representation (a student leader, a union representative and a local government representative) and professional skill sets (in finance, auditing, law, accounting, management, business and higher education). The 60–40 ratio of external to internal members should be retained in a reduced council.

However, a smaller governing body in and of itself does not mean that ethical governance will emerge within dysfunctional universities. This leads to another critical observation that emerged from the study. A council stands or falls by the quality of its membership and the strength of its leadership. Disregard this simple recommendation, and dysfunction is assured. It is very important that stringent criteria of appointment be applied in nominating and electing council members. These criteria must include demonstrated competence in a relevant professional field, a track record of success in the workplace, and a clean slate when it comes to personal ethics.

A nominee for council who is blacklisted for debt should under no circumstances be considered for appointment to the highest decision-making body of a university; this implies that credit checks on candidates should be conducted. A nominee with a record of consistently failing businesses should not be elected. A manager from a municipality that regularly receives qualified audits should also not enjoy consideration for council membership. Most university councils have some qualifying criteria, but many simply ignore them in the political pressure for one or other candidate. This is the point at which councils capitulate, with the result that lasting damage is done to management functionality and sustainable governance.

Of course, it is impossible to take politics out of public (or, for that matter, private) sector appointments in a highly politicised country like South Africa. It is important, nevertheless, to depoliticise councils at every level of appointment. By politicisation I mean the recruitment, nomination and selection of members because of partisan or party-political affiliations above all other considerations, such as experience and expertise. The commitment to depoliticising council appointment should apply as much to the ministerial appointees as it does to other external members of the governing body. It would help in this regard if ministerial appointees were limited to no more than two members in the smaller, reconstituted councils proposed.

The strength and support of the chairperson of council is crucial to the success of a university. Chairs are selected by the ordinary members of council. In the present, this means that a popular choice, political ally or even a corrupt figure can rise to the chair with little regard for competence, ethics and experience. Here, too, guidelines should stipulate the qualities of a desirable chairperson of a university as a public institution, including demonstrated leadership experience at board level or equivalent governance authority. A university council, especially in dysfunctional institutions, cannot be the training ground for a new chairperson of council.

In this regard, the question of eminence should feature prominently in the choice of chairpersons of council. Functional universities tend to choose a senior judge from the highest courts, a distinguished academic leader who enjoys emeritus status, a prominent executive of a successful bank, or the head of a large and respected non-profit organisation. These are accomplished people in their fields, with considerable executive experience and, crucially, an appreciation for the place that a university occupies within society.

In dysfunctional universities, esteemed chairs often resign when the balance of forces in a contested council tilts towards the noisily corrupt members of the body. It is therefore important to ensure that the supporting structures of council are also ethical and competent, such as the executive committee of council (exco), and that the relationship between the chair of council and the vice-chancellor of the university remains solid.

The attempt to break the relationship between chair and vice-chancellor is key to the goal of institutional incapacitation on the part of corrupt forces within a university. That bond between the two leaders is of the utmost importance. When it breaks, dysfunction thrives. There are, of course, instances of collusion between these two powerful positions, but that kind of corrupt relationship is rare when the persons involved hold each other to account as they pursue the best interests of the university.

Naturally, in a democratic environment members of council would choose their own leaders, whether that be the vice-chancellor or the chair of council. What these proposals suggest is a series of measures that push the decision-making towards acceptable outcomes. To emphasise, those measures include firm criteria for selection; strong bonds among key members; and reduced opportunities for corruption by creating smaller councils.

Now, to return to the principal thesis of this inquiry. If the resources of a university and the power to influence their distribution lie at the heart of institutional dysfunctionality, then there are additional interventions that must be made to break that circuitry of control.

One simple but necessary action would be to exclude students and unions from tender processes. As players in multimillion-rand decisions, the involvement of bodies representing students and workers make them especially vulnerable to pressure to assume proxy roles in campus politics. Most universities exclude these stakeholders from procurement processes, while some may allow unions as observers in such meetings. But the decision-making on multimillion-rand tenders should be led by a combination of external experts, one or two external council members, and the line function departments relevant to the decisions (for instance, the deputy-vice chancellor for operations and the head of the finance department).

In chronically dysfunctional universities, it is vitally important that allocative decisions on mega-projects like infrastructural funding be handed to an independent, external firm with a reputation for competence and objectivity in adjudications of this kind. Until a university can demonstrate capacity and integrity in large-scale funding decisions, such a function should reside outside it. The risk to the institution is simply too high, and the chances of malfeasance too great, given the many loopholes in a broken system for corruption to seep in.

When systems nevertheless fail and dysfunction sets in, it is important to reset the terms for external intervention. It is obvious that in situations of deep dysfunction and repeated intervention, the term of appointment of an administrator must extend beyond three years, and ideally to five. That administrator must be able to bring in an expert team from outside to fulfil key functions, such as finance, audit and planning, and to bolster the administration.

Why there needs to be an extended administration is that the underlying reasons for dysfunction are not only technical but also social and cultural. Informal institutional rules need to be identified, destroyed and replaced. This takes time, as new administrative rules and routines slowly embed themselves in, and are reinforced through, institutional practice. New rules are not enough, though. In severe cases of dysfunction, new people may need to be brought in to staff critical functions on a permanent basis. This means that external intervention should allow for the replacement of corrupt and incompetent staff in the most important management and administrative roles required for high functionality.

The interventions required are political as well. A positive politics means investing in the social and cultural reorientation of the dysfunctional university towards its academic mandate. Rebuilding, or even instating for the first time, a sense of the academic project takes time, but it is vitally important for the steering vision of an institution of higher learning. That is why the administrator must be a strong academic, or the team must include those with outstanding management skills and insights.

These are the kinds of interventions that build academic cultures at the heart of a university's mandate. The senate is strengthened with senior academicians and enjoys prominence in every academic decision, such as appointments to the professoriate, promotions and approval of new academic faculties, centres or units. Even the closing or reopening of a campus in times of turmoil must include consultation with senate.

One critical intervention lies in the leadership role of the vice-chancellor. In highly functional institutions, staff as well students and the broader community are reminded all the time of what matters to the university – its academic mandate. No leadership message should pass without reminding campus citizens of the pursuit of high academic standards, the achievements of accomplished scholars, the breakthroughs made in scientific work, the innovations in technology, and so forth. In other words, academic cultures are built through academic practices that are made visible in the lives of those inside and outside the university.

When a university begins to resemble in its institutional practices the kinds of actions that are typical of the external political world, then the academic project begins to lose its shine. When buildings or campus streets are named primarily after politicians; when most of an institution's awards go to political activists; when the campus becomes the major staging ground for high-profile political gatherings; when activists without solid academic grounding or managerial accomplishments enjoy senior appointments – this is when the academic project diminishes in everyday campus life.

This certainly does not mean that social activism and political recognition should not be part and parcel of a university's civic obligations. The critique here is about a dominant orientation towards the political in the university's understanding of itself and its posture towards the outside world. In this respect, the University of the Western Cape is an ideal counter-example of an institution with a profound sense of its political history and obligations but which at the same time places the academic project at the centre of its institutional endeavours.

Academic re-acculturation means rebuilding the agendas of meetings, including those of those of executive management, senate and council, to place matters of teaching, learning and research at the centre of institutional decision-making. When the leadership of a university takes on this exercise in academic re-acculturation, there will be instant and sustained resistance. The lifting of academic admission standards will bring reaction. The demand for high-level teaching will be questioned. More stringent promotion criteria will elicit a fierce response. Even something as simple as showing up for academic work will encounter opposition in the more dysfunctional universities. In brief, there is no shortcut to academic re-acculturation inside dysfunctional universities. The truth is that for some institutions, there may never have been an academic culture since its inception. Re-acculturation requires hard, consistent work, best led by someone with unquestioned academic credibility and no shortage of political acumen.

This leads to the final act in turning around dysfunctional institutions. It is crystal clear from a political economy analysis of universities that the question of power is central to the resolution of dysfunction. The effectiveness of the policy and planning actions proposed here depend also on the politics of intervention. How can universities recapture the management terrain lost to rogue unions and student politics in dysfunctional institutions?

This will require political intervention at three levels. First, by changing the rules of the game. In other words, there should be different rules for the new engagement, for example, the clear delineation of roles for the various stakeholders. Unions represent workers. Student leaders act on behalf of students. Managers manage the university. Council governs the institution.

Second, by enforcing the rules of the game through a strong council that mandates management to execute its functions in accordance with those rules. Such decisiveness in leadership must become part of the performance indicators that mark effective management at the head of a university. This means that management acts quickly and firmly in the very first cases that ignore, threaten or override the agreed-upon rules, regardless of the political standing of the persons involved. Until there are consequences for non-compliance, from the top down, enforcing the new rules will be like sweeping porridge uphill.

Third, by regularising the rules of the game, so that, over time, those alternative norms guide institutional practice as the new common sense. This requires the normalisation of the new rules in every academic and administrative unit of the university. There needs to be an officer in each unit whose work it is to ensure compliance with the new rules. It implies returning to the rules on a regular basis, by reminding students, workers and academics about the importance of the new ways of doing things, until through observance they become everyday practice.

CONCLUSION

The book has sought deep(er) explanations for institutional dysfunction through a political economy perspective on South African universities. It offered, first, a microscopic view of the inner workings of dysfunctional universities, followed more briefly by a telescopic view of the outer workings of society that condition what happens inside these institutions. In the course of the inquiry, it became clear that there exists in South African higher education a subsystem of dysfunctional universities where corruption thrives and criminality has become commonplace. To ignore this reality is to be complicit in acts of wilful blindness.

This reality once moved the 26 heads of universities to make a joint public statement in which they acknowledged that 'corruption had reached endemic levels in the country' and declared an undertaking 'to root out corruption in all its forms from the higher education sector'.[30] The dysfunction in the studied sample has, however, been overshadowed by the stable and sometimes outstanding performances of the functional universities in the larger system.

In the course of this study, it also became evident that political economy has a knowledge problem. Thus far, political economy has been inattentive to the relationship between politics and resources in corrupt and dysfunctional institutions. The overriding deployment of political economy by the left has framed the concept in relation to its Marxist roots, directing attention to the exploitative nature of capitalist relations generally and labour relations in particular. On the other hand, the more liberal uses of the concept are often descriptive, and even sometimes merely decorative, to suggest sophistication in analysis merely by invoking the term rather than pursuing its systematic application.

In researching the dark side of political economy in dysfunctional universities, one thing has stood out: the wilful exercise of corruption in full knowledge of the rules.[31] People do not act on the basis of ignorance inside dysfunctional universities, for 'corruption ... [is] a product of a learning process'.[32] They know the system and use that knowledge to achieve illicit ends.

What we do not know, from a political economy perspective, is the origins, nature and purposes of that knowledge of the corrupt in universities. Where does corrupted knowledge come from? How is such knowledge acquired and dispersed? In what ways does 'the curse of knowledge' influence behavioural choices?[33] Under what conditions would 'anti-corruption knowledge' be effective in stemming the tide of corrupt behaviours?[34] And can the knowledge of corruption be unlearned?[35]

In other words, what is the knowledge that informs the decisions of human actors to participate in the corruption of public institutions? By framing the problem as epistemological, and not simply economic or political in the narrow senses of these terms, the resolution of these problems suggests a pedagogical intervention as well, if disruption is to be disrupted. This makes sense, of course, in the context of educational institutions – the changing of minds through critical engagement with resident knowledge.

That surely is one of the next steps for further research on a more informed political economy in the rebuilding of chronically dysfunctional institutions: one that finds vital connections between knowledge, power and resources.

APPENDICES

APPENDIX A.1
Independent assessors' investigations of South African universities

No.	Year	Institution	Minister	Independent assessor	Administrator	Gazette details
1	1998	**University of Transkei**	Prof. S. M. E. Bengu	Adv T. L. Skweyiya	Morley Nkosi, then Nicky Morgan, then Molapo Qhobela	20 Nov. 1998: Notice no. 1512 Gazette no. 19501
2	1998	**Vaal Triangle Technikon**	Prof. S. M. E. Bengu	Prof. J. J. F. Durand	No administrator appointed	11 Sept. 1998: Notice no. 2015 Gazette no. 19239
3	1999	**Fort Hare University**	Prof. S. M. E. Bengu	Prof. S. J. Saunders	No administrator appointed	12 Mar. 1999: Notice no. 346 Gazette no. 19842
4	1999	**Mangosuthu Technikon**	Prof. Kader Asmal	Prof. J. J. F. Durand	No administrator appointed	17 Sept. 1999: Notice no. 2132 Gazette no. 20486
5	2000	**University of the North** (now University of Limpopo)	Prof. Kader Asmal	Prof. Thandabantu Nhlapo	Prof. Patrick Fitzgerald	16 Oct. 2000: Notice no. 21645 Gazette no. 21654
6	2003	**University of Durban-Westville** (now Durban-Westville Campus of the University of KwaZulu-Natal)	Prof. Kader Asmal	Dr B. Aug Khumalo; Mr Hugh Amoore	No administrator appointed	4 Nov. 2003: Notice no. 3195 Gazette no. 25671
7	2006	**Durban University of Technology**	Mrs Naledi Pandor	Prof. N. C. Manganyi	Prof. J. D. Jansen	20 Oct. 2006: Notice no. 1055 Gazette no. 29315
8	2007	**University of Limpopo**	Mrs Naledi Pandor	Prof. Bennie Khoapa	No administrator appointed	13 Aug. 2007: Notice no. 709 Gazette no. 30169

continued

9	2008	**Mangosuthu University of Technology**	Mrs Naledi Pandor	Dr Vincent Maphai	Prof. J. D. Jansen, then Dr Mashupye Kgapola	10 Dec. 2008: Notice no. 1340 Gazette no. 31689
10	2010	**Tshwane University of Technology**	Dr B. E. Nzimande	Dr Vincent Maphai	Prof. Themba Mosia	22 Nov. 2010: Notice no. 1076 Gazette no. 33787
11	2011	**Walter Sisulu University**	Dr B. E. Nzimande	Prof. Daniel J. Ncayiyana	Prof. Lourens van Staden	28 Sept. 2011: Notice no. 822 Gazette no. 34641
12	2011	**University of Zululand**	Dr B. E. Nzimande	Prof. Hugh Africa	Prof. Chris de Beer	25 Mar. 2011: Notice no. 172 Gazette no. 34156
13	2012	**Vaal University of Technology**	Dr B. E. Nzimande	Adv M. F. Sikhakhane	Prof. Patrick Fitzgerald	11 May 2012: Notice no. 365 Gazette no. 35332
14	2012	**Central University of Technology**	Dr B. E. Nzimande	Prof. Julian Smith	Prof. Stan Ridge (prevented from taking up position)	11 May 2012: Notice no. 366 Gazette no. 35332
15	2018	**Mangosuthu University of Technology**	Dr Naledi Pandor	Prof. Barney Pityana; Ms Judy Favish	No administrator (Acting Vice-Chancellor Marcus Ramogale)	23 Nov. 2018: Notice no. 1286 Gazette no. 42053
16	2019	**Vaal University of Technology**	Dr Naledi Pandor	Prof. Barney Pityana; Prof. Rocky Ralebipi-Simela	Prof. Ihron Rensburg	31 Oct. 2019: Notice no. 127 Gazette no. 43015
17	2019	**University of Fort Hare**	Dr BE Nzimande	Prof. Chris Brink; Prof. Louis Molamu	Prof. Loyiso Nongxa, then Dr Nhlanganiso Dladla	13 Dec. 2019: Notice no.1592 Gazette no. 42902

APPENDIX A.2
Some non-assessor-type ministerial interventions

No.	Year	Institution	Presidential commission of inquiry	Persons responsible
18.	1996	**University of Durban-Westville**	Gautschi Commission	Adv. Johan Gautschi, Adv. Linda Zama
19.	2006	**University of Venda**	Replacement vice-chancellor (acting)	Dr Jim Leatt
20.	2015	**Sefako Makgatho Health Sciences University**	Interim vice-chancellor (2015); vice-chancellor (2017)	Prof. Chris de Beer
21.	2020	**University of South Africa**	Task team	Prof. Vincent Maphai (chair)

APPENDIX B

A brief summation of the origins, evolution and current status of South African universities

Current name (2021)	Origins and change	Impact of mergers & incorporations (2002–2005)
1. University of South Africa (Unisa)	The first South African university. Origins as the University of the Cape of Good Hope (1873), an examining agency for all the university colleges. Renamed Unisa (1916) and much later started to offer postal tuition (1946).	Unisa merged with Technikon South Africa and incorporated Vudec, the Vista University Distance Education Centre of Vista University.
2. University of Cape Town (UCT)	Started as a university college called the South African College in 1829; became the autonomous University of Cape Town in 1918.	Unaffected by the mergers.
3. Stellenbosch University (SU)	Started as a university college called Victoria College in 1887 and became the autonomous University of Stellenbosch in 1918.	Unaffected by the mergers except that its School of Oral Health became part of the Faculty of Dentistry at the University of the Western Cape (UWC).
4. University of the Witwatersrand (Wits)	Started as the Transvaal University College (1906), became the South African School of Mines and Technology (1910) and the autonomous University of the Witwatersrand (1922).	Unaffected by the mergers.
5. University of Pretoria	Started as the Pretoria Centre of the Transvaal University College in Johannesburg (the forerunner of Wits) in 1908, but became the Transvaal University College (1910) at the point that Wits became the School of Mines (etc.), and was named the autonomous University of Pretoria in 1930.	Unaffected by the mergers except that it incorporated the Mamelodi campus of Vista University.

continued

257

Current name (2021)	Origins and change	Impact of mergers & incorporations (2002–2005)
6. North West University	North West University (NWU) was established in 2004.	NWU is a product of the merger of three entities: Potchefstroom University for Christian Higher Education (1951); the University of the North West (1996), itself the former homeland University of Bophuthatswana established in 1980 in Mafikeng; and the Vaal Triangle campus of the Potchefstroom University.
7. University of the Free State	Started as Grey University College in 1906, became the University College of the Orange Free State, then the University of the Orange Free State (1950), and the University of the Free State (2001).	Largely unaffected by the mergers except that the UFS incorporated the QwaQwa campus from the University of the North (now University of Limpopo) and the Bloemfontein campus of the former Vista University.
8. Nelson Mandela University (NMU)	The Nelson Mandela Metropolitan University was established in 2005 and renamed the Nelson Mandela University in 2017.	NMU is the product of a merger between the University of Port Elizabeth (1964), the Port Elizabeth Technikon with its Saasveld campus in George, and the Port Elizabeth campus of Vista University.
9. University of the Western Cape (UWC)	Started in 1959 as the University College of the Western Cape before becoming the University of the Western Cape (1970), but only gained full autonomy as UWC in 1983.	Unaffected by the mergers except that the School of Oral Health of Stellenbosch University was incorporated into UWC's Faculty of Dentistry (2004).
10. University of Fort Hare (UFH)	Started as the South African Native College (1916), which became the University College of Fort Hare (1951) and the University of Fort Hare (1970).	Unaffected by the mergers except that UFH incorporated the East London campus of Rhodes University in 2004.
11. University of KwaZulu-Natal (UKZN)	Established in 2004.	UKZN was a merger of the former University of Natal (1949) and the University of Durban-Westville (1972), each of which also started as university colleges (1910 and 1961, respectively).

continued

Current name (2021)	Origins and change	Impact of mergers & incorporations (2002–2005)
12. Walter Sisulu University (WSU)	Established in 2005.	WSU is a product of the 2005 merger of the old University of Transkei, the Eastern Cape Technikon, and the Border Technikon.
13. University of Venda (UV)	Established as the University of Venda in 1982 but became a comprehensive university in 1995 with the change of its name to the University of Venda for Science and Technology in 1995.	Unaffected by the mergers.
14. Sefako Makgatho University (SMU)	Established in 2015 as the Sefako Makgatho Health Sciences University.	SMU is formed in part from the so-called de-merger or delinking of the Medical University of South Africa (Medunsa, 1976) from its earlier incorporation as the health sciences campus of the University of Limpopo in 2005.
15. University of Limpopo (UL)	Established in 1959 as the University College of the North, gained autonomy as the University of the North in 1970, and renamed the University of Limpopo in 2005.	UL is a product of the merger between the University of the North and the Medical University of South Africa (2005), with the medical campus de-merging from the larger university (UL) in 2015 to become part of the new health sciences university, SMU.
16. University of Zululand (UZ)	Established in 1960 as the University College of Zululand, became the University of Zululand in 1970, and gained autonomy in 1984 with the same name.	Unaffected by the mergers.
17. University of Johannesburg (UJ)	Established in 2005.	UJ is the product of a merger between the Rand Afrikaans University (1966), the Witwatersrand Technikon, and the Soweto and East Rand campuses of Vista University.
18. Rhodes University	Started as Rhodes University College in 1904 and became the autonomous Rhodes University in 1951.	Unaffected by the mergers.

continued

Current name (2021)	Origins and change	Impact of mergers & incorporations (2002–2005)
19. Sol Plaatje University (SPU)	Established in 2014.	Came into existence long after the mergers.
20. University of Mpumalanga (UM)	Established in 2014.	Came into existence long after the mergers.
21. Durban University of Technology (DUT)	Established as the Durban Institute of Technology in 2002 and then renamed as the Durban University of Technology in 2007.	DUT is the product of a merger of two large technikons, the Technikon Natal (1907) and the ML Sultan Technikon (1979).
22. Tshwane University of Technology (TUT)	Established in 2004.	TUT is the merger of Technikon Pretoria (1968), Technikon Northern Gauteng (1980), and Technikon North West (1976).
23. Cape Peninsula University of Technology (CPUT)	Established in 2005.	CPUT came about through the merger in 2005 of the Cape Technikon (1920) and the Peninsula Technikon (1962).
24. Vaal University of Technology (VUT)	Started as the Vaal Triangle College for Advanced Technical Education (1966), became the Vaal Triangle Technikon (1979) and was renamed the Vaal University of Technology (2004).	Unaffected by the mergers.
25. Mangosuthu University of Technology (MUT)	Established in 1979.	Unaffected by the mergers.
26. Central University of Technology	Started as Technikon Free State in 1981 and changed status to the Central University of Technology in 2004.	Unaffected by the mergers but did incorporate the Welkom campus of the old Vista University in 2004.

Note: This table must be read as a very brief and incomplete sketch of origins and changes in university naming and identification over time. For example, several of the university colleges had earlier origins as units or departments or even embryonic faculties before their university college status.

APPENDIX C

Remuneration of university council members, 2020 (overall per university and individually per meeting)

Institution	Total rem per annum	Rem OCM	Rem CC	Rem DCC	Rem CCC	Rem OMCC
University of South Africa	R2 084 250	R2 500	R4 250	R2 800	R3 200	R2 500
University of Venda	R1 329 093		R6 250	R5 250	R5 250	R4 550
University of KwaZulu-Natal	R967 460	R3 700	R5 300	R4 700	R3 700	R3 700
North West University	R848 162	R3 467	R6 929	R3 467	R4 364	R3 467
University of Johannesburg	R848 000	R4 240	R90 000 (pa)	R69 000 (pa)	R354 000 (pa)	R335 000 (pa)
University of Pretoria	R666 179	R4 223	R6 078	R4 223	R6 078	R4 223
Central University of Technology	R637 260	R2 135	R2 810	R2 470	R2 470	R2 135
Cape Peninsula University of Technology	R610 000	R1 500	R2 000	R1 750	R1 750	R1 500
Durban University of Technology	R550 562	R3 500	R5 000	R4 500	R4 000	R3 500
Walter Sisulu University	R510 000	R3 000	R5 000	R3 750	R3 750	R3 000
University of Mpumalanga	R449 830	R2 789	R3 951	R3 489	R3 489	R2 789
Sefako Makgatho University	R345 000	R3 500	R5 300	R4 500	R4 000	R3 500
Tshwane University of Technology	R295 000	R4 000	R4 800	R4 500	R4 500	R4 000
Sol Plaatje University	R222 800	R1 675	R2 000	R1 650	R1 675	R1 350
Nelson Mandela University	R98 500	R750	R1 000	R850	R850	R750
University of the Free State	R55 800	R1 400	R2 000	R1 800	R1 600	R1 400

continued

Vaal University of Technology	–	R4 000	R5 000	R4 000	R4 500	R4 000
University of Limpopo	–	R3 700	R5 200	R4 700	R3 700	R3 700
Mangosuthu University of Technology	–	R2 500	R4 000	R3 500	R3 000	R2 500
University of Fort Hare	–	R2 500	R4 000	R3 500	R3 000	R2 500
University of Zululand	–	R2 500	R3 500	R2 500	R3 000	R2 500
Rhodes University	Does not remunerate council members					
Stellenbosch University	Does not remunerate council members					
University of Cape Town	Does not remunerate council members					
University of the Witwatersrand	Does not remunerate council members					
University of the Western Cape	Does not remunerate council members					

Note: Rem: remuneration; OCM: ordinary council member; CC: chair of council; DCC: deputy chair of council; CCC: chairs of council committees; OMCC: ordinary member of council committees.

APPENDIX D
Income streams by institutional type (2020)

Institutions (per DHET type)	Total	State subsidy	Tuition and accommodation fees	Third-stream income
	R'000	R'000	R'000	R'000
Traditional universities				
North West University	5 145 573	2 212 570	1 764 442	1 168 561
Rhodes University	1 572 501	686 579	565 382	320 540
University of the Free State	3 995 353	1 559 072	1 448 130	988 151
University of Pretoria	7 284 560	3 109 830	2 282 156	1 892 574
Stellenbosch University	6 447 844	1 350 150	1 612 531	3 485 163
University of Cape Town	6 785 372	2 294 036	1 442 389	3 048 947
University of the Witwatersrand	9 010 948	2 334 938	2 246 494	4 429 516
University of Limpopo	2 190 799	1 108 313	740 323	342 163
University of Fort Hare	1 689 967	960 977	590 768	138 222
University of the Western Cape	2 517 783	1 469 103	583 652	465 028
University of KwaZulu-Natal	6 124 014	2 768 631	2 148 423	1 206 960
Subtotal	**52 764 714**	**19 854 199**	**15 424 690**	**17 485 825**
Comprehensive universities				
University of Zululand	1 275 294	689 024	438 739	147 531
Nelson Mandela University	3 026 537	1 335 311	908 241	782 985
University of South Africa	9 815 633	4 501 846	4 752 909	560 878
University of Johannesburg	5 575 391	2 572 792	1 974 901	1 027 698

continued

Sol Plaatje University	613 730	449 044	132 594	32 092
University of Mpumalanga	748 157	549 023	163 035	36 099
Walter Sisulu University	2 541 005	1 072 870	1 247 949	220 186
University of Venda	–	–	–	–
Sefako Makgatho Health Sciences University	1 278 486	809 269	338 295	130 922
Subtotal	**24 874 233**	**11 979 179**	**9 956 663**	**2 938 391**
Universities of technology				
Central University of Technology	1 377 720	796 661	471 623	109 436
Durban University of Technology	3 007 281	1 257 623	1 481 415	268 243
Tshwane University of Technology	–	–	–	–
Cape Peninsula University of Technology	2 973 078	1 614 975	1 135 395	222 708
Mangosuthu University of Technology	–	–	–	–
Vaal University of Technology	1 762 519	874 291	725 014	163 214
Subtotal	**9 120 598**	**4 543 550**	**3 813 447**	**763 601**
Total	**86 759 545**	**36 376 928**	**29 194 800**	**21 187 817**

Sources: The 'sources of income' data were derived mainly from the financial statements of the different universities, which are public documents submitted annually to the DHET. These numbers were cross-checked against DHET subsidy allocations to each university, as well as the annual NSFAS allocations for the year in question. The annual University State Budgets and the Ministerial Statements on University Funding were some of the specific documents scrutinised, along with the annual reports of universities, which, in most cases, were available for this reporting year.

NOTES

CHAPTER 1: A STUDY OF CHRONIC DYSFUNCTION IN UNIVERSITIES

1   Bongekile Macupe, 'Is the Vaal University of Technology an Institution Bewitched?', *News24*, 25 July 2021, https://www.news24.com/citypress/news/is-the-vaal-university-of-technology-an-institution-bewitched-20210725.

2   Nithaya Chetty and Christopher Merrett, *The Struggle for the Soul of a South African University: The University of KwaZulu-Natal: Academic Freedom, Corporatisation and Transformation* (self-published, 2014).

3   Aubrey Mokadi, *A Portrait of Governance in Higher Education: Taking a Stand for Transformation* (Johannesburg: Sedibeng, 2002).

4   Nhlanhla P. Maake, *Barbarism in Higher Education: Once upon a Time in a University* (Johannesburg: Ekaam Book, 2011).

5   Ahmed Essop, *Institutional Governance in the Higher Education System in South Africa* (Pretoria: Council on Higher Education, 2015).

6   Tembile Kulati, *Analysis of Recent Assessor Reports of Universities in SA* (Pretoria: Higher Education South Africa, 2012), http://www.usaf.ac.za/wp-content/uploads/2017/08/2012_HESA_Analysis-of-Assessor-Reports-of-Universities-in-SA_Oct.pdf.

7   Department of Higher Education and Training, *Summary of Recent Assessor Reports and CHE Publications on the Governance of Universities* (Pretoria: Department of Higher Education and Training, 2016).

8   See John Harris et al., 'Power, Politics, and Influence in Organizations', in *International Encyclopedia of the Social and Behavioral Sciences*, ed. James D. Wright (Amsterdam: Elsevier, 2015), 770.

9   Karl Marx, 'Eighteenth Brumaire of Louis Bonaparte', https://www.marxists.org/archive/marx/works/1852/18th-brumaire/ch01.htm. What Marx actually said was: 'Men make their own history, but they do not make it as they please; they do not make it under self-selected circumstances, but under circumstances existing already, given and transmitted from the past.'

10 See James Leatt, *Conjectures: Living with Questions* (Cape Town: Karavan Press, 2021), 102–105; Omphile Tomoso and Lindikaya W. Myeki, 'Estimating South African Higher Education Productivity and Its Determinants Using Färe Primont

Index: Are Historically Disadvantaged Universities Catching Up?', *Research in Higher Education*, 27 May 2022, https://doi.org/10.1007/s11162-022-09699-3.

11 See Jonathan D. Jansen and Cyrill A. Walters, *The Decolonization of Knowledge: Radical Ideas and the Shaping of Institutions in South Africa and Beyond* (Cambridge: Cambridge University Press, 2022).

12 Chris Brink, Louis Molamu, and Bulelani Mahlangu, *Report of the Independent Assessor Regarding the University of Fort Hare (UFH)* (Pretoria: Department of Higher Education and Training, 2019), 5–6, https://www.gov.za/sites/default/files/gcis_document/201912/42902gon1592.pdf.

13 Njabulo S. Ndebele, 'The University of the North in the New Era: What the Mosquito Thinks (1994)', in *Fine Lines from the Box: Further Thoughts about Our Country* (Cape Town: Umuzi, 2007), 55.

14 A. Keet, interview, 23 June 2021.

15 Jonathan D. Jansen, *Knowledge in the Blood: Confronting Race and the Apartheid Past* (Stanford: Stanford University Press, 2009); Johann Mouton and Astrid Valentine, 'The Extent of South African Authored Articles in Predatory Journals', *South African Journal of Science* 113, no. 7–8 (2017), https://doi.org/10.17159/sajs.2017/20170010; Sharlene Swartz et al., *Studying While Black: Race, Education and Emancipation in South African Universities* (Cape Town: HSRC Press, 2018).

16 State capture entered the South African political lexicon during the years of the Zuma presidency (May 2009 – February 2018) and refers to the collusion between private interests (both companies and individuals) and politicians, with the goal of commandeering state resources for themselves and, in the process, hollowing out important institutions (such as the prosecution authorities) that were supposed to prevent this kind of corruption in the first place. There is an abundance of excellent books by academics and journalists alike describing the operations of state capture in South Africa; see, for example, Ivor Chipkin and Mark Swilling, eds, *Shadow State: The Politics of State Capture* (Johannesburg: Wits University Press, 2018) and Pieter-Louis Myburgh, *The Republic of Gupta: A Story of State Capture* (Cape Town: Penguin Books, 2017).

17 Johan Gautschi, Linda Zama, and Hoosen Jerry Coovadia, *Report of the Presidential Commission of Inquiry with Respect to the University of Durban-Westville* (Pretoria: Department of Education, 1996). Although, strangely, no entity reported possessing the Gautschi Commission report – from the Presidency to the Department of Higher Education and Training – at least ten interviews were conducted with knowledgeable persons who were at Durban-Westville in that period of upheaval, including some named in the report. Also, summaries of the report appeared in various media, and these too were studied. In 2004 the University of Durban-Westville merged with the University of Natal to form the University of KwaZulu-Natal.

18 Department of Higher Education and Training, *Report of the Ministerial Task Team to Conduct an Independent Review of the University of South Africa* (Pretoria: Department of Higher Education and Training, 2021).

19 See, for example, Cheryl Goodenough, 'Mangosuthu Technikon', *Focus*, no. 16 (1999), https://hsf.org.za/publications/focus/issue-16-fourth-quarter-1999/mangosuthu-technikon.

20   The Preamble to the Act (No. 16, 26 June 1873) that established South Africa's first university, reads: 'Whereas it is expedient, for the better advancement of sound learning amongst all classes of Her Majesty's subjects in this Colony, to establish and incorporate an University at the Cape of Good Hope ...' Maurice Boucher, *Spes in Arduis: A History of the University of South Africa* (Pretoria: University of South Africa, 1973); the opening chapters of this substantial work derive mainly from the author's master's thesis, 'The University of the Cape of Good Hope and the University of South Africa, 1873–1946: A Study in National and *Imperial Perspective*' (Master's thesis, University of South Africa, 1970; emphasis added). The founding of 'a colonial university' in the Cape, however, goes back decades before, when a government commission considered such an institution, to be modelled on London University and Queen's University in Ireland (*Spes in Arduis*, 8).

CHAPTER 2: HISTORICAL ROOTS OF DYSFUNCTION

1   The authoritative work on Unisa since its founding as the University of the Cape of Good Hope is still Maurice Boucher's doctoral thesis, 'The University of the Cape of Good Hope and the University of South Africa, 1873–1946: A Study in National and Imperial Perspective' (PhD thesis, University of South Africa, 1970); it has been published in various forms, including as *The University of the Cape of Good Hope and the University of South Africa, 1873–1946: A Study in National and Imperial Perspective* (Pretoria: Government Printer, 1974).

2   Maurice Boucher, 'A Brief History of the South African University System', *Historia* 18, no. 1 (1973), https://upjournals.up.ac.za/index.php/historia/article/view/2773/2612.

3   It is important to note that several of these 'university colleges' had name changes between the time of their original naming as colleges and when they obtained full university status. For example, the original Transvaal University College (TUC) was so named in 1906, and its Pretoria Centre was established in 1908. In 1910, the Pretoria Centre became the new TUC; it was this institution that became the University of Pretoria in 1930. Also in 1910, the original TUC of 1906 was renamed the South African School of Mines and Technology, which became the University of the Witwatersrand in 1922.

4   Zacharia Keodirelang Matthews, 'University College of Fort Hare', *South African Outlook*, April–May (1957), https://uir.unisa.ac.za/bitstream/handle/10500/5795/ZKM_C4_13.pdf?sequence=1&isAllowed=y.

5   A. P. Hunter, 'South Africa's Crisis in Education', Senate special lecture, University of the Witwatersrand, 1978, quoted in Mokubung O. Nkomo, *Student Culture and Activism in Black South African Universities: The Roots of Resistance* (Westport, CT: Greenwood Press, 1984), 65.

6   See Martin Hall, 'Institutional Culture of Mergers and Alliances in South Africa', in *Mergers and Alliances in Higher Education: International Practice and Emerging Opportunities*, ed. Adrian Curaj, Luke Georghiou, and Jennifer Casenga Harper (Cham: Springer, 2015).

7   Sean Morrow, 'Fort Hare in Its Local Context: A Historical View', in *Within the Realm of Possibility: From Disadvantage to Development at the University of Fort*

Hare and the University of the North, ed. Mokubung O. Nkomo, Derrick Swartz, and Botshabelo Maja (Pretoria: HSRC Press, 2006), 93.

8   Matthews, 'University College of Fort Hare'; see also Donovan Williams, *A History of the University College of Fort Hare, South Africa: The 1950s; The Waiting Years* (Lewiston, NY: E. Mellen Press, 2001).

9   Boucher, 'A Brief History of the South African University System'.

10   Maurice Boucher, 'Some Observations upon the Influence of Scotland in South African University Education', *Historia* 14, no. 2 (1969), https://journals.co.za/doi/pdf/10.10520/AJA0018229X_1159; see also Boucher, 'A Brief History of the South African University System'.

11   See Jonathan D. Jansen and Cyrill A. Walters, *The Decolonization of Knowledge: Radical Ideas and the Shaping of Institutions in South Africa and Beyond* (Cambridge: Cambridge University Press, 2022).

12   Bronwyn Strydom, 'South African University History: A Historiographical Overview', *African Historical Review* 48, no. 1 (2016): 77, https://doi.org/10.1080/17532523.2016.1236886.

13   Ministry of Education, 'Standard Institutional Statute', *Government Gazette* 41, no. 23065 (27 March 2002), https://www.gov.za/sites/default/files/gcis_document/201409/230650.pdf.

CHAPTER 3: DYSFUNCTIONALITY IN UNIVERSITIES

1   Vincent Mosco, *The Political Economy of Communication* (London: Sage Publications, 2009), 24.

2   Adrian Leftwich, *Drivers of Change: Refining the Analytical Framework*. Part 1: *Conceptual and Theoretical Issues* (York: University of York, 2006), 10, http://www.gsdrc.org/docs/open/doc103.pdf.

3   Michelle Lokot and Amiya Bhatia, 'Unequal and Invisible: A Feminist Political Economy Approach to Valuing Women's Care Labor in the COVID-19 Response', *Frontiers in Sociology* 5 (2020), https://doi.org/10.3389/fsoc.2020.588279.

4   James K. Boyce, 'Political Economy of the Environment: A Look Back and Ahead', in *The Routledge Handbook of the Political Economy of the Environment*, ed. Éloi Laurent and Klara Zwickl (London: Routledge, 2021).

5   Federica Carugati and Margaret Levi, *A Moral Political Economy: Present, Past, and Future* (Cambridge: Cambridge University Press, 2021).

6   Mario Novelli et al., *The Political Economy of Education Systems in Conflict-Affected Contexts: A Rigorous Literature Review* (London: Department for International Development, 2014), http://eppi.ioe.ac.uk/cms/Portals/0/PDF%20reviews%20and%20summaries/Political%20Economy%20Education%202014%20Novelli%20report.pdf?ver=2014-11-24-104035-650; Geeta Gandhi Kingdon et al., *A Rigorous Review of the Political Economy of Education Systems in Developing Countries* (London: Department for International Development, 2014), https://eppi.ioe.ac.uk/cms/Portals/0/PDF%20reviews%20and%20summaries/Political%20economy%202014Kingdon.pdf?ver=2014-04-24-141259-443.

7   Samuel Bowles and Herbert Gintis, *Schooling in Capitalist America: Educational Reform and the Contradictions of Economic Life* (New York: Basic Books, 1976).

8   Meenai Shrivastava and Sanjiv Shrivastava, 'Political Economy of Higher Education: Comparing South Africa to Trends in the World', *Higher Education* 67, no. 6 (2014), https://doi.org/10.1007/s10734-013-9709-6; Ben W. Ansell, *From the Ballot to the Blackboard: The Redistributive Political Economy of Education* (New York: Cambridge University Press, 2010); Carlos A. Torres and Daniel Schugurensky, 'The Political Economy of Higher Education in the Era of Neoliberal Globalization: Latin America in Comparative Perspective', *Higher Education* 43, no. 4 (2002), https://doi.org/10.1023/A:1015292413037; David Robertson, 'The Emerging Political Economy of Higher Education', *Studies in Higher Education* 23, no. 2 (1998), https://doi.org/10.1080/03075079812331380414.

9   Carugati and Levi, *A Moral Political Economy*, 4.

10   Alina Rocha Menocal et al., *Thinking and Working Politically through Applied Political Economy Analysis: A Guide for Practitioners* (Washington DC: United States Agency for International Development, 2018), 1, https://usaidlearninglab. org/sites/default/files/resource/files/pea_guide_final.pdf.

11   Mosco, *The Political Economy of Communication*, 2.

12   Harold D. Lasswell, *Politics: Who Gets What, When, How* (New York: Whittlesey, 1936).

13   Elena Denisova-Schmidt, *Corruption in Higher Education: Global Challenges and Responses* (Boston: Brill, 2020).

14   Monica Kirya, 'Corruption in Universities: Paths to Integrity in the Higher Education Subsector' (Bergen: Chr. Michelsen Institute, 2019), https://www. u4.no/publications/corruption-in-universities-paths-to-integrity-in-the-higher-education-subsector.pdf.

15   Tobias Schulze-Cleven et al., 'The New Political Economy of Higher Education: Between Distributional Conflicts and Discursive Stratification', *Higher Education* 73, no. 6 (2017), https://doi.org/10.1007/s10734-017-0114-4.

16   See Bertha Z. Osei-Hwedie and Kwaku Osei-Hwedie, 'The Political, Economic, and Cultural Bases of Corruption in Africa', in *Corruption and Development in Africa: Lessons from Country Case-Studies*, ed. Kempe R. Hope and Bornwell C. Chikulo (London: Palgrave, 2000).

17   Department of Higher Education and Training, *Report of the Ministerial Task Team to Conduct an Independent Review of the University of South Africa* (Pretoria: Department of Higher Education and Training, 2021).

18   Simone Bohn, 'Justifying Corrupt Exchanges: Rational-Choice Corruptors', in *(Dys-)Functionalities of Corruption: Comparative Perspectives and Methodological Pluralism*, ed. Tobias Debiel and Andrea Gawrich (Wiesbaden: Springer, 2014).

19   Carugati and Levi, *A Moral Political Economy*.

20   Taabo Mugume and Thierry Luescher, 'Student Politics at Makerere University in the Lens of Schmitter and Streeck's Framework: Student Leaders and Political Parties', *Makerere Journal of Higher Education* 9, no. 1 (2017): 133–160.

21   Nikolas Kirby, 'An "Institution-First" Conception of Public Integrity', *British Journal of Political Science* 51, no. 4 (2021): 1621, https://doi.org/10.1017/S000712342000006X.

22   Agata Gurzawska, *Principles and Approaches in Ethics Assessment: Institutional Integrity* (Enschede: Satori, 2015), 1621, https://satoriproject.eu/media/1.e-Institutional-Integrity.pdf.

23 Statistics South Africa, *Financial Statistics of Higher Education Institutions* (Pretoria: Statistics South Africa, 2019), 8, http://www.statssa.gov.za/publications/ P91031/P910312019.pdf.

24 Jonathan D. Jansen, *Leading for Change: Race, Intimacy and Leadership on Divided University Campuses* (London: Routledge, 2016).

25 Ngai-Ling Sum and Bob Jessop, *Towards a Cultural Political Economy: Putting Culture in Its Place in Political Economy* (Cheltenham: Edward Elgar Publishing, 2013), viii.

26 Lynley Donnelly, 'Rise of the New Construction "Mafia"', *Mail & Guardian*, 12 April 2019, https://mg.co.za/article/2019-04-12-00-rise-of-the-new-construction-mafia/.

27 Schulze-Cleven et al., 'The New Political Economy of Higher Education', 797.

28 Linda Ronnie and Suki Goodman, 'People Are Buying Fake Degrees Now More Than Ever', *The Citizen*, 5 February 2019, https://www.citizen.co.za/news/south-africa/education/2077568/people-are-buying-fake-degrees-now-more-than-ever/; Lebo Tleane, 'South Africans Who Made Millions from Faking Their Qualifications', *Youth Village*, October 2019, https://youthvillage.co.za/2019/10/south-africans-who-made-millions-from-faking-their-qualifications/; Siyabonga Mkhwanazi, 'State Cracking Down on Officials with Fake Qualifications', *Independent Online*, 1 December 2018, https://www.iol.co.za/news/politics/state-cracking-down-on-officials-with-fake-qualifications-18344271; Tamar Kahn, 'Naming and Shaming Fake Degrees', *TimesLIVE*, 1 August 2018, https://www.timeslive.co.za/news/south-africa/2018-08-01-naming-and-shaming-fake-degrees/; 'Massive Fake Degrees Scandal Uncovered at South African University', *BusinessTech*, 31 July 2016, https://businesstech.co.za/news/business/132052/massive-fake-degrees-scandal-uncovered-at-south-african-university/.

29 Johann Mouton and Astrid Valentine, 'The Extent of South African Authored Articles in Predatory Journals', *South African Journal of Science* 113, no. 7–8 (2017), https://doi.org/10.17159/sajs.2017/20170010.

30 Ismael Gómez, Jorge Costa Delgado, and Johannes Angermüller, 'How to Become an Academic Philosopher: Academic Discourse as a Multileveled Positioning Practice', *Sociología Histórica*, no. 2 (2013): 263.

31 Department of Higher Education and Training, *Report on the Evaluation of 2018 Universities' Research Output* (Pretoria: Department of Higher Education and Training, 2020), 2, https://www.up.ac.za/media/shared/1/2020/May%202020/report-on-the-evaluation-of-the-2018-universities-research-output_april_2020. doc.zp189504.pdf.

32 Richard F. Elmore, 'Backward Mapping: Implementation Research and Policy Decisions', in *Studying Implementation: Methodological and Administrative Issues*, ed. Walter Williams (Chatham, NJ: Chatham House Publishers, 1982).

33 See Ahmed Essop, *Institutional Governance in the Higher Education System in South Africa* (Pretoria: Council on Higher Education, 2015).

34 'Negative resources' are those assets targeted for corrupt ends that lie at the heart of dysfunction in institutions. 'Positive resources' are not targets of the corrupt but are invaluable assets in sustaining functionality in universities.

35 IGI Global, 'What Is Cultural Resources', 2022, https://www.igi-global.com/dictionary/cultural-management-for-multinational-enterprises/44712.

36 See Jonathan D. Jansen, *Knowledge in the Blood: Confronting Race and the Apartheid Past* (Stanford: Stanford University Press, 2009).

37 Vishnu Padayachee, 'Can Progressive Macroeconomic Policy Address Growth and Employment While Reducing Inequality in South Africa?', *Economic and Labour Relations Review* 30, no. 1 (2019): 8, https://doi.org/10.1177/1035304619826862.

38 The principal policy document produced by MERG at this time (1993) was *Making Democracy Work: A Framework for Macroeconomic Policy in South Africa; A Report to Members of the Democratic Movement of South Africa* (Bellville: Centre for Development Studies, University of the Western Cape, 1993); see Rob Davies, *Towards a New Deal: A Political Economy of the Times of My Life* (Johannesburg: Jonathan Ball Publishers, 2021), 54.

39 Sarah Meny-Gibert, 'State "Infrastructural Power" and the bantustans: The Case of School Education in the Transkei and Ciskei', *African Historical Review* 50, no. 1–2 (2018), https://www.tandfonline.com/doi/abs/10.1080/17532523.2019.15 80422; Shireen Ally and Arianna Lissoni, 'Let's Talk about bantustans', in *New Histories of South Africa's Apartheid-Era bantustans*, ed. Shireen Ally and Arianna Lissoni (New York: Routledge, 2017); Linda Chisholm, 'Late-Apartheid Education Reforms and bantustan Entanglements', *African Historical Review* 50, no. 1–2 (2018), https://doi.org/10.1080/17532523.2019.1588496.

40 John W. Meyer and Brian Rowan, 'Institutionalized Organizations: Formal Structure as Myth and Ceremony', *American Journal of Sociology* 83, no. 2 (1977), https://doi.org/10.1086/226550; Njabulo S. Ndebele, 'Creative Instability: The Case of the South African Higher Education System', *Journal of Negro Education* 66, no. 4 (1997), https://doi.org/10.2307/2668171; Magda Fourie, 'Institutional Transformation at South African Universities: Implications for Academic Staff', *Higher Education* 38, no. 3 (1999), https://doi.org/10.1023/A:1003768229291.

41 At the time of writing, this facility had been renamed the Sibusiso Bengu Development Grant.

42 Department of Higher Education and Training, *Ministerial Statement on University Funding: 2015/16 and 2016/17* (Pretoria: Department of Higher Education and Training, 2014), 9 (Table 11), https://www.dhet.gov.za/Financial%20and%20 Physical%20Planning/Ministerial%20Statement%20at%20University%20 funding. %202015-16%20and%202016-2017,%20November%202014.pdf.

43 Angelique Wildschut, email to author, 7 June 2021, indicating an increase in students funded from 452 002 in 2016 to 755 116 in 2020, a significant growth of 67.1 per cent.

44 It is worth noting that the funding of disadvantaged students through the NSFAS facility accounts for 38.4 per cent of the total state budget for the university sector (R29.4 million out of R76.7 million in the 2022/23 allocation); see Department of Higher Education and Training, *Ministerial Statement on University Funding: 2021/22 and 2022/23* (Pretoria: Department of Higher Education and Training, 2020), 3 (Table 1), https://www.dhet.gov.za/Institutional%20Funding/ Ministerial%20Statement%20on%20University%20Funding,%20Dec%202020. pdf.

45 This is called the institutional factor sub-block grant, which has two factors: proportion of disadvantaged students and the size of the university.

46 Meny-Gibert, 'State "Infrastructural Power" and the bantustans', 48, quoting Michael Mann, 'The Autonomous Power of the State: Its Origins, Mechanisms, and Results', in *States in History*, ed. John A. Hall (Oxford: Blackwell, 1986) and

Michael Mann, *The Sources of Social Power*, vol. 2: *The Rise of Classes and Nation States, 1760–1914* (Cambridge: Cambridge University Press, 1993).

47 Jonathan Hyslop, 'Political Corruption: Before and after Apartheid', *Journal of Southern African Studies* 31, no. 4 (2005), https://doi.org/10.1080/03057070500370555.

48 Senior official in DHET, email to author, 8 June 2021.

49 Meny-Gibert, 'State "Infrastructural Power" and the bantustans'.

CHAPTER 4: A PERSONAL JOURNEY THROUGH THE POLITICAL ECONOMY OF UNIVERSITIES

1   Ellen Hartigan-O'Connor, 'The Personal Is Political Economy', *Journal of the Early Republic* 36, no. 2 (2016), https://doi.org/10.1353/jer.2016.0026.

2   Vincent Maphai, *Report of the Independent Assessor, Dr. Vincent Maphai, to the Honourable Minister of Education G. N. M. Pandor, M.P.: Investigation into the Mangosuthu University of Technology* (Pretoria: Government Printer, 2008), 16.

3   John Carlin, 'Tough Talk from ANC's Man in Inkatha Territory: In Zululand, a Defiant Aaron Ndlovu Is Ready for Any Conflict to Come', *The Independent*, 22 July 1993, https://www.independent.co.uk/news/world/tough-talk-from-anc-s-man-in-inkatha-territory-in-zululand-a-defiant-aaron-ndlovu-is-ready-for-any-conflict-to-come-writes-john-carlin-in-empangeni-1486545.html.

4   Mangosuthu University of Technology, 'Rectors and Vice-Chancellor', https://www.mut.ac.za/mut40/rectors-and-vice-chancellor/.

5   Afrikaans; an ox-hide whip.

6   My informant was the head of finance at the Mangosuthu University of Technology at the time I acted as administrator there.

7   Primarashni Gower and Monako Dibetle, 'The Vice in VC', *Mail & Guardian*, 5 November 2008, https://mg.co.za/article/2008-11-05-the-vice-in-vc/.

8   Mzilikazi wa Afrika, 'Top Diplomat Axed after Running High Commission "Like a Spaza Shop"', *Sunday Times*, 24 September 2017, https://www.timeslive.co.za/sunday-times/news/2017-09-23-top-diplomat-axed-after-running-high-commission-like-a-spaza-shop/.

9   Amelia Naidoo, 'DUT Students Threaten Mass Action', *Independent Online*, 16 August 2006, https://www.iol.co.za/news/south-africa/dut-students-threaten-mass-action-289554.

10 'Why SABC Boss Loves Meetings', *News24*, 12 October 2014, https://www.news24.com/News24/Why-SABC-boss-loves-meetings-20150429.

11 Londiwe Buthelezi, 'Police Looking for Ex-SABC Chair Ellen Tshabalala', *News24*, 18 March 2020, https://www.news24.com/fin24/companies/ict/police-looking-for-ex-sabc-chair-ellen-tshabalala-20200318.

12 'Sociology Head Is Forced into Hiding', *Times Higher Education Supplement*, no. 1192 (8 September 1995), https://www.timeshighereducation.com/news/sociology-head-is-forced-into-hiding/95116.article.

13 'It's Spy vs Spy at UDW', *Mail & Guardian*, 13 October 1995, https://mg.co.za/article/1995-10-13-its-spy-vs-spy-at-udw/.

14 Kader Asmal, 'Terms of Reference of the Minister of Education to the Independent Assessor to Conduct an Investigation into the Affairs of the University of

Durban-Westville', in Bongani Augustine Khumalo, *Independent Assessor's Report on the Investigation at the University of Durban Westville* (Pretoria: Department of Education, 2003)

15 Jonathan D. Jansen, *Knowledge in the Blood: Confronting Race and the Apartheid Past* (Stanford: Stanford University Press, 2009).

16 See Ian Bunting, 'Funding', in *Transformation in Higher Education: Global Pressures and Local Realities in South Africa*, ed. Nico Cloete et al. (Cape Town: Juta, 2002), 65–69.

17 Jonathan D. Jansen and Cyrill A. Walters, *The Decolonization of Knowledge: Radical Ideas and the Shaping of Institutions in South Africa and Beyond* (Cambridge: Cambridge University Press, 2022).

18 Jansen, *Knowledge in the Blood.*

19 See Bunting, 'Funding', 69.

20 Jonathan D. Jansen, *Leading for Change: Race, Intimacy and Leadership on Divided University Campuses* (London: Routledge, 2016).

21 The apt phrase of John Samuel, who at one stage was my adviser as vice-chancellor at the UFS.

22 Lawrence V. Weill, *Out in Front: The College President as the Face of the Institution* (Lanham, MD: Rowman and Littlefield, 2009).

23 Nic Spaull and Jonathan D. Jansen, *South African Schooling: The Enigma of Inequality; A Study of the Present Situation and Future Possibilities* (Cham: Springer, 2019), 28–29.

24 Cathy Dlodlo, 'FS Health Stays under Administration', *OFM News*, 9 November 2016, https://www.ofm.co.za/article/local-news/208775/fs-health-stays-under-administration.

25 'How the Free State Health System Is Being Destroyed', *GroundUp*, 27 February 2015, https://www.groundup.org.za/media/features/freestatehealth/freestate-health.html.

26 'Free State MEC Killed in Crash', *Independent Online*, 2 December 2012, https://www.iol.co.za/news/politics/free-state-mec-killed-in-crash-1434213.

27 'Free State MEC in Court', eNCA, 29 November 2013, https://www.enca.com/south-africa/free-state-mec-court.

CHAPTER 5: CASTING LONG SHADOWS

1 In his book *The Mind of South Africa* (New York: Ballantine, 1991) the veteran journalist Allister Sparks tells the story of the two young lead negotiators for their parties, Cyril Ramaphosa of the African National Congress (ANC) and Roelf Meyer of the National Party (NP), long sworn enemies, going fishing together during the difficult negotiations to end apartheid. Meyer gets a trout hook caught in his hand, and Ramaphosa, the skilled fisherman, extracts it from his partner's hand. There is a humorous exchange between the men that reflects on the broader symbolic import of this moment of care and interdependence. The story of the fish hook took on multiple meanings in the many apocryphal versions that arose after the incident. See the review of the book by David Honigmann, 'The Roelf 'n' Cyril show', *The Independent,* 10 June 1995, https://www.independent.co.uk/arts-entertainment/the-roelf-n-cyril-show-1586014.html.

2   Mokubung O. Nkomo, *Student Culture and Activism in Black South African Universities: The Roots of Resistance* (Westport, CT: Greenwood Press, 1984).

3   Nkomo, *Student Culture and Activism in Black South African Universities*, xix.

4   Njabulo S. Ndebele, 'Creative Instability: The Case of the South African Higher Education System', *Journal of Negro Education* 66, no. 4 (1997): 443, https://doi.org/10.2307/2668171.

5   Heike Becker, 'South African Student Protests, 1968 to 2016: Dissent, Disruption, Decolonization', *International Socialist Review*, no. 111 (2018), https://isreview.org/issue/111/south-african-student-protests-1968-2016/.

6   'To the gate!' (the entrance to the university).

7   University of the Western Cape, *Hek Toe! UWC in the 1980s* (Bellville: University of the Western Cape, 2004).

8   Ndebele, 'Creative Instability', 445.

9   Julian Brown, 'An Experiment in Confrontation: The Pro-Frelimo Rallies of 1974', *Journal of Southern African Studies* 38, no. 1 (2012), https://doi.org/10.1080/03057070.2012.644978.

10 Saleem Badat, *Black Student Politics: Higher Education and Apartheid from SASO to SANSCO, 1968–1990* (London: Routledge, 2016); Becker, 'South African Student Protests, 1968 to 2016'; Julian Brown, *The Road to Soweto: Resistance and the Uprising of 16 June 1976* (Woodbridge, UK: James Currey, 2016); Anne Heffernan, *Limpopo's Legacy: Student Politics and Democracy in South Africa* (Woodbridge, UK: Boydell and Brewer, 2019).

11 Brown, *The Road to Soweto*, 20–39.

12 Graeme Moodie, 'The State and the Liberal Universities in South Africa: 1948–1990', *Higher Education* 27, no. 1 (1994), https://doi.org/10.1007/BF01383758.

13 Gail Morlan, 'The Student Revolt against Racism in South Africa', *Africa Today* 17, no. 3 (1970).

14 Johannes Degenaar, 'The Concept of a Volksuniversiteit', in *The Future of the University in South Africa*, ed. H. W. van der Merwe and David Welsh (Cape Town: David Philip, 1977).

15 Pierre J. Hugo, 'Academic Dissent and Apartheid in South Africa', *Journal of Black Studies* 7, no. 3 (1977), https://doi.org/10.1177/002193477700700301.

16 See Fred Hendricks, 'The Mafeje Affair: The University of Cape Town and Apartheid', *African Studies* 67, no. 3 (2008), https://doi.org/10.1080/00020180802505061.

17 Jonathan D. Jansen, *Knowledge in the Blood: Confronting Race and the Apartheid Past* (Stanford: Stanford University Press, 2009).

18 Brown, *The Road to Soweto*, 34.

19 Brian H. King and Brent McCusker, 'Environment and Development in the Former South African bantustans', *Geographical Journal* 173, no. 1 (2007), https://doi.org/10.1111/j.1475-4959.2007.00229.x.

20 Nkosinathi Gwala, 'State Control, Student Politics and the Crisis in Black Universities', in *Popular Struggles in South Africa*, ed. William Cobbett and Robin Cohen (London: James Currey, 1988), 172.

21 Adam Habib, *Structural Disadvantage, Leadership Ineptitude, and Stakeholder Complicity: A Study of the Institutional Crisis of the University of the Transkei* (Rondebosch: Centre for Higher Education Transformation, 2000), 11.

22 Clive Napier, 'The Transkei bantustan and Its University: A Crisis of Legitimacy', *Reality* 18, no. 2 (1985), https://www.sahistory.org.za/sites/default/files/DC/

remar85.5/remar85.5.pdf; Linda Vergnani, 'South African Homeland Deports 3 Professors', *Chronicle of Higher Education*, 6 January 1993, https://www.chronicle.com/article/south-african-homeland-deports-3-professors/?cid2=gen_login_refresh&cid=gen_sign_in; Gwala, 'State Control, Student Politics and the Crisis in Black Universities', 170.

23 Gwala, 'State Control, Student Politics and the Crisis in Black Universities', 171.

24 John Davies, 'The State and the South African University System under Apartheid', *Comparative Education* 32, no. 3 (1996): 327, https://doi.org/10.1080/03050069628740; see also Francine de Clercq, 'Black Universities as Contested Terrains: The Politics of Progressive Engagement', *Perspectives in Education* 12, no. 2 (1991) and William Beinart, 'Beyond "Homelands": Some Ideas about the History of African Rural Areas in South Africa', in *New Histories of South Africa's Apartheid-Era bantustans*, ed. Shireen Ally and Arianna Lissoni (New York: Routledge, 2017), 7–8.

25 Gwala, 'State Control, Student Politics and the Crisis in Black Universities', 175.

26 Leslie Witz, 'Misplaced Ideals? The Case of Unibo: A Reply to J. F. de V. Graaff', *Reality*, January 1986, https://disa.ukzn.ac.za/sites/default/files/pdf_files/rejul86.7.pdf.

27 Gwala, 'State Control, Student Politics and the Crisis in Black Universities'.

28 Vergnani, 'South African Homeland Deports 3 Professors'.

29 Witz, 'Misplaced Ideals?', 11.

30 Habib, *Structural Disadvantage, Leadership Ineptitude, and Stakeholder Complicity*, 9.

31 Amnesty International, 'Fear of Extrajudicial Execution. South Africa (Bophuthatswana): Solomon (Solly) Bokaba, Age 27, President of the Student Representative Council (SRC) at the University of Bophuthatswana (UNIBO), AI Index: AFR 53/20/93 Distr: UA/SC, 25 May 1993, https://www.amnesty.org/en/wp-content/uploads/2021/06/afr530201993en.pdf.

32 Gwala, 'State Control, Student Politics and the Crisis in Black Universities', 181.

33 See Habib, *Structural Disadvantage, Leadership Ineptitude, and Stakeholder Complicity*, 10.

34 Jonathan Hyslop, 'Political Corruption: Before and After Apartheid', *Journal of Southern African Studies* 31, no. 4 (2005): 783, https://doi.org/10.1080/03057070500370555; see also Sarah Meny-Gibert, 'State "Infrastructural Power" and the bantustans: The Case of School Education in the Transkei and Ciskei', *African Historical Review* 50, no. 1–2 (2018), https://www.tandfonline.com/doi/abs/10.1080/17532523.2019.1580422.

35 Lulamile Feni, 'King Dalindyebo Vows to Shut Down WSU, Take Back the Land', *HeraldLIVE*, 27 February 2021, https://www.heraldlive.co.za/news/2021-02-27-king-dalindyebo-vows-to-shut-down-wsu-take-back-the-land/.

36 Jim Leatt, interview, 29 March 2021.

37 Napier, 'The Transkei bantustan and Its University', 17.

38 Napier, 'The Transkei bantustan and Its University', 18.

39 Padraig O'Malley, *National Education Coordinating Committee (NECC)* (1991), https://omalley.nelsonmandela.org/omalley/index.php/site/q/03lv02424/04lv02730/05lv03188/06lv03208.htm.

40   Gabriel Cele and Charlton Koen, 'Student Politics in South Africa. An Overview of Key Developments', *Cahiers de la Recherche sur l'Éducation et les Savoirs* 2 (2003), https://journals.openedition.org/cres/1517#tocto2n8.

41   Department of Education, *Education White Paper 3: A Programme for the Transformation of Higher Education* (Pretoria: Department of Education, 1997), 7, https://www.gov.za/sites/default/files/gcis_document/201409/18207gen11960. pdf.

42   Nico Cloete and N. Mohamed, 'Transformation Forums as Revolutionary Councils: Midwives to Democracy or Advisory Councils for Restructuring and Innovation' (discussion paper, Union of Democratic University Staff Associations, 1995).

43   Cloete and Mohamed, 'Transformation Forums as Revolutionary Councils'.

44   Magda Fourie, 'Institutional Transformation at South African Universities: Implications for Academic Staff', *Higher Education* 38, no. 3 (1999): 280, https://doi.org/10.1023/A:1003768229291.

45   Magda Fourie-Malherbe, interview, 8 July 2021.

46   Former University of Western Cape-based policy researcher, Zoom interview, 13 July 2021.

47   Fourie, 'Institutional Transformation at South African Universities', 281.

48   Martin Hall, Ashley Symes, and Thierry M. Luescher, *Governance in South African Higher Education: Research Report Prepared for the Council on Higher Education* (Pretoria: Council on Higher Education, 2002), 38.

49   National Commission on Higher Education, *NCHE Report: A Framework for Transformation* (Pretoria: National Commission on Higher Education, 1996), 199.

50   Department of Education, *Education White Paper 3*, 32, https://www.gov.za/sites/default/files/gcis_document/201409/18207gen11960.pdf.

51   Republic of South Africa, *Higher Education Act 101 of 1997* (Pretoria: Government Printer, 1997), 26, https://www.gov.za/sites/default/files/gcis_document/201409/a101-97.pdf.

52   Hall, Symes, and Luescher, *Governance in South African Higher Education*, 38.

53   Ann Harper et al., *Institutional Forums: An Overview of Their Establishment and Functioning at South African Public Higher Education Institutions* (Pretoria: Centre for Higher Education Transformation, 2002); Anne-Marea Griffin, 'Toward Deliberative Democracy: The Institutional Forum as an Innovative Shared Governance Mechanism in South African Higher Education', *African Journal of Business Ethics* 12, no. 1 (2018), https://doi.org/10.15249/12-1-160.

54   Nico Cloete et al., *Transformation in Higher Education: Global Pressures and Local Realities in South Africa* (Cape Town: Juta, 2002), 234.

55   National Commission on Higher Education, *NCHE Report*, 23.

56   Hall, Symes, and Luescher, *Governance in South African Higher Education*, 86.

57   Hall, Symes, and Luescher, *Governance in South African Higher Education*, 86.

58   National Commission on Higher Education, *NCHE Report*, section 7.3.

59   Fourie, 'Institutional Transformation at South African Universities', 281.

60   Jonathan D. Jansen, *As by Fire: The End of the South African University* (Cape Town: Tafelberg, 2017), 118.

CHAPTER 6: THE UNIVERSITY AS A CONCENTRATED AND EXPLOITABLE RESOURCE

1 'With R14m "She Should Have Built Me a House!"', *News24*, 3 September 2017, https://www.news24.com/News24/with-r14m-she-should-have-built-me-a-house-20170903-2.

2 Malibongwe Dayimani, 'Sibongile Mani Sentenced to 5 Years' Imprisonment for Theft of NSFAS Funds', *News24*, 30 March 2022, https://www.news24.com/news24/newsletters/icymi/featured/sibongile-mani-sentenced-to-5-years-imprisonment-for-theft-of-nsfas-funds-20220330.

3 Former NSFAS administrator, sharing a cryptic message that came via the NSFAS hotline, Zoom interview, 24 September 2021.

4 Table detailing the different streams of income for universities in 2020, namely, state subsidy, tuition and accommodation, and third-stream income. Department of Higher Education and Training, email message to author, 23 September 2021.

5 Department of Higher Education and Training, *Ministerial Statement on University Funding: 2021/22 and 2022/23* (Pretoria: Department of Higher Education and Training, 2020), 3, Table 1, https://www.dhet.gov.za/Institutional%20Funding/Ministerial%20Statement%20on%20University%20Funding,%20Dec%202020.pdf.

6 University of Cape Town, *Annual Report 2020* (Cape Town: University of Cape Town, 2020), 60, https://www.uct.ac.za/sites/default/files/image_tool/images/431/finance/operations/statements/afs2020.pdf.

7 Department of Higher Education and Training, *University State Budgets* (Pretoria: Department of Higher Education and Training, 2021), 2, 20, https://www.dhet.gov.za/Institutional%20Funding/University%20State%20budgets,%20March%202021.xls.

8 Vincent Maphai, *Developing a Culture of Good Governance: Report of the Presidential Review Commission on the Reform and Transformation of the Public Service in South Africa* (Pretoria: Presidential Review Commission, 1998), https://www.gov.za/documents/report-presidential-review-commission-reform-and-transformation-public-service-south.

9 Walter Sisulu University, *Annual Report 2020* (Mthatha: Walter Sisulu University, 2020), https://www.wsu.ac.za/images/annualreport/WSU_Annual_Report_2020_compressed.pdf.

10 Ewert P. J. Kleynhans and David Dyason, 'A University in a Small City: Discovering Which Sectors Benefit', *Acta Commercii* 17, no. 1 (2017), https://doi.org/10.4102/ac.v17i1.513.

11 Bureau for Economic Research, *Economic Impact Assessment of Stellenbosch University on the Local Municipal Area* (Stellenbosch: Stellenbosch University, 2018), https://www.sun.ac.za/english/Documents/Economic%20Impact%20Study/BER-Final-EIA-new.PDF.

12 Stellenbosch University registrar, email to author, 4 October 2021.

13 Bureau for Economic Research, *Economic Impact Assessment of Stellenbosch University on the Local Municipal Area*, 74.

14 Sarah Wild, 'Rhodes "on the Brink of Closure" Due to Lack of Water', *Mail & Guardian*, 14 August 2013, https://mg.co.za/article/2013-08-14-rhodes-on-the-brink-of-closure-says-vice-chancellor/; see also the unprecedented open letter of

the then vice-chancellor, Professor Saleem Badat, to the municipal authorities concerning the breakdown in water supply and its impact on the university, 'An Open Letter to the Mayor, the Municipal Manager and the Makana Municipality Councillors', 14 August 2013, http://vital.seals.ac.za:8080/vital/access/manager/PdfViewer/vital:7941/SOURCEPDF?viewPdfInternal=1.

15 Badat, 'An Open Letter to the Mayor, the Municipal Manager and the Makana Municipality Councillors', 14 August 2013.

16 Department of Higher Education and Training, *Ministerial Statement on University Funding: 2021/22 and 2022/23*, 3, Table 1.

17 This number was given in response to parliamentary questions about how many students NSFAS funded: 452 002 in 2016; 538 780 in 2017; 611 261 in 2018; 659 863 in 2019; and 755 116 in 2020. Angelique Wildschut-February, email message to Randall Carolissen, NSFAS administrator, 7 June 2021; Randall Carolissen, email to author, 11 June 2021.

18 Rob Adam, Zoom interview, 27 September 2021.

19 National Student Financial Aid Scheme, 'Performance of NSFAS under Administration: Handover Report from the Executive Administrator' (Cape Town: National Student Financial Aid Scheme, 2020).

20 Former NSFAS administrator, Zoom interview, 24 September 2021.

21 The NSFAS N+2 rule means that a student has only two years added to the normal time (N) required to complete the degree.

22 Randall Carolissen, email to author, 27 September 2021.

23 Former NSFAS administrator, Zoom interview, 24 September 2021.

24 Msindisi Fengu, 'VUT Embroiled in R20m Laptop Tender Scandal after Going "Independent Procurement Route"', *News24*, 4 August 2021, https://www.news24.com/citypress/news/vut-embroiled-in-r20m-laptop-tender-scandal-after-going-independent-procurement-route-20210804.

25 Rapula Moatshe, 'R17m Sefako Makgatho Health Sciences University Laptop Tender "Delayed by Management Feud"', *Independent Online*, 17 September 2021, https://www.iol.co.za/pretoria-news/news/r17m-sefako-makgatho-health-sciences-university-laptop-tender-delayed-by-management-feud-61d6c923-fad2-4305-986c-06e563d4c27e.

26 Note that this reported funding from the state in 2021/22 is based on an N-2 calculation; that is, it actually accounts for research units submitted two years earlier, in this case in 2019.

27 Department of Higher Education and Training, *University State Budgets*, Table 3.17.

28 University of Cape Town, *Annual Report 2020*, 91.

29 A government–academic–private sector partnership initiative to produce high-level skills for industry using advanced technologies.

30 Former National Research Foundation vice-president, Zoom interview, 14 September 2021.

31 Johann Mouton and Astrid Valentine, 'The Extent of South African Authored Articles in Predatory Journals', *South African Journal of Science* 113, no. 7–8 (2017), https://doi.org/10.17159/sajs.2017/20170010.

32 Other 'outputs' are weighed differently, for example, 3 units for doctoral graduates; 1 unit for master's graduates; 0.5 unit for conference proceedings; and up to 10 units for a full book.

33 Department of Higher Education and Training, email to author, 30 September 2021.

34 Mouton and Valentine, 'The Extent of South African Authored Articles in Predatory Journals', 85.

35 Andrew Kerr and Phillip Jager, 'A Description of Predatory Publishing in South African Economics Departments', *South African Journal of Economics* 89, no. 3 (2021), https://doi.org/10.1111/saje.12278.

36 Johann Mouton et al., *The Quality of South Africa's Research Publications: Final Report to the DHET* (Stellenbosch: Centre for Research on Evaluation, Science and Technology, 2019), https://www.researchgate.net/publication/348658730_THE_QUALITY_OF_SOUTH_AFRICA%27S_RESEARCH_PUBLICATIONS_Final_report_to_the_DHET.

37 Department of Higher Education and Training, *Ministerial Statement on University Funding: 2021/22 and 2022/23*, Table 9. The amount for 23 universities is R2.3 million and as capital funds for the two new universities, R461 474 (SPU) and R692 210 (UMP).

38 Lourens van Staden, Zoom interview, 6 May 2021.

39 Walter Sisulu University, *Annual Report 2020*, 42; University of Fort Hare, *Annual Report 2020* (Alice: University of Fort Hare, 2020), 43.

40 University of Fort Hare vice-chancellor, Zoom interview, 4 May 2021.

CHAPTER 7: THE UNIVERSITY AS A CRIMINAL ENTERPRISE

1   Long-standing senior member of the Unisa council, interview, 11 June 2021.

2   Athandiwe Saba, 'Deadly Twist to University Dispute', *Mail & Guardian,* 7 December 2018, https://mg.co.za/article/2018-12-07-00-deadly-twist-to-university-dispute/.

3   Sen Muller, 'The Murder of Prof Kamwendo at UniZulu', *Mail & Guardian*, 8 December 2018, https://mg.co.za/article/2018-12-08-letter-the-murder-of-prof-kamwendo-at-unizulu/.

4   Mzilikazi wa Afrika and Kyle Cowan, 'Degrees-for-Sale Scam Rocks Zululand Varsity', *Sunday Times*, 31 July 2016, https://www.timeslive.co.za/sunday-times/news/2016-07-31-degrees-for-sale-scam-rocks-zululand-varsity.

5   Chris de Beer, interview, 9 March 2021.

6   University of Fort Hare vice-chancellor, Zoom interview, 4 May 2021.

7   Thobile Mlangeni, 'No Degree of Success in UMP Negotiations with Taxi Associations', *Mpumalanga News*, 17 June 2021, https://mpumalanganews.co.za/397491/no-degree-of-success-in-ump-negotiations-with-taxi-associations/.

8   Thobile Mlangeni, 'Taxi Associations Protest, Demand to Transport Students', *Mpumalanga News*, 11 June 2021, https://mpumalanganews.co.za/397097/taxi-associations-protest-demand-to-transport-students/.

9   Mlangeni, 'No Degree of Success in UMP Negotiations with Taxi Associations'.

10 Mlangeni, 'Taxi Associations Protest, Demand to Transport Students'.

11 A rural university's chair of council, Zoom interview, 16 July 2021.

12 Helen Swingler, 'Taxis Protest Jammie Shuttle Route', *UCT News*, 28 August 2007, https://www.news.uct.ac.za/article/-2007-08-28-taxis-protest-jammie-shuttle-route.

13   James G. R. Simpson, 'Boipatong: The Politics of a Massacre and the South African Transition', *Journal of Southern African Studies* 38, no. 3 (2012), https://doi.org/10. 1080/03057070.2012.711674.

14   Marius Pieterse, 'How Structural Flaws Contribute to the Crisis in South Africa's Municipalities', *The Conversation*, 29 August 2018, https://theconversation. com/how-structural-flaws-contribute-to-the-crisis-in-south-africas-municipalities-102136.

15   Vaal University of Technology administrator, Zoom interview, 7 July 2021.

16   Mabel Jansen, Ben Khoapa, and Seth Radebe, *Report of the Commission of Inquiry: Vaal University of Technology* (Vanderbijlpark: Vaal University of Technology, 2006).

17   Aubrey Mokadi, *A Portrait of Governance in Higher Education: Taking a Stand for Transformation* (Johannesburg: Sedibeng, 2002).

18   Jansen, Khoapa, and Radebe, *Report of the Commission of Inquiry*, 43.

19   Former deputy vice-chancellor of Vaal University of Technology, Zoom interview, 21 June 2021.

20   Jansen, Khoapa, and Radebe, *Report of the Commission of Inquiry*, 52–53.

21   Jansen, Khoapa, and Radebe, *Report of the Commission of Inquiry*, 64.

22   Jansen, Khoapa, and Radebe, *Report of the Commission of Inquiry*, 58.

23   Jansen, Khoapa, and Radebe, *Report of the Commission of Inquiry*, 391.

24   Jansen, Khoapa, and Radebe, *Report of the Commission of Inquiry*, 393.

25   N. Barney Pityana and M. D. Rocky Ralebipi-Simela, 'Report of the Independent Assessors on the State of the Vaal University of Technology', *Government Gazette no. 43015*, 14 February 2020, https://www.gov.za/sites/default/files/gcis_document/ 202002/43015gon127.pdf.

26   Former Unisa vice-chancellor, Zoom interview, 13 May 2021.

27   Former Unisa council member, Zoom interview, 11 June 2021.

28   Former Unisa council member, Zoom interview, 11 June 2021.

29   It is not, however, without historical precedent, as some recall. Stellenbosch University at one time had an office for its chair of council under Rector Thom, as did the University of the Orange Free State under Rector Kok.

30   Former Unisa vice-chancellor, Zoom interview, 13 May 2021.

31   Former Unisa vice-chancellor, Zoom interview, 13 May 2021.

32   Former Vaal University of Technology senior deputy vice-chancellor, Zoom interview, 16 June 2021.

33   Former Unisa vice-chancellor, Zoom interview, 13 May 2021.

34   Former Unisa vice-chancellor, Zoom interview, 13 May 2021.

35   Former Unisa vice-chancellor, Zoom interview, 13 May 2021.

36   Former Unisa vice-chancellor, Zoom interview, 13 May 2021.

37   Afrikaans; a meeting of leaders at a remote retreat.

38   Former Unisa council member, Zoom interview, 11 June 2021.

39   Jacobus S. Wessels, Makhosandile H. Kwaza, and Edwin Ijeoma, 'Sustained Poor Audit Outcomes: The Case of the Amathole District Municipality', in *Public Administration Challenges: Cases from Africa*, ed. Jacobus S. Wessels, Thean Potgieter, and Thevan Naidoo (Cape Town: Juta, 2021).

40   University of Fort Hare vice-chancellor, Zoom interview, 4 May 2021.

41   University of Fort Hare vice-chancellor, Zoom interview, 4 May 2021.

42   University of Fort Hare vice-chancellor, Zoom interview, 4 May 2021.

43   University of Fort Hare vice-chancellor, Zoom interview, 4 May 2021.

44   Former University of Natal deputy vice-chancellor, Zoom interview, 10 August 2021.

45   Malibongwe Dayimani, 'Fort Hare University Lays Charges against Fugitive Professor Linked to Premier Oscar Mabuyane', *News24*, 25 March 2021, https://www.news24.com/news24/southafrica/news/fort-hare-university-lays-charges-against-premier-oscar-mabuyanes-fugitive-nigerian-professor-20210325.

46   Malibongwe Dayimani and Sino Majangaza, 'Oscar Slams Fort Hare VC over Crisis of Killings', *Daily Dispatch*, 24 February 2020, https://www.dispatchlive.co.za/news/2020-02-24-oscar-slams-fort-hare-vc-over-crisis-of-killings/.

47   Former University of Limpopo vice-chancellor, Zoom interview, 4 August 2021.

48   Peter Mbati, Zoom interview, 4 August 2021.

49   Peter Mbati, Zoom interview, 4 August 2021.

50   Former Walter Sisulu University vice-chancellor and University of Zululand deputy vice-chancellor, Zoom interview, 5 May 2021.

51   Former University of Fort Hare deputy vice-chancellor and former Walter Sisulu University vice-chancellor, Zoom interview, 5 May 2021.

52   Former University of Zululand deputy vice-chancellor, Zoom interview, 5 May 2021.

53   Former University of Limpopo acting deputy vice-chancellor, interview, 24 February 2021.

54   Former University of Fort Hare administrator, Zoom interview, 25 March 2021.

55   Former University of the North acting deputy vice-chancellor, interview, 24 February 2021.

56   Nico Cloete, interview, 21 May 2021.

57   V. J. Reddy, Zoom interview, 25 May 2021.

CHAPTER 8: THE MICROPOLITICS OF CORRUPTION IN UNIVERSITIES

1   Senior HR consultant working for administrators and on invitation from vice-chancellors in higher education, interview, 17 June 2021.

2   Lourens van Staden, Zoom interview, 6 May 2022.

3   Former University of the North vice-chancellor and former University of Cape Town vice-chancellor, Zoom interview, 3 May 2021.

4   Jacky Lumby, *In the Wings and Backstage: Exploring the Micropolitics of Leadership in Higher Education* (London: Leadership Foundation for Higher Education, 2015), 29, https://eprints.soton.ac.uk/386161/.

5   Lumby, *In the Wings and Backstage*, 29.

6   Joseph J. Blase, 'The Micropolitical Orientation of Teachers toward Closed School Principals', *Education and Urban Society* 23, no. 4 (1991), https://doi.org/10.1177/0013124591023004002; Lumby, *In the Wings and Backstage*; Lisa Rogers et al., 'The Micropolitics of Implementation: A Qualitative Study Exploring the Impact of Power, Authority, and Influence When Implementing Change in Healthcare Teams', *BMC Health Services Research* 20, no. 1 (2020), https://doi.org/10.1186/s12913-020-05905-z.

7   Monica Kirya, 'Corruption in Universities: Paths to Integrity in the Higher Education Subsector' (Bergen: Chr. Michelsen Institute, 2019), https://www.u4.no/publications/corruption-in-universities-paths-to-integrity-in-the-higher-education-subsector.pdf.

8   Geeta Gandhi Kingdon et al., *A Rigorous Review of the Political Economy of Education Systems in Developing Countries* (London: Department for International Development, 2014), https://eppi.ioe.ac.uk/cms/Portals/0/PDF%20reviews%20and%20summaries/Political%20economy%202014Kingdon.pdf?ver=2014-04-24-141259-443.

9   Financial consultant and adviser to higher education institutions, Zoom interview, 11 May 2021.

10 A rural university's chair of council, Zoom interview, 16 July 2022.

11 Jacky Lumby, 'Let's Shine a Light on the Dark Art of Micropolitics in Universities', *The Guardian*, 15 October 2015, https://www.theguardian.com/higher-education-network/2015/oct/15/lets-shine-a-light-on-the-dark-art-of-micropolitics-in-universities.

12 Qaanitah Hunter, Jeff Wicks, and Kaveel Singh, *Eight Days in July: Inside the Zuma Unrest That Set South Africa Alight* (Cape Town: Tafelberg, 2021).

13 Blake E. Ashforth and Vikas Anand, 'The Normalization of Corruption in Organizations', *Research in Organizational Behavior* 25 (2003), https://doi.org/10.1016/S0191-3085(03)25001-2.

14 Ashforth and Anand, 'The Normalization of Corruption in Organizations', 9; see also Alison Taylor, *What Do Corrupt Firms Have in Common? Red Flags of Corruption in Organizational Culture* (New York: Columbia University, 2016), https://web.law.columbia.edu/sites/default/files/microsites/public-integrity/files/what_do_corrupt_firms_have_in_common_-_capi_issue_brief_-_april_2016.pdf.

15 Barney Pityana, Zoom interview, 6 April 2022.

16 Thierry Luescher et al., *The State of Transformation in South Africa's Public Universities: A Research Report Prepared by the Human Sciences Research Council on Behalf of the Ministerial Oversight Committee on Transformation in the South African Public Universities* (Pretoria: Human Sciences Research Council, 2021).

17 Margaret Heffernan, *Willful Blindness: Why We Ignore the Obvious at Our Peril* (New York: Simon and Schuster, 2011).

18 Yavuz Selim Düger, '"Willful Blindness" as a Dark Side of Organizational Behavior: Can Effective Leadership Overcomes This Challenge?', in *Studies on Interdisciplinary Economics and Business*, ed. Özer Özçelik and Adil Akinci (Pieterlen: Peter Lang, 2020), 304.

19 Administrator, Zoom interview, 8 March 2021.

20 Department of Higher Education and Training, *Report of the Ministerial Task Team to Conduct an Independent Review of the University of South Africa* (Pretoria: Department of Higher Education and Training, 2021), 55.

21 Former Unisa council member, Zoom interview, 11 June 2021.

22 Former Vaal University of Technology deputy vice-chancellor, Zoom interview, 21 June 2021.

23 Sarah Meny-Gibert, 'State "Infrastructural Power" and the bantustans: The Case of School Education in the Transkei and Ciskei', *African Historical Review* 50, no. 1–2 (2018), https://www.tandfonline.com/doi/abs/10.1080/17532523.2019.1580422.

24 Malibongwe Dayimani and Sino Majangaza, 'Oscar Slams Fort Hare VC over Crisis of Killings', *Daily Dispatch*, 24 February 2020, https://www.dispatchlive.co.za/news/2020-02-24-oscar-slams-fort-hare-vc-over-crisis-of-killings/.

25 Former Unisa council member, Zoom interview, 11 June 2021.

26 Sadly, Peter died shortly after I conducted this lengthy lunch-time interview with him about his experiences as manager and rescuer of dysfunctional universities.

27 Former senior management consultant who advised administrators of dysfunctional universities, interview, 17 June 2021.

28 Former University of Johannesburg deputy vice-chancellor, Zoom interview, 28 July 2021.

29 Former University of Johannesburg deputy vice-chancellor, Zoom interview, 28 July 2021.

30 Former Unisa vice-chancellor, Zoom interview, 13 May 2021.

31 Former University of Cape Town deputy vice-chancellor and senior researcher on institutional governance in higher education in South Africa, interview, 22 July 2021.

32 Former Unisa vice-chancellor, Zoom interview, 13 May 2021.

33 Former Mangosuthu University of Technology assessor, Zoom interview, 8 April 2022.

34 See, for example, Katherine Levine Einstein, Maxwell Palmer, and David M. Glick, 'Who Participates in Local Government? Evidence from Meeting Minutes', *Perspectives on Politics* 17, no. 1 (2019), https://doi.org/10.1017/S153759271800213X.

35 Former Cape Peninsula University of Technology senior manager who subsequently served as an HR specialist advising administrators of dysfunctional universities, Zoom interview, 11 June 2021.

36 Former Sefako Makgatho Health Sciences University vice-chancellor, Zoom interview, 9 March 2021.

37 Former Sefako Makgatho Health Sciences University vice-chancellor, Zoom interview, 9 March 2021.

38 Former Walter Sisulu University administrator, Zoom interview, 30 March 2021.

39 Various interviews, including with a former Unisa vice-chancellor, 13 May 2021, and a former Unisa council member, 11 June 2021.

40 Former University of Zululand deputy vice-chancellor, Zoom interview, 5 May 2021.

41 Head of assessor's team, emailed response to questions, 11 April 2021.

42 I detail the role of a local newspaper in the politics of universities in the chapter 'The Intimate Observer', in my book *Leading for Change: Race, Intimacy and Leadership on Divided University Campuses* (London: Routledge, 2016).

43 Patrick Fitzgerald, Zoom interview, 7 April 2022.

44 Peter Mbati, Zoom interview, 4 August 2021.

45 Former Unisa council member, Zoom interview, 11 June 2021.

46 Charles King, 'The Micropolitics of Social Violence', *World Politics* 56, no. 3 (2004): 439, https://doi.org/10.1353/wp.2004.0016.

47 Department of Higher Education and Training, *Report of the Ministerial Task Team to Conduct an Independent Review of the University of South Africa*.

48 Former University of the Western Cape deputy vice-chancellor, Zoom interview, 25 May 2021.

49   Former Vaal University of Technology administrator, Zoom interview, 28 June 2021.
50   Former Tshwane University of Technology administrator, Zoom interview, 8 April 2021.
51   Department of Higher Education and Training, *Report of the Ministerial Task Team to Conduct an Independent Review of the University of South Africa*.
52   Former Vaal University of Technology administrator, Zoom interview, 28 June 2021.
53   Former University of Venda vice-chancellor, interview, 29 March 2021.

CHAPTER 9: THE TWIN ROOTS OF CHRONIC DYSFUNCTIONALITY IN UNIVERSITIES

1   In July 2017, the NMMU was renamed Nelson Mandela University (NMU).
2   Nthabiseng Ogude tells this story in her forthcoming memoir, provisionally titled *The Making of a Sharpeville Girl: Narratives of Exile and Return to South Africa*.
3   Agata Gurzawska, *Principles and Approaches in Ethics Assessment: Institutional Integrity* (Enschede: Satori, 2015), 4, https://satoriproject.eu/media/1.e-Institutional-Integrity.pdf.
4   Nikolas Kirby, 'An "Institution-First" Conception of Public Integrity', *British Journal of Political Science* 51, no. 4 (2021): 1631, https://doi.org/10.1017/S000712342000006X.
5   Gordon K. Davies, 'General Threats to Institutional Integrity', *New Directions for Community Colleges*, no. 52 (1985): 29, https://doi.org/10.1002/cc.36819855205.
6   Kirby, 'An "Institution-First" Conception of Public Integrity', 1621.
7   Former vice-chancellor and administrator of universities, Zoom interview, 30 March 2021.
8   Former Department of Education senior official responsible for higher education, Zoom interview, 23 March 2021.
9   Makhenkesi Stofile was a senior member of the ANC who served variously as cabinet minister, ambassador, and the second premier of the Eastern Cape, from 1997 to 2004.
10   Former Department of Education senior official responsible for higher education, Zoom interview, 23 March 2021.
11   Former Department of Education senior official responsible for higher education, Zoom interview, 23 March 2021.
12   Former Department of Education senior official responsible for higher education, Zoom interview, 23 March 2021.
13   Former adviser to the minister of education and deputy director-general responsible for higher education, interview, 23 March 2021.
14   Vincent Maphai, Zoom interview, 22 March 2021.
15   Martin Hall, Zoom interview, 22 July 2021.
16   Jonathan D. Jansen, *Knowledge in the Blood: Confronting Race and the Apartheid Past* (Stanford: Stanford University Press, 2009).
17   Jonathan Jansen, 'Medical Varsity Is Dying from Protests, Is in Dire Need of Life-Saving Surgery', *TimesLIVE*, 10 November 2021, https://www.timeslive.co.za/sunday-times-daily/opinion-and-analysis/2021-11-10-jonathan-jansen--medical-varsity-is-dying-from-protests-is-in-dire-need-of-life-saving-surgery/.
18   Department of Higher Education and Training, *Report of the Ministerial Task Team to Conduct an Independent Review of the University of South Africa* (Pretoria: Department of Higher Education and Training, 2021), 21.

19 James Leatt, *Conjectures: Living with Questions* (Cape Town: Karavan Press, 2021), 103.

20 Jonathan Jansen, 'When Does a University Cease to Exist?', *Mail & Guardian*, 3 February 2005, https://repository.up.ac.za/bitstream/handle/2263/340/Jansen%20%282005%29d.pdf?sequence=1&isAllowed=y.

21 Gurzawska, *Principles and Approaches in Ethics Assessment*, 5.

22 S. J. Saunders, *Report to the Minister of Education, the Honourable S. M. E. Bengu by Emeritus Professor S. J. Saunders, Appointed as Independent Assessor to Investigate the Affairs of the University of Fort Hare in Terms of Chapter 6 of the Higher Education Act, 1997* (Pretoria: Department of Education, 1999), 12, https://cisp.cachefly.net/assets/articles/attachments/10763_notice326.pdf.

23 Former Vaal University of Technology deputy vice-chancellor, Zoom interview, 21 June 2021.

24 I have written about this problem often: see 'Unisa Has a Race Problem: If You're Black, Promotion's a Walk in the Park', *TimesLIVE*, 15 August 2019, https://www.timeslive.co.za/ideas/2019-08-15-unisa-has-a-race-problem-if-youre-black-promotions-a-walk-in-the-park/; see also Sharon Dell, 'University Split over "Racist" Academic Promotion Criteria', *University World News*, 31 August 2019, https://www.universityworldnews.com/post.php?story=20190829125153963.

25 Former Mangosuthu University of Technology deputy vice-chancellor, Zoom interview, 29 April 2021.

26 Former Vaal University of Technology deputy vice-chancellor, Zoom interview, 21 June 2021.

27 Universities South Africa, 'Higher Education Leadership and Management', 2021 https://www.usaf.ac.za/higher-education-leadership-and-management-helm-programme/.

28 Former advisor to the minister of education and deputy director-general responsible for higher education, interview, 23 March 2021.

29 Kate Cox et al., *Understanding the Drivers of Organisational Capacity* (Santa Monica, CA: RAND Corporation, 2018), 7, https://www.rand.org/content/dam/rand/pubs/research_reports/RR2100/RR2189/RAND_RR2189.pdf.

30 Robert Price, *The Politics of Organizational Change* (New York: Routledge, 2019).

31 Higher Education Leadership and Management Programme director Oliver Seale, interview, 7 July 2021.

32 Nico Cloete, 'Performance Figures Show Unisa's Downward Trend', *Sunday Times*, 31 October 2021, https://www.timeslive.co.za/sunday-times/opinion-and-analysis/opinion/2021-10-31-performance-figures-show-unisas-downward-trend/.

33 Department of Higher Education and Training, *Report of the Ministerial Task Team to Conduct an Independent Review of the University of South Africa*.

34 Former University of Zululand administrator, Zoom interview, 9 March 2021.

35 Former Sefako Makgatho Health Sciences University administrator, Zoom interview, 9 March 2021.

36 Former University of Fort Hare administrator, Zoom interview, 25 March 2021.

37 Dr Jim Leatt, interim vice-chancellor of Univen at the time, interview, 29 March 2021.

38 From an article by the outstanding sociologist and opposition parliamentarian, the late Belinda Bozzoli, 'Campus Clean-Up: How the DA Would Improve SA's Universities', *Daily Maverick*, 19 February 2018, https://www.dailymaverick.co.za/opinionista/2018-02-19-campus-clean-up-how-the-da-would-improve-sas-universities/.

39   Chris Brink, Louis Molamu, and Bulelani Mahlangu, *Report of the Independent Assessor Regarding the University of Fort Hare (UFH)* (Pretoria: Department of Higher Education and Training, 2019), 13, https://www.gov.za/sites/default/files/gcis_document/201912/42902gon1592.pdf.

40   University of Fort Hare vice-chancellor, Zoom interview, 5 May 2021.

41   Chris Brink, Louis Molamu and Bulelani Mahlangu, *Report of the Independent Assessor Regarding the University of Fort Hare (UFH)* (Pretoria: Department of Higher Education and Training, 2019), https://www.gov.za/sites/default/files/gcis_document/201912/42902gon1592.pdf, 14.

42   University of Fort Hare vice-chancellor, Zoom interview, 5 May 2021.

43   Larry Pokpas, Loïs Dippenaar, and Nasima Badsha, 'The University of the Western Cape: Educating towards and for a Changed Society', in *The Responsive University and the Crisis in South Africa*, ed. Chris Brink (Boston: Brill, 2021), 322.

CHAPTER 10: RETHINKING AND REBUILDING DYSFUNCTIONAL SOUTH AFRICAN UNIVERSITIES

1   In the mid-1990s, there was a single ministry of education, responsible for both universities and schools.

2   See, for example, the somewhat dramatic headline that appeared on the front page of a major Sunday paper in the 1990s above an article by Cornia Pretorius, 'Black Students March to Pretoria', *Sunday Times*, 28 March 1999.

3   The Freedom Charter of the African National Congress, considered a foundational vision for a free South Africa, proclaimed that 'The doors of learning and of culture shall be opened'. See https://www.sahistory.org.za/article/freedom-charter.

4   Former Department of Education senior director responsible for higher education, Zoom interview, 23 March 2021.

5   Called TEFSA, the Tertiary Education Fund of South Africa, which was the forerunner of what today is called NSFAS, the National Student Financial Aid Scheme.

6   Former Department of Education senior official responsible for higher education, Zoom interview, 23 March 2021.

7   Igea Troiani and Claudia Dutson, 'The Neoliberal University as a Space to Learn/Think/Work in Higher Education', *Architecture and Culture* 9, no. 1 (2021), https://doi.org/10.1080/20507828.2021.1898836.

8   Shireen Ally and Arianna Lissoni, 'Let's Talk about bantustans', in *New Histories of South Africa's Apartheid-Era bantustans*, ed. Shireen Ally and Arianna Lissoni (New York: Routledge, 2017).

9   Linda   Chisholm,   'Late-Apartheid   Education   Reforms   and   bantustan Entanglements', *African Historical Review* 50, no. 1–2 (2018), https://doi.org/10.1080/17532523.2019.1588496.

10   From Melissa E. Steyn and Mikki van Zyl, *Like That Statue at Jammie Stairs: Some Student Perceptions and Experiences of Institutional Culture at the University of Cape Town in 1999* (Cape Town: Institute for Intercultural and Diversity Studies of Southern Africa, 2001), to Cyril K. Adonis and Fortunate Silinda, 'Institutional Culture and Transformation in Higher Education in Post-1994 South Africa: A Critical Race Theory Analysis', *Critical African Studies* 13, no. 1 (2021), https://doi.org/10.1080/21681392.2021.1911448.

11   See Jonathan D. Jansen and Cyrill A. Walters, *The Decolonization of Knowledge: Radical Ideas and the Shaping of Institutions in South Africa and Beyond* (Cambridge: Cambridge University Press, 2022).

12   Student theses contain studies of Sadtu's role and impacts in school dysfunction, such as Kathlyn McClure Pattillo, 'Quiet Corruption: Teachers' Unions and Leadership in South African Township Schools' (Honors thesis, Wesleyan University, 2012), https://digitalcollections.wesleyan.edu/object/ir-542; and Gabrielle Wills, 'An Economic Perspective on School Leadership and Teachers' Unions in South Africa' (PhD dissertation, Stellenbosch University, 2016), https://resep.sun.ac.za/wp-content/uploads/2017/10/2016-02-21-G-Wills-PhD-School-leadership-and-teachers-unions-in-South-Africa-FINAL.pdf.

13   The only major investigation of union corruption was the so-called Volmink Report on Sadtu. John Volmink et al., *Report of the Ministerial Task Team Appointed by Minister Angie Motshekga to Investigate Allegations into the Selling of Posts of Educators by Members of Teachers Unions and Departmental Officials in Provincial Education Departments: Final Report* (Pretoria: Department of Basic Education, 2016).

14   Gretchen Helmke and Steven Levitsky, 'Informal Institutions and Comparative Politics: A Research Agenda', *Perspectives on Politics* 2, no. 4 (2004): 727, https://doi.org/10.1017/S1537592704040472.

15   Former vice-chancellor and administrator of dysfunctional universities, Zoom interview, 30 March 2021.

16   One way to understand this ambivalence is to consider another South African institution, rugby, which was not only an all-white sport in terms of official recognition but also a means for expressing white supremacy. While more and more black South Africans have come round to supporting the national team, not least because of Nelson Mandela's example, many still support the once superior All Blacks with Maori players in its touring teams.

17   Malaika wa Azania, *Corridors of Death: The Struggle to Exist in Historically White Institutions* (Polokwane: Blackbird Books, 2020).

18   Sharlene Swartz et al., *Studying While Black: Race, Education and Emancipation in South African Universities* (Cape Town: HSRC Press, 2018); Lis Lange, 'South African Universities between Decolonisation and the Fourth Industrial Revolution', in *The Responsive University and the Crisis in South Africa*, ed. Chris Brink (Boston: Brill, 2021), 283.

19   Lionel Thaver, '"At Home", Institutional Culture and Higher Education: Some Methodological Considerations', *Perspectives in Education* 24, no. 1 (2006), https://journals.co.za/doi/10.10520/EJC87360.

20   See Jonathan D. Jansen, *Leading for Change: Race, Intimacy and Leadership on Divided University Campuses* (London: Routledge, 2016).

21   Department of Higher Education and Training, *Report of the Ministerial Task Team to Conduct an Independent Review of the University of South Africa* (Pretoria: Department of Higher Education and Training, 2021).

22   Department of Higher Education senior official, Zoom interview, 7 October 2021.

23   See Adam Habib, *Rebels and Rage: Reflecting on #FeesMustFall* (Johannesburg: Jonathan Ball Publishers, 2019).

24 Christiaan van der Merwe, '"Historically Black" Universities See More Student Debt', *Research Professional News*, 1 April 2021, https://www.researchprofessional news.com/rr-news-africa-south-2021-4-disadvantaged-universities-bear-brunt-of-south-africa-s-student-debt/.

25 Former University of Cape Town deputy vice-chancellor, Zoom interview, 30 September 2021.

26 Some recent incidents concerning academic freedom include the 2016 disinvitation of Danish editor Flemming Rose, who had published the controversial 'Mohammed cartoons', to deliver the T. B. Davie Memorial Lecture at UCT – see David Benatar, *The Fall of the University of Cape Town: Africa's Leading University in Decline* (Johannesburg: Politicsweb Publishing, 2021), 82–89; or the fierce debates in 2019 around the boycott of Israeli academics and universities in the light of the Palestinian struggle for justice.

27 Stuart Saunders, *Vice-Chancellor on a Tightrope: A Personal Account of Climactic Years in South Africa* (Cape Town: David Philip, 2000), 182.

28 Margaret Heffernan, *Willful Blindness: Why We Ignore the Obvious at Our Peril* (New York: Simon and Schuster, 2011).

29 Chris Brink, Louis Molamu, and Bulelani Mahlangu, *Report of the Independent Assessor Regarding the University of Fort Hare (UFH)* (Pretoria: Department of Higher Education and Training, 2019), 21, https://www.gov.za/sites/default/files/gcis_document/201912/42902gon1592.pdf.

30 Universities South Africa, 'The USAf Board Takes a Stand on Corruption', 29 October 2020, https://www.usaf.ac.za/the-usaf-board-takes-a-stand-on-corruption/.

31 Anne Heffernan, *Limpopo's Legacy: Student Politics and Democracy in South Africa* (Woodbridge, UK: Boydell and Brewer, 2019).

32 Hendi Yogi Prabowo, Jaka Sriyana, and Muhammad Syamsudin, 'Forgetting Corruption: Unlearning the Knowledge of Corruption in the Indonesian Public Sector', *Journal of Financial Crime* 25, no. 1 (2018), 29, https://doi.org/10.1108/JFC-07-2016-0048.

33 Mattias Agerberg, 'The Curse of Knowledge? Education, Corruption, and Politics', *Political Behavior* 41, no. 2 (2018), https://doi.org/10.1007/s11109-018-9455-7.

34 Harald Mathisen and Nick Duncan, *Knowledge Management for Anti-corruption* (Bergen: Ch. Michelsen Institute, 2006), https://www.cmi.no/publications/file/2561-knowledge-management-for-anti-corruption.pdf.

35 Prabowo, Sriyana, and Syamsudin, 'Forgetting Corruption'.

REFERENCES

Adonis, Cyril K., and Fortunate Silinda. 'Institutional Culture and Transformation in Higher Education in Post-1994 South Africa: A Critical Race Theory Analysis'. *Critical African Studies* 13, no. 1 (2021): 73–94. https://doi.org/10.1080/21681392.2021.1 911448.

Agerberg, Mattias. 'The Curse of Knowledge? Education, Corruption, and Politics'. *Political Behavior* 41, no. 2 (2018): 369–399. https://doi.org/10.1007/s11109-018-9455-7.

Ally, Shireen, and Arianna Lissoni. 'Let's Talk about bantustans'. In *New Histories of South Africa's Apartheid-Era bantustans*, edited by Shireen Ally and Arianna Lissoni, xi–xiv. New York: Routledge, 2017.

Amnesty International. 'Fear of Extrajudicial Execution. South Africa (Bophuthatswana): Solomon (Solly) Bokaba, Age 27, President of the Student Representative Council (SRC) at the University of Bophuthatswana (UNIBO)', AI Index: Afr 53/20/93 Distr: UA/SC. 25 May 1993. https://www.amnesty.org/en/wp-content/uploads/2021/06/afr530201993en.pdf.

Ansell, Ben W. *From the Ballot to the Blackboard: The Redistributive Political Economy of Education.* New York: Cambridge University Press, 2010.

Ashforth, Blake E., and Vikas Anand. 'The Normalization of Corruption in Organizations'. *Research in Organizational Behavior* 25 (2003): 1–52. https://doi.org/10.1016/S0191-3085(03)25001-2.

Kader, Asmal. 'Terms of Reference of the Minister of Education to the Independent Assessor to Conduct an Investigation into the Affairs of the University of Durban-Westville', in Bongani Augustine Khumalo, *Independent Assessor's Report on the Investigation at the University of Durban Westville.* Pretoria: Department of Education, 2003.

Badat, Saleem. *Black Student Politics: Higher Education and Apartheid from SASO to SANSCO, 1968–1990.* London: Routledge, 2016.

Badat, Saleem. 'An Open Letter to the Mayor, the Municipal Manager and the Makana Municipality Councillors', 14 August 2013. http://Vital.Seals.Ac.Za:8080/Vital/Access/Manager/Pdfviewer/Vital:7941/Sourcepdf?Viewpdfinternal=1.

Becker, Heike. 'South African Student Protests, 1968 to 2016: Dissent, Disruption, Decolonization'. *International Socialist Review*, no. 111 (2018). https://isreview.org/issue/111/south-african-student-protests-1968-2016/.

Beinart, William. 'Beyond "Homelands": Some Ideas about the History of African Rural Areas in South Africa'. In *New Histories of South Africa's Apartheid-Era bantustans*, edited by Shireen Ally and Arianna Lissoni, 1–17. New York: Routledge, 2017.

Benatar, David. *The Fall of the University of Cape Town: Africa's Leading University in Decline*. Johannesburg: Politicsweb Publishing, 2021.

Blase, Joseph J. 'The Micropolitical Orientation of Teachers toward Closed School Principals'. *Education and Urban Society* 23, no. 4 (1991): 356–378. https://doi.org/10.1177/0013124591023004002.

Bohn, Simone. 'Justifying Corrupt Exchanges: Rational-Choice Corruptors'. In *(Dys-) Functionalities of Corruption: Comparative Perspectives and Methodological Pluralism*, edited by Tobias Debiel and Andrea Gawrich, 159–182. Wiesbaden: Springer, 2014.

Boucher, Maurice. 'A Brief History of the South African University System'. *Historia* 18, no. 1 (1973): 59–66. https://upjournals.up.ac.za/index.php/historia/article/view/2773/2612.

Boucher, Maurice. 'Some Observations upon the Influence of Scotland in South African University Education'. *Historia* 14, no. 2 (1969): 98–106. https://journals.co.za/doi/pdf/10.10520/AJA0018229X_1159.

Boucher, Maurice. *Spes in Arduis: A History of the University of South Africa*. Pretoria: University of South Africa, 1973.

Boucher, Maurice. 'The University of the Cape of Good Hope and the University of South Africa, 1873–1946: A Study in National and Imperial Perspective'. PhD thesis, University of South Africa, 1970.

Boucher, Maurice. *The University of the Cape of Good Hope and the University of South Africa, 1873–1946: A Study in National and Imperial Perspective*. Pretoria: Government Printer, 1974.

Bowles, Samuel, and Herbert Gintis. *Schooling in Capitalist America: Educational Reform and the Contradictions of Economic Life*. New York: Basic Books, 1976.

Boyce, James K. 'Political Economy of the Environment: A Look Back and Ahead'. In *The Routledge Handbook of the Political Economy of the Environment*, edited by Éloi Laurent and Klara Zwickl, 13–25. London: Routledge, 2021.

Bozzoli, Belinda. 'Campus Clean-Up: How the DA Would Improve SA's Universities'. *Daily Maverick*, 19 February 2018. https://www.dailymaverick.co.za/opinionista/2018-02-19-campus-clean-up-how-the-da-would-improve-sas-universities/.

Brink, Chris, Louis Molamu, and Bulelani Mahlangu. *Report of the Independent Assessor Regarding the University of Fort Hare (UFH)*. Pretoria: Department of Higher Education and Training, 2019. https://www.gov.za/sites/default/files/gcis_document/201912/42902gon1592.pdf.

Brown, Julian. 'An Experiment in Confrontation: The Pro-Frelimo Rallies of 1974'. *Journal of Southern African Studies* 38, no. 1 (2012): 55–71. https://doi.org/10.1080/03057070.2012.644978.

Brown, Julian. *The Road to Soweto: Resistance and the Uprising of 16 June 1976*. Woodbridge, UK: James Currey, 2016.

Bunting, Ian. 'Funding'. In *Transformation in Higher Education: Global Pressures and Local Realities in South Africa*, edited by Nico Cloete, Richard Fehnel, Peter Maassen, Teboho Moja, Helene Perold, and Trish Gibbon, 73–94. Cape Town: Juta, 2002.

Bureau for Economic Research. *Economic Impact Assessment of Stellenbosch University on the Local Municipal Area*. Stellenbosch: Stellenbosch University, 2018. https://www.sun.ac.za/english/Documents/Economic%20Impact%20Study/BER-Final-EIA-new.pdf.

BusinessTech. 'Massive Fake Degrees Scandal Uncovered at South African University'. 31 July 2016. https://businesstech.co.za/news/business/132052/massive-fake-degrees-scandal-uncovered-at-south-african-university/.

Buthelezi, Londiwe. 'Police Looking for Ex-SABC Chair Ellen Tshabalala'. *News24*, 18 March 2020. https://www.news24.com/fin24/companies/ict/police-looking-for-ex-sabc-chair-ellen-tshabalala-20200318.

Carlin, John. 'Tough Talk from ANC's Man in Inkatha Territory: In Zululand, a Defiant Aaron Ndlovu Is Ready for Any Conflict to Come'. *The Independent*, 22 July 1993. https://www.independent.co.uk/news/world/tough-talk-from-anc-s-man-in-inkatha-territory-in-zululand-a-defiant-aaron-ndlovu-is-ready-for-any-conflict-to-come-writes-john-carlin-in-empangeni-1486545.html.

Carugati, Federica, and Margaret Levi. *A Moral Political Economy: Present, Past, and Future*. Cambridge: Cambridge University Press, 2021.

Cele, Gabriel, and Charlton Koen. 'Student Politics in South Africa. An Overview of Key Developments'. *Cahiers de la Recherche sur l'Éducation et les Savoirs* 2 (2003): 201–223.

Chetty, Nithaya, and Christopher Merrett. *The Struggle for the Soul of a South African University: The University of KwaZulu-Natal; Academic Freedom, Corporatisation and Transformation*. Self-published, 2014.

Chipkin, Ivor, and Mark Swilling, eds. *Shadow State: The Politics of State Capture*. Johannesburg: Wits University Press, 2018.

Chisholm, Linda. 'Late-Apartheid Education Reforms and bantustan Entanglements'. *African Historical Review* 50, no. 1–2 (2018): 27–45. https://doi.org/10.1080/17532523.2019.1588496.

Cloete, Nico. 'Performance Figures Show Unisa's Downward Trend'. *Sunday Times*, 31 October 2021. https://www.timeslive.co.za/sunday-times/opinion-and-analysis/opinion/2021-10-31-performance-figures-show-unisas-downward-trend/.

Cloete, Nico, and N. Mohamed. 'Transformation Forums as Revolutionary Councils: Midwives to Democracy or Advisory Councils for Restructuring and Innovation'. Unpublished discussion paper, Union of Democratic University Staff Associations, 1995.

Cloete, Nico, Richard Fehnel, Peter Maassen, Teboho Moja, Helene Perold, and Trish Gibbon, eds. *Transformation in Higher Education: Global Pressures and Local Realities in South Africa*. Cape Town: Juta, 2002.

Cox, Kate, Stephen Jolly, Simon van der Staaij, and Christian van Stolk. *Understanding the Drivers of Organisational Capacity*. Santa Monica, CA: RAND Corporation, 2018. https://www.rand.org/content/dam/rand/pubs/research_reports/RR2100/RR2189/RAND_RR2189.pdf.

Davies, Gordon K. 'General Threats to Institutional Integrity'. *New Directions for Community Colleges*, no. 52 (1985): 29–36. https://doi.org/10.1002/cc.36819855205.

Davies, John. 'The State and the South African University System under Apartheid'. *Comparative Education* 32, no. 3 (1996): 319–332. https://doi.org/10.1080/03050069628740.

Davies, Rob. *Towards a New Deal: A Political Economy of the Times of My Life*. Johannesburg: Jonathan Ball, 2021.

Dayimani, Malibongwe. 'Fort Hare University Lays Charges against Fugitive Professor Linked to Premier Oscar Mabuyane'. *News24*, 25 March 2021. https://www.news24.com/news24/southafrica/news/fort-hare-university-lays-charges-against-premier-oscar-mabuyanes-fugitive-nigerian-professor-20210325.

Dayimani, Malibongwe. 'Sibongile Mani Sentenced to 5 Years' Imprisonment for Theft of NSFAS Funds'. *News24*, 30 March 2022. https://www.news24.com/news24/newsletters/icymi/featured/sibongile-mani-sentenced-to-5-years-imprisonment-for-theft-of-nsfas-funds-20220330.

Dayimani, Malibongwe. 'Two Senior University of Fort Hare Officials Quit amid Hawks Probe into Alleged NSFAS Corruption.' News24, 21 October 2021. https://www.news24.com/news24/southafrica/news/two-senior-university-of-fort-hare-officials-quit-amid-hawks-probe-into-alleged-nsfas-corruption-20211021.

Dayimani, Malibongwe, and Sino Majangaza. 'Oscar Slams Fort Hare VC over Crisis of Killings'. Daily Dispatch, 24 February 2020. https://www.dispatchlive.co.za/news/2020-02-24-oscar-slams-fort-hare-vc-over-crisis-of-killings/.

De Clercq, Francine. 'Black Universities as Contested Terrains: The Politics of Progressive Engagement'. Perspectives in Education 12, no. 2 (1991): 49–64. https://www.researchgate.net/profile/Francine-De-Clercq/publication/271846181_Black_Universities_as_contested_terrains_the_politics_of_progressive_engagement/links/60e327cd92851ca944aaf2f9/Black-Universities-as-contested-terrains-the-politics-of-progressive-engagement.pdf.

Degenaar, Johannes. 'The Concept of a Volksuniversiteit'. In The Future of the University in South Africa, edited by H. W. van der Merwe and David Welsh, 148–171. Cape Town: David Philip, 1977.

Dell, Sharon. 'University Split over "Racist" Academic Promotion Criteria'. University World News, 31 August 2019. https://www.universityworldnews.com/post.php?story=20190829125153963.

Denisova-Schmidt, Elena. Corruption in Higher Education: Global Challenges and Responses. Boston: Brill, 2020.

Department of Education. Education White Paper 3: A Programme for the Transformation of Higher Education. Pretoria: Department of Education, 1997. https://www.gov.za/sites/default/files/gcis_document/201409/18207gen11960.pdf.

Department of Higher Education and Training. Ministerial Statement on University Funding: 2015/16 and 2016/17. Pretoria: Department of Higher Education and Training, 2014. https://www.dhet.gov.za/Financial%20and%20Physical%20Planning/Ministerial%20Statement%20at%20University%20funding;%202015-16%20and%20 2016-2017,%20November%202014.pdf.

Department of Higher Education and Training. Ministerial Statement on University Funding: 2021/22 and 2022/23. Pretoria: Department of Higher Education and Training, 2020. https://www.dhet.gov.za/Institutional%20Funding/Ministerial%20 Statement%20on%20University%20Funding,%20Dec%202020.pdf.

Department of Higher Education and Training. Report of the Ministerial Task Team to Conduct an Independent Review of the University of South Africa. Pretoria: Department of Higher Education and Training, 2021.

Department of Higher Education and Training. Report on the Evaluation of 2018 Universities' Research Output. Pretoria: Department of Higher Education and Training, 2020. https://www.up.ac.za/media/shared/1/2020/May%202020/report-on-the-evaluation-of-the-2018-universities-research-output_april_2020.doc.zp189504.pdf.

Department of Higher Education and Training. Summary of Recent Assessor Reports and CHE Publications on the Governance of Universities. Pretoria: Department of Higher Education and Training, 2016.

Department of Higher Education and Training. University State Budgets. Pretoria: Department of Higher Education and Training, 2021. https://www.dhet.gov.za/Institutional%20Funding/University%20State%20budgets,%20March%202021.xls.

Dlodlo, Cathy. 'FS Health Stays under Administration'. OFM News, 9 November 2016. https://www.ofm.co.za/article/local-news/208775/fs-health-stays-under-administration.

Donnelly, Lynley. 'Rise of the New Construction "Mafia"'. *Mail & Guardian*, 12 April 2019. https://mg.co.za/article/2019-04-12-00-rise-of-the-new-construction-mafia/.

Düger, Yavuz Selim. '"Willful Blindness" as a Dark Side of Organizational Behavior: Can Effective Leadership Overcome This Challenge?' In *Studies on Interdisciplinary Economics and Business*, edited by Özer Özçelik and Adil Akinci, 303–312. Pieterlen: Peter Lang, 2020.

Einstein, Katherine Levine, Maxwell Palmer, and David M. Glick. 'Who Participates in Local Government? Evidence from Meeting Minutes'. *Perspectives on Politics* 17, no. 1 (2019): 28–46. https://doi.org/10.1017/S153759271800213X.

Elmore, Richard F. 'Backward Mapping: Implementation Research and Policy Decisions'. In *Studying Implementation: Methodological and Administrative Issues*, edited by Walter Williams, 1982, 18–35. Chatham, NJ: Chatham House Publishers, 1982.

eNCA. 'Free State MEC in Court'. 29 November 2013. https://www.enca.com/south-africa/free-state-mec-court.

Essop, Ahmed. *Institutional Governance in the Higher Education System in South Africa*. Pretoria: Council on Higher Education, 2015.

Fengu, Msindisi. 'VUT Embroiled in R20m Laptop Tender Scandal after Going "Independent Procurement Route"'. *News24*, 4 August 2021. https://www.news24.com/citypress/news/vut-embroiled-in-r20m-laptop-tender-scandal-after-going-independent-procurement-route-20210804.

Feni, Lulamile. 'King Dalindyebo Vows to Shut Down WSU, Take Back the Land'. *HeraldLIVE*, 27 February 2021. https://www.heraldlive.co.za/news/2021-02-27-king-dalindyebo-vows-to-shut-down-wsu-take-back-the-land/.

Fourie, Magda. 'Institutional Transformation at South African Universities: Implications for Academic Staff'. *Higher Education* 38, no. 3 (1999): 275–290. https://doi.org/10.1023/A:1003768229291.

Gautschi, Johan, Linda Zama, and Hoosen Jerry Coovadia. *Report of the Presidential Commission of Inquiry with Respect to the University of Durban-Westville*. Pretoria: Department of Education, 1996.

Gómez, Ismael, Jorge Costa Delgado, and Johannes Angermüller. 'How to Become an Academic Philosopher: Academic Discourse as a Multileveled Positioning Practice'. *Sociología Histórica*, no. 2 (2013): 263–320.

Goodenough, Cheryl. 'Mangosuthu Technikon'. *Focus*, no. 16 (1999). https://hsf.org.za/publications/focus/issue-16-fourth-quarter-1999/mangosuthu-technikon.

Gower, Primarashni, and Monako Dibetle. 'The Vice in VC'. *Mail & Guardian*, 5 November 2008. https://mg.co.za/article/2008-11-05-the-vice-in-vc/.

Griffin, Anne-Marea. 'Toward Deliberative Democracy: The Institutional Forum as an Innovative Shared Governance Mechanism in South African Higher Education'. *African Journal of Business Ethics* 12, no. 1 (2018). https://doi.org/10.15249/12-1-160.

GroundUp. 'How the Free State Health System Is Being Destroyed'. *GroundUp*, 27 February 2015. https://www.groundup.org.za/media/features/freestatehealth/freestatehealth.html.

Gurzawska, Agata. *Principles and Approaches in Ethics Assessment: Institutional Integrity*. Enschede: Satori, 2015. https://satoriproject.eu/media/1.e-Institutional-Integrity.pdf.

Gwala, Nkosinathi. 'State Control, Student Politics and the Crisis in Black Universities'. In *Popular Struggles in South Africa*, edited by William Cobbett and Robin Cohen, 163–182. London: James Currey, 1988.

Habib, Adam. 'The Institutional Crisis of the University of the Transkei'. *Politikon* 28, no. 2 (2001): 157–179. https://doi.org/10.1080/02589340120091637.

Habib, Adam. *Rebels and Rage: Reflecting on #FeesMustFall*. Johannesburg: Jonathan Ball Publishers, 2019.

Habib, Adam. *Structural Disadvantage, Leadership Ineptitude, and Stakeholder Complicity: A Study of the Institutional Crisis of the University of the Transkei*. Rondebosch: Centre for Higher Education Transformation, 2000.

Hall, Martin. 'Institutional Culture of Mergers and Alliances in South Africa'. In *Mergers and Alliances in Higher Education: International Practice and Emerging Opportunities*, edited by Adrian Curaj, Luke Georghiou, and Jennifer Casenga Harper, 145–173. Cham: Springer, 2015.

Hall, Martin, Ashley Symes, and Thierry M. Luescher. *Governance in South African Higher Education: Research Report Prepared for the Council on Higher Education*. Pretoria: Council on Higher Education, 2002.

Harper, A., N. Olivier, S. Thobakgale, and Z. Tshwete. *Institutional Forums: An Overview of Their Establishment and Functioning at South African Public Higher Education Institutions*. Pretoria: Centre for Higher Education Transformation, 2002.

Harris, John, Liam Maher, Gerald Ferris, and Zachary Russell. 'Power, Politics, and Influence in Organizations'. In *International Encyclopedia of the Social and Behavioral Sciences*, edited by James D. Wright, 770–775. Amsterdam: Elsevier, 2015.

Hartigan-O'Connor, Ellen. 'The Personal Is Political Economy'. *Journal of the Early Republic* 36, no. 2 (2016): 335–341. https://doi.org/10.1353/jer.2016.0026.

Heffernan, Anne. *Limpopo's Legacy: Student Politics and Democracy in South Africa*. Woodbridge, UK: Boydell and Brewer, 2019.

Heffernan, Margaret. *Willful Blindness: Why We Ignore the Obvious at Our Peril*. New York: Simon and Schuster, 2011.

Helmke, Gretchen, and Steven Levitsky. 'Informal Institutions and Comparative Politics: A Research Agenda'. *Perspectives on Politics* 2, no. 4 (2004): 725–740. https://doi.org/10.1017/S1537592704040472.

Hendricks, Fred. 'The Mafeje Affair: The University of Cape Town and Apartheid'. *African Studies* 67, no. 3 (2008): 423–451. https://doi.org/10.1080/00020180802505061.

Honigmann, David. 'The Roelf 'n' Cyril Show'. *The Independent*, 10 June 1995. https://www.independent.co.uk/arts-entertainment/the-roelf-n-cyril-show-1586014.html.

Hugo, Pierre J. 'Academic Dissent and Apartheid in South Africa'. *Journal of Black Studies* 7, no. 3 (1977): 243–262. https://doi.org/10.1177/002193477700700301.

Hunter, A. P. 'South Africa's Crisis in Education'. Senate Special Lecture, University of the Witwatersrand, 1978.

Hunter, Qaanitah, Jeff Wicks, and Kaveel Singh. *Eight Days in July: Inside the Zuma Unrest That Set South Africa Alight*. Cape Town: Tafelberg, 2021.

Hyslop, Jonathan. 'Political Corruption: Before and after Apartheid'. *Journal of Southern African Studies* 31, no. 4 (2005): 773–789. https://doi.org/10.1080/03057070500370555.

IGI Global. 'What Is Cultural Resources'. 2022. https://www.igi-global.com/dictionary/cultural-management-for-multinational-enterprises/44712.

Independent Online. 'Free State MEC Killed in Crash'. 2 December 2012. https://www.iol.co.za/news/politics/free-state-mec-killed-in-crash-1434213.

Jacob, Bhongo. '"Millionaire NSFAS Student" Sibongile Mani Fails to Have Case Discharged'. *TimesLIVE*, 20 October 2021. https://www.timeslive.co.za/news/south-africa/2021-10-20-millionaire-nsfas-student-sibongile-mani-fails-to-have-case-discharged/.

Jansen, Jonathan D. *As by Fire: The End of the South African University.* Cape Town: Tafelberg, 2017.

Jansen, Jonathan D. *Knowledge in the Blood: Confronting Race and the Apartheid Past.* Stanford: Stanford University Press, 2009.

Jansen, Jonathan D. *Leading for Change: Race, Intimacy and Leadership on Divided University Campuses.* London: Routledge, 2016.

Jansen, Jonathan D. 'Medical Varsity Is Dying from Protests, Is in Dire Need of Life-Saving Surgery'. *TimesLIVE*, 10 November 2021. https://www.timeslive.co.za/sunday-times-daily/opinion-and-analysis/2021-11-10-jonathan-jansen--medical-varsity-is-dying-from-protests-is-in-dire-need-of-life-saving-surgery/.

Jansen, Jonathan D. 'UNISA Has a Race Problem: If You're Black, Promotion's a Walk in the Park'. *TimesLIVE*, 15 August 2019. https://www.timeslive.co.za/ideas/2019-08-15-unisa-has-a-race-problem-if-youre-black-promotions-a-walk-in-the-park/.

Jansen, Jonathan D. 'When Does a University Cease to Exist?' *Mail & Guardian*, 3 February 2005. https://repository.up.ac.za/bitstream/handle/2263/340/Jansen%20%282005%29d.pdf?sequence=1&isAllowed=y.

Jansen, Jonathan D., and Cyrill A. Walters. *The Decolonization of Knowledge: Radical Ideas and the Shaping of Institutions in South Africa and Beyond.* Cambridge: Cambridge University Press, 2022.

Jansen, Mabel, Ben Khoapa, and Seth Radebe. *Report of the Commission of Inquiry: Vaal University of Technology.* Vanderbijlpark: Vaal University of Technology, 2006.

Kahn, Tamar. 'Naming and Shaming Fake Degrees'. *TimesLIVE*, 1 August 2018. https://www.timeslive.co.za/news/south-africa/2018-08-01-naming-and-shaming-fake-degrees/.

Kerr, Andrew, and Phillip Jager. 'A Description of Predatory Publishing in South African Economics Departments'. *South African Journal of Economics* 89, no. 3 (2021): 439–456. https://doi.org/10.1111/saje.12278.

Khumalo, Bongani Augustine. *Report to the Minister of Education, Professor K. Asmal, M.P.: Independent Assessor's Report on the Investigation at the University of Durban Westville.* Pretoria: Government Printer, 2003.

King, Brian H., and Brent McCusker. 'Environment and Development in the Former South African bantustans'. *Geographical Journal* 173, no. 1 (2007): 6–12. https://doi.org/10.1111/j.1475-4959.2007.00229.x.

King, Charles. 'The Micropolitics of Social Violence'. *World Politics* 56, no. 3 (2004): 431–455. https://doi.org/10.1353/wp.2004.0016.

Kingdon, Geeta Gandhi, Angela Little, Monazza Aslam, Shenila Rawal, Terry Moe, Harry Patrinos, Tara Beteille, Rukmini Banerji, Brent Parton, and Shailendra K. Sharma. *A Rigorous Review of the Political Economy of Education Systems in Developing Countries.* London: Department for International Development, 2014. https://eppi.ioe.ac.uk/cms/Portals/0/PDF%20reviews%20and%20summaries/Political%20economy%202014Kingdon.pdf?ver=2014-04-24-141259-443.

Kirby, Nikolas. 'An "Institution-First" Conception of Public Integrity'. *British Journal of Political Science* 51, no. 4 (2021): 1620–1635. https://doi.org/10.1017/S000712342000006X.

Kirya, Monica. 'Corruption in Universities: Paths to Integrity in the Higher Education Subsector'. Bergen: Chr. Michelsen Institute, 2019. https://www.u4.no/publications/

corruption-in-universities-paths-to-integrity-in-the-higher-education-subsector.
pdf.

Kleynhans, Ewert P. J., and David Dyason. 'A University in a Small City: Discovering Which Sectors Benefit'. *Acta Commercii* 17, no. 1 (2017): 1–13. https://doi.org/10.4102/ac.v17i1.513.

Kulati, Tembile. *Analysis of Recent Assessor Reports of Universities in SA*. Pretoria: Higher Education South Africa, 2012. http://www.usaf.ac.za/wp-content/uploads/2017/08/2012_HESA_Analysis-of-Assessor-Reports-of-Universities-in-SA_Oct.pdf.

Lange, Lis. 'South African Universities between Decolonisation and the Fourth Industrial Revolution'. In *The Responsive University and the Crisis in South Africa*, edited by Chris Brink, 272–299. Boston: Brill, 2021.

Lasswell, Harold D. *Politics: Who Gets What, When, How*. New York: Whittlesey, 1936.

Leatt, James. *Conjectures: Living with Questions*. Cape Town: Karavan Press, 2021.

Leftwich, Adrian. *Drivers of Change: Refining the Analytical Framework*. Part 1: *Conceptual and Theoretical Issues*. York: University of York, 2006. http://www.gsdrc.org/docs/open/doc103.pdf.

Lokot, Michelle, and Amiya Bhatia. 'Unequal and Invisible: A Feminist Political Economy Approach to Valuing Women's Care Labor in the Covid-19 Response'. *Frontiers in Sociology* 5 (2020): 1–4. https://doi.org/10.3389/fsoc.2020.588279.

Luescher, Thierry. *The State of Transformation in South Africa's Public Universities: A Research Report Prepared by the Human Sciences Research Council on Behalf of the Ministerial Oversight Committee on Transformation in the South African Public Universities*. Pretoria: Human Sciences Research Council, 2021.

Lumby, Jacky. *In the Wings and Backstage: Exploring the Micropolitics of Leadership in Higher Education*. London: Leadership Foundation for Higher Education, 2015. https://eprints.soton.ac.uk/386161/.

Lumby, Jacky. 'Let's Shine a Light on the Dark Art of Micropolitics in Universities'. *The Guardian*, 15 October 2015. https://www.theguardian.com/higher-education-network/2015/oct/15/lets-shine-a-light-on-the-dark-art-of-micropolitics-in-universities.

Maake, Nhlanhla P. *Barbarism in Higher Education: Once upon a Time in a University*. Johannesburg: Ekaam Book, 2011.

Macroeconomic Research Group. *Making Democracy Work: A Framework for Macroeconomic Policy in South Africa; A Report to Members of the Democratic Movement of South Africa*. Bellville: Centre for Development Studies, University of the Western Cape, 1993.

Macupe, Bongekile. 'Is the Vaal University of Technology an Institution Bewitched?' *News24*, 25 July 2021. https://www.news24.com/citypress/news/is-the-vaal-university-of-technology-an-institution-bewitched-20210725.

Mail & Guardian. 'It's Spy vs Spy at UDW'. 13 October 1995. https://mg.co.za/article/1995-10-13-its-spy-vs-spy-at-udw/.

Mangosuthu University of Technology. 'Rectors and Vice-Chancellor'. 2022. https://www.mut.ac.za/mut40/rectors-and-vice-chancellor/.

Mann, Michael. 'The Autonomous Power of the State: Its Origins, Mechanisms, and Results'. In *States in History*, edited by John A. Hall, 109–136. Oxford: Blackwell, 1986.

Mann, Michael. *The Sources of Social Power*, vol. 2: *The Rise of Classes and Nation States, 1760–1914*. Cambridge: Cambridge University Press, 1993.

Maphai, Vincent. *Developing a Culture of Good Governance: Report of the Presidential Review Commission on the Reform and Transformation of the Public Service in South Africa*. Pretoria: Presidential Review Commission, 1998. https://www.gov.za/documents/report-presidential-review-commission-reform-and-transformation-public-service-south.

Maphai, Vincent. *Report of the Independent Assessor, Dr. Vincent Maphai, to the Honourable Minister of Education G. N. M. Pandor, M.P.: Investigation into the Mangosuthu University of Technology*. Pretoria: Government Printer, 2008.

Marx, Karl. 'Eighteenth Brumaire of Louis Bonaparte'. https://www.marxists.org/archive/marx/works/1852/18th-brumaire/ch01.htm.

Mathisen, Harald, and Nick Duncan. *Knowledge Management for Anti-corruption*. Bergen: Ch. Michelsen Institute, 2006. https://www.cmi.no/publications/file/2561-knowledge-management-for-anti-corruption.pdf.

Matthews, Zacharia Keodirelang. 'University College of Fort Hare'. *South African Outlook*, April–May 1957: 1–35. https://uir.unisa.ac.za/bitstream/handle/10500/5795/ZKM_C4_13.pdf?sequence=1&isAllowed=y.

Mawasha, Abram L. 'Turfloop: Where an Idea Was Expressed, Hijacked and Redeemed'. In *Within the Realm of Possibility: From Disadvantage to Development at the University of Fort Hare and the University of the North*, edited by Mokubung O. Nkomo, Derrick Swartz, and Botshabelo Maja, 65–84. Pretoria: HSRC Press, 2006.

Menocal, Alina Rocha, Marc Cassidy, Sarah Swift, David Jacobstein, Corinne Rothblum, and Ilona Tservil. *Thinking and Working Politically through Applied Political Economy Analysis: A Guide for Practitioners*. Washington DC: United States Agency for International Development, 2018. https://usaidlearninglab.org/sites/default/files/resource/files/pea_guide_final.pdf.

Meny-Gibert, Sarah. 'State "Infrastructural Power" and the bantustans: The Case of School Education in the Transkei and Ciskei'. *African Historical Review* 50, no. 1–2 (2018): 46–77. https://www.tandfonline.com/doi/abs/10.1080/17532523.2019.1580422.

Meyer, John W., and Brian Rowan. 'Institutionalized Organizations: Formal Structure as Myth and Ceremony'. *American Journal of Sociology* 83, no. 2 (1977): 340–363. https://doi.org/10.1086/226550.

Ministry of Education. 'Standard Institutional Statute'. *Government Gazette* 41, no. 23065 (27 March 2002). https://www.gov.za/sites/default/files/gcis_document/201409/230650.pdf.

Mkhwanazi, Siyabonga. 'State Cracking Down on Officials with Fake Qualifications'. *Independent Online*, 1 December 2018. https://www.iol.co.za/news/politics/state-cracking-down-on-officials-with-fake-qualifications-18344271.

Mlangeni, Thobile. 'No Degree of Success in UMP Negotiations with Taxi Associations'. *Mpumalanga News*, 17 June 2021. https://mpumalanganews.co.za/397491/no-degree-of-success-in-ump-negotiations-with-taxi-associations/.

Mlangeni, Thobile. 'Taxi Associations Protest, Demand to Transport Students'. *Mpumalanga News*, 11 June 2021. https://mpumalanganews.co.za/397097/taxi-associations-protest-demand-to-transport-students/.

Moatshe, Rapula. 'R17m Sefako Makgatho Health Sciences University Laptop Tender "Delayed by Management Feud"'. *Independent Online*, 17 September 2021. https://www.iol.co.za/pretoria-news/news/r17m-sefako-makgatho-health-sciences-university-laptop-tender-delayed-by-management-feud-61d6c923-fad2-4305-986c-06e563d4c27e.

Mokadi, Aubrey. *A Portrait of Governance in Higher Education: Taking a Stand for Transformation*. Johannesburg: Sedibeng, 2002.

Moodie, Graeme. 'The State and the Liberal Universities in South Africa: 1948–1990'. *Higher Education* 27, no. 1 (1994): 1–40. https://doi.org/10.1007/BF01383758.

Morlan, Gail. 'The Student Revolt against Racism in South Africa'. *Africa Today* 17, no. 3 (1970): 12–20.

Morrow, Sean. 'Fort Hare in Its Local Context: A Historical View'. In *Within the Realm of Possibility: From Disadvantage to Development at the University of Fort Hare and the University of the North*, edited by Mokubung O. Nkomo, Derrick Swartz, and Botshabelo Maja, 85–103. Pretoria: HSRC Press, 2006.

Mosco, Vincent. *The Political Economy of Communication*. London: Sage Publications, 2009.

Mouton, Johann, and Astrid Valentine. 'The Extent of South African Authored Articles in Predatory Journals'. *South African Journal of Science* 113, no. 7–8 (2017): 79–87. https://doi.org/10.17159/sajs.2017/20170010.

Mouton, Johann, Herman Redelinghuys, Johann Spies, Jaco Blanckenberg, Lynn Lorenzen, Kyle Ford, Annemarie Visagie, and Marthie van Niekerk. *The Quality of South Africa's Research Publications: Final Report to the DHET*. Stellenbosch: Centre for Research on Evaluation, Science and Technology, 2019. https://www.researchgate.net/publication/348658730_THE_QUALITY_OF_SOUTH_AFRICA%27S_RESEARCH_PUBLICATIONS_Final_report_to_the_DHET.

Mugume, Taabo, and Thierry Luescher. 'Student Politics at Makerere University in the Lens of Schmitter and Streeck's Framework: Student Leaders and Political Parties'. *Makerere Journal of Higher Education* 9, no. 1 (2017): 133–160.

Muller, Sen. 'The Murder of Prof Kamwendo at UniZulu'. *Mail & Guardian*, 8 December 2018. https://mg.co.za/article/2018-12-08-letter-the-murder-of-prof-kamwendo-at-unizulu/.

Myburgh, Pieter-Louis. *The Republic of Gupta: A Story of State Capture*. Cape Town: Penguin Books, 2017.

Naidoo, Amelia. 'DUT Students Threaten Mass Action'. *Independent Online*, 16 August 2006. https://www.iol.co.za/news/south-africa/dut-students-threaten-mass-action-289554.

Napier, Clive. 'The Transkei bantustan and Its University: A Crisis of Legitimacy'. *Reality* 18, no. 2 (1985): 15–18. https://www.sahistory.org.za/sites/default/files/DC/remar85.5/remar85.5.pdf.

National Commission on Higher Education. *NCHE Report: A Framework for Transformation*. Pretoria: National Commission on Higher Education, 1996.

National Student Financial Aid Scheme. 'Performance of NSFAS under Administration: Handover Report from the Executive Administrator'. Cape Town: National Student Financial Aid Scheme, 2020.

Ndebele, Njabulo S. 'Creative Instability: The Case of the South African Higher Education System'. *Journal of Negro Education* 66, no. 4 (1997): 443–448. https://doi.org/10.2307/2668171.

Ndebele, Njabulo S. 'The University of the North in the New Era: What the Mosquito Thinks (1994)'. In *Fine Lines from the Box: Further Thoughts about Our Country*. Cape Town: Umuzi, 2007.

News24. 'Why SABC Boss Loves Meetings'. *News24*, 12 October 2014. https://www.news24.com/News24/Why-SABC-boss-loves-meetings-20150429.

News24. 'With R14m "She Should Have Built Me a House!"' *News24*, 3 September 2017. https://www.news24.com/News24/with-r14m-she-should-have-built-me-a-house-20170903-2.

Njilo, Nonkululeko. 'Up to R2bn Paid by NSFAS to Wrong Students "Could Be Irrecoverable"'. *TimesLIVE*, 12 March 2020. https://www.timeslive.co.za/news/south-africa/2020-03-12-up-to-r2bn-paid-by-nsfas-to-wrong-students-could-be-irrecoverable/.

Nkomo, Mokubung O. *Student Culture and Activism in Black South African Universities: The Roots of Resistance*. Westport, CT: Greenwood Press, 1984.

Novelli, Mario, Sean Higgins, Mehmet Ugur, and Oscar Valiente. *The Political Economy of Education Systems in Conflict-Affected Contexts: A Rigorous Literature Review*. London: Department for International Development, 2014. http://eppi.ioe.ac.uk/cms/Portals/0/PDF%20reviews%20and%20summaries/Political%20Economy%20Education%202014%20Novelli%20report.pdf?ver=2014-11-24-104035-650.

Ogude, Nthabiseng. *The Making of a Sharpeville Girl: Narratives of Exile and Return to South Africa*. Forthcoming.

Omal, Felix. 'Micro-politics of Student Participation in University Leadership across the Historically Black Universities'. *World Studies in Education* 20, no. 1 (2019): 67–82.

O'Malley, Padraig. *National Education Coordinating Committee (NECC)*. 1991. https://omalley.nelsonmandela.org/omalley/index.php/site/q/03lv02424/04lv02730/05lv03188/06lv03208.htm.

Osei-Hwedie, Bertha Z., and Kwaku Osei-Hwedie. 'The Political, Economic, and Cultural Bases of Corruption in Africa'. In *Corruption and Development in Africa: Lessons from Country Case-Studies*, edited by Kempe R. Hope and Bornwell C. Chikulo, 40–56. London: Palgrave, 2000.

Padayachee, Vishnu. 'Can Progressive Macroeconomic Policy Address Growth and Employment While Reducing Inequality in South Africa?' *Economic and Labour Relations Review* 30, no. 1 (2019): 3–21. https://doi.org/10.1177/1035304619826862.

Pattillo, Kathlyn McClure. 'Quiet Corruption: Teachers' Unions and Leadership in South African Township Schools'. Honors thesis, Wesleyan University, 2012. https://digitalcollections.wesleyan.edu/object/ir-542.

Pieterse, Marius. 'How Structural Flaws Contribute to the Crisis in South Africa's Municipalities'. *The Conversation*, 29 August 2018. https://theconversation.com/how-structural-flaws-contribute-to-the-crisis-in-south-africas-municipalities-102136.

Pityana, N. Barney, and M. D. Rocky Ralebipi-Simela. 'Report of the Independent Assessors on the State of the Vaal University of Technology'. *Government Gazette*, no. 43015, 14 February 2020: 43–115. https://www.gov.za/sites/default/files/gcis_document/202002/43015gon127.pdf.

Pokpas, Larry, Loïs Dippenaar, and Nasima Badsha. 'The University of the Western Cape: Educating towards and for a Changed Society'. In *The Responsive University and the Crisis in South Africa*, edited by Chris Brink, 312–338. Boston: Brill, 2021.

Prabowo, Hendi Yogi, Jaka Sriyana, and Muhammad Syamsudin. 'Forgetting Corruption: Unlearning the Knowledge of Corruption in the Indonesian Public

Sector'. *Journal of Financial Crime* 25, no. 1 (2018): 28–56. https://doi.org/10.1108/JFC-07-2016-0048.

Pretorius, Cornia. 'Black Students March to Pretoria'. *Sunday Times*, 28 March 1999.

Price, Robert. *The Politics of Organizational Change*. New York: Routledge, 2019.

Republic of South Africa. Higher Education Act 101 of 1997. Pretoria: Government Printer, 1997. https://www.gov.za/sites/default/files/gcis_document/201409/a101-97.pdf.

Robertson, David. 'The Emerging Political Economy of Higher Education'. *Studies in Higher Education* 23, no. 2 (1998): 221–228. https://doi.org/10.1080/03075079812331380414.

Rogers, Lisa, Aoife de Brún, Sarah A. Birken, Carmel Davies, and Eilish McAuliffe. 'The Micropolitics of Implementation: A Qualitative Study Exploring the Impact of Power, Authority, and Influence When Implementing Change in Healthcare Teams'. *BMC Health Services Research* 20, no. 1 (2020): 1–13. https://doi.org/10.1186/s12913-020-05905-z.

Ronnie, Linda, and Suki Goodman. 'People Are Buying Fake Degrees Now More Than Ever'. *The Citizen*, 5 February 2019. https://www.citizen.co.za/news/south-africa/education/2077568/people-are-buying-fake-degrees-now-more-than-ever/.

Saba, Athandiwe. 'Deadly Twist to University Dispute'. *Mail & Guardian*, 7 December 2018. https://mg.co.za/article/2018-12-07-00-deadly-twist-to-university-dispute/.

Saunders, S. J. *Report to the Minister of Education, the Honourable S. M. E. Bengu by Emeritus Professor S. J. Saunders, Appointed as Independent Assessor to Investigate the Affairs of the University of Fort Hare in Terms of Chapter 6 of the Higher Education Act, 1997*. Pretoria: Department of Education, 1999. https://cisp.cachefly.net/assets/articles/attachments/10763_notice326.pdf.

Saunders, S. J. *Vice-Chancellor on a Tightrope: A Personal Account of Climactic Years in South Africa*. Cape Town: David Philip, 2000.

Schulze-Cleven, Tobias, Tilman Reitz, Jens Maesse, and Johannes Angermuller. 'The New Political Economy of Higher Education: Between Distributional Conflicts and Discursive Stratification'. *Higher Education* 73, no. 6 (2017): 795–812. https://doi.org/10.1007/s10734-017-0114-4.

Shrivastava, Meenai, and Sanjiv Shrivastava. 'Political Economy of Higher Education: Comparing South Africa to Trends in the World'. *Higher Education* 67, no. 6 (2014): 809–822. https://doi.org/10.1007/s10734-013-9709-6.

Simpson, James G. R. 'Boipatong: The Politics of a Massacre and the South African Transition'. *Journal of Southern African Studies* 38, no. 3 (2012): 623–647. https://doi.org/10.1080/03057070.2012.711674.

Sparks, Allister Haddon. *The Mind of South Africa*. New York: Ballantine, 1991.

Spaull, Nic, and Jonathan D. Jansen. *South African Schooling: The Enigma of Inequality; A Study of the Present Situation and Future Possibilities*. Cham: Springer, 2019.

Statistics South Africa. *Financial Statistics of Higher Education Institutions*. Pretoria: Statistics South Africa, 2019. http://www.statssa.gov.za/publications/P91031/P910312019.pdf.

Steyn, Melissa E., and Mikki van Zyl. *Like That Statue at Jammie Stairs: Some Student Perceptions and Experiences of Institutional Culture at the University of Cape Town in 1999*. Cape Town: Institute for Intercultural and Diversity Studies of Southern Africa, 2001.

Strydom, Bronwyn. 'South African University History: A Historiographical Overview'. *African Historical Review* 48, no. 1 (2016): 56–82. https://doi.org/10.1080/17532523.2016.1236886.

Sum, Ngai-Ling, and Bob Jessop. *Towards a Cultural Political Economy: Putting Culture in Its Place in Political Economy.* Cheltenham, UK: Edward Elgar, 2013. doi:10.4337/9780857930712.

Swartz, Sharlene, Alude Mahali, Relebohile Moletsane, Emma Arogundade, Nene Ernest Khalema, Adam Cooper, and Candice Groenewald. *Studying While Black: Race, Education and Emancipation in South African Universities.* Cape Town: HSRC Press, 2018.

Swingler, Helen. 'Taxis Protest Jammie Shuttle Route'. *UCT News*, 28 August 2007. https://www.news.uct.ac.za/article/-2007-08-28-taxis-protest-jammie-shuttle-route.

Taylor, Alison. *What Do Corrupt Firms Have in Common? Red Flags of Corruption in Organizational Culture.* New York: Columbia University, 2016. https://web.law.columbia.edu/sites/default/files/microsites/public-integrity/files/what_do_corrupt_firms_have_in_common_-_capi_issue_brief_-_april_2016.pdf.

Thaver, Lionel. '"At Home", Institutional Culture and Higher Education: Some Methodological Considerations'. *Perspectives in Education* 24, no. 1 (2006): 15–26.

Times Higher Education Supplement. 'Sociology Head Is Forced into Hiding'. No. 1192 (8 September 1995): 10. https://www.timeshighereducation.com/news/sociology-head-is-forced-into-hiding/95116.article.

Tleane, Lebo. 'South Africans Who Made Millions from Faking Their Qualifications'. *Youth Village*, October 2019. https://youthvillage.co.za/2019/10/south-africans-who-made-millions-from-faking-their-qualifications/.

Tomoso, Omphile, and Lindikaya W. Myeki. 'Estimating South African Higher Education Productivity and Its Determinants Using FärePrimont Index: Are Historically Disadvantaged Universities Catching Up?' *Research in Higher Education*, 27 May 2022. https://doi.org/10.1007/s11162-022-09699-3.

Torres, Carlos A., and Daniel Schugurensky. 'The Political Economy of Higher Education in the Era of Neoliberal Globalization: Latin America in Comparative Perspective'. *Higher Education* 43, no. 4 (2002): 429–455. https://doi.org/10.1023/A:1015292413037.

Troiani, Igea, and Claudia Dutson. 'The Neoliberal University as a Space to Learn/Think/Work in Higher Education'. *Architecture and Culture* 9, no. 1 (2021): 5–23. https://doi.org/10.1080/20507828.2021.1898836.

Universities South Africa. 'Higher Education Leadership and Management'. 2021. https://www.usaf.ac.za/higher-education-leadership-and-management-helm-programme/.

Universities South Africa. 'The USAf Board Takes a Stand on Corruption, 29 October 2020'. News release. https://www.usaf.ac.za/the-usaf-board-takes-a-stand-on-corruption/.

University of Cape Town. *Annual Report 2020.* Cape Town: University of Cape Town, 2020. https://www.uct.ac.za/sites/default/files/image_tool/images/431/finance/operations/statements/afs2020.pdf.

University of Fort Hare. *Annual Report 2020.* Alice: University of Fort Hare, 2020.

University of the Western Cape. *Hek Toe! UWC in the 1980s.* Bellville: University of the Western Cape, 2004.

Van der Merwe, Christiaan. '"Historically Black" Universities See More Student Debt'. *Research Professional News*, 1 April 2021. https://www.researchprofessionalnews.com/rr-news-africa-south-2021-4-disadvantaged-universities-bear-brunt-of-south-africas-student-debt/.

Vergnani, Linda. 'South African Homeland Deports 3 Professors'. *Chronicle of Higher Education*, 6 January 1993. https://www.chronicle.com/article/south-african-homeland-deports-3-professors/?cid2=gen_login_refresh&cid=gen_sign_in.

Volmink, John, Michael Gardiner, Siyabonga Msimang, Paul Nel, Amelia Moleta, Gerhard Scholtz, and Tommy Prins. *Report of the Ministerial Task Team Appointed by Minister Angie Motshekga to Investigate Allegations into the Selling of Posts of Educators by Members of Teachers Unions and Departmental Officials in Provincial Education Departments: Final Report*. Pretoria: Department of Basic Education, 2016.

Wa Afrika, Mzilikazi. 'Top Diplomat Axed after Running High Commission "Like a Spaza Shop"'. *Sunday Times*, 24 September 2017. https://www.timeslive.co.za/sunday-times/news/2017-09-23-top-diplomat-axed-after-running-high-commission-like-a-spaza-shop/'. 2017.

Wa Afrika, Mzilikazi, and Kyle Cowan. 'Degrees-for-Sale Scam Rocks Zululand Varsity. *Sunday Times*, 31 July 2016. https://www.timeslive.co.za/sunday-times/news/2016-07-31-degrees-for-sale-scam-rocks-zululand-varsity.

Wa Azania, Malaika. *Corridors of Death: The Struggle to Exist in Historically White Institutions*. Polokwane: Blackbird Books, 2020.

Walter Sisulu University. *Annual Report 2020*. Mthatha: Walter Sisulu University, 2020. https://www.wsu.ac.za/images/annualreport/WSU_Annual_Report_2020_compressed.pdf.

Weill, Lawrence V. *Out in Front: The College President as the Face of the Institution*. Lanham, MD: Rowman and Littlefield, 2009.

Wessels, Jacobus S., Makhosandile H. Kwaza, and Edwin Ijeoma. 'Sustained Poor Audit Outcomes: The Case of the Amathole District Municipality'. In *Public Administration Challenges: Cases from Africa*, edited by Jacobus S. Wessels, Thean Potgieter, and Thevan Naidoo, 246–412. Cape Town: Juta, 2021.

Wild, Sarah. 'Rhodes "on the Brink of Closure" Due to Lack of Water'. *Mail & Guardian*, 14 August 2013. https://mg.co.za/article/2013-08-14-rhodes-on-the-brink-of-closure-says- vice-chancellor/.

Williams, Donovan. *A History of the University College of Fort Hare, South Africa: The 1950s; The Waiting Years*. Lewiston, NY: E. Mellen Press, 2001.

Wills, Gabrielle. 'An Economic Perspective on School Leadership and Teachers' Unions in South Africa'. PhD dissertation, Stellenbosch University, 2016. https://resep.sun.ac.za/wp-content/uploads/2017/10/2016-02-21-G-Wills-PhD-School-leadership-and-teachers-unions-in-South-Africa-FINAL.pdf.

Witz, Leslie. 'Misplaced Ideals? The Case of Unibo: A Reply to J. F. de V. Graaff'. *Reality*, January 1986: 10–12. https://disa.ukzn.ac.za/sites/default/files/pdf_files/rejul86.7.pdf.